SUBJECT MATTER

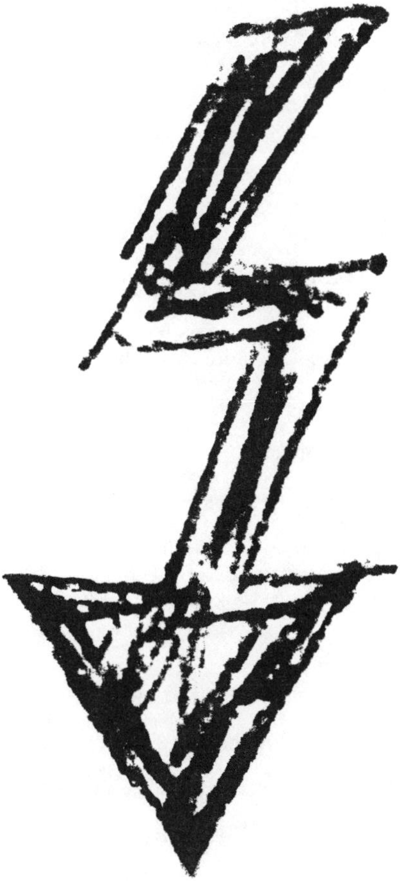

SHORT CIRCUITS

Mladen Dolar, Alenka Zupančič, and Slavoj Žižek, editors

The Puppet and the Dwarf: The Perverse Core of Christianity, by Slavoj Žižek

The Shortest Shadow: Nietzsche's Philosophy of the Two, by Alenka Zupančič

Is Oedipus Online? Siting Freud after Freud, by Jerry Aline Flieger

Interrogation Machine: Laibach and NSK, by Alexei Monroe

The Parallax View, by Slavoj Žižek

A Voice and Nothing More, by Mladen Dolar

Subjectivity and Otherness: A Philosophical Reading of Lacan, by Lorenzo Chiesa

The Odd One In: On Comedy, by Alenka Zupančič

The Monstrosity of Christ: Paradox or Dialectic?, by Slavoj Žižek and John Milbank, edited by Creston Davis

Interface Fantasy: A Lacanian Cyborg Ontology, by André Nusselder

Lacan at the Scene, by Henry Bond

Laughter: Notes on a Passion, by Anca Parvulescu

All for Nothing: Hamlet's Negativity, by Andrew Cutrofello

The Not-Two: Logic and God in Lacan, by Lorenzo Chiesa

The Trouble with Pleasure: Deleuze and Psychoanalysis, by Aaron Schuster

What IS Sex?, by Alenka Zupančič

Liquidation World: On the Art of Living Absently, by Alexi Kukuljevic

Incontinence of the Void: Economico-Philosophical Spandrels, by Slavoj Žižek

The Dash: The Other Side of Absolute Knowing, by Rebecca Comay and Frank Ruda

Subject Matter: The Anaesthetics of Habit and the Logic of Breakdown, by Aron Vinegar

What's That Smell? A Philosophy of the Olfactory, by Simon Hajdini

How to Research Like a Dog: Kafka's New Science, by Aaron Schuster

SUBJECT MATTER

THE ANAESTHETICS OF HABIT AND THE LOGIC OF BREAKDOWN

Aron Vinegar

THE MIT PRESS CAMBRIDGE, MASSACHUSETTS LONDON, ENGLAND

This book was set in Copperplate Gothic Std and Joanna MT Pro by New Best-set Typesetters Ltd. Printed and bound in the United States of America.

Library of Congress Cataloging-in-Publication Data

Names: Vinegar, Aron, author.
Title: Subject matter : the anaesthetics of habit and the logic of breakdown / Aron Vinegar.
Description: Cambridge, Massachusetts : The MIT Press, [2023] | Series: Short circuits | Includes bibliographical references and index.
Identifiers: LCCN 2022050352 (print) | LCCN 2022050353 (ebook) | ISBN 9780262546362 (paperback) | ISBN 9780262375924 (epub) | ISBN 9780262375917 (pdf)
Subjects: LCSH: Habit. | Adaptability (Psychology)
Classification: LCC BF335 .V564 2023 (print) | LCC BF335 (ebook) | DDC 155.2/4—dc23/eng/20230607
LC record available at https://lccn.loc.gov/2022050352
LC ebook record available at https://lccn.loc.gov/2022050353

10 9 8 7 6 5 4 3 2 1

CONTENTS

SERIES FOREWORD

A short circuit occurs when there is a faulty connection in the network—faulty, of course, from the standpoint of the network's smooth functioning. Is not the shock of short-circuiting, therefore, one of the best metaphors for a critical reading? Is not one of the most effective critical procedures to cross wires that do not usually touch: to take a major classic (text, author, notion) and read it in a short-circuiting way, through the lens of a "minor" author, text, or conceptual apparatus ("minor" should be understood here in Deleuze's sense: not "of lesser quality," but marginalized, disavowed by the hegemonic ideology, or dealing with a "lower," less dignified topic)? If the minor reference is well chosen, such a procedure can lead to insights which completely shatter and undermine our common perceptions. This is what Marx, among others, did with philosophy and religion (short-circuiting philosophical speculation through the lens of political economy, that is to say, economic speculation); this is what Freud and Nietzsche did with morality (short-circuiting the highest ethical notions through the lens of the unconscious libidinal economy). What such a reading achieves is not a simple "desublimation," a reduction of the higher intellectual content to its lower economic or libidinal cause; the aim of such an approach is, rather, the inherent decentering of the interpreted text, which brings to light its "unthought," its disavowed presuppositions and consequences.

And this is what Short Circuits wants to do, again and again. The underlying premise of the series is that Lacanian psychoanalysis is a privileged instrument of such an approach, whose purpose is to illuminate a standard text or ideological formation, making it readable in a totally new way—the long history of Lacanian interventions in philosophy, religion, the arts (from the visual arts to the cinema, music, and literature), ideology, and politics justifies this premise. This, then, is not a new series of books on psychoanalysis, but a series of "connections in the Freudian field"—of short Lacanian interventions in art, philosophy, theology, and ideology.

Short Circuits intends to revive a practice of reading which confronts a classic text, author, or notion with its own hidden presuppositions, and thus reveals its disavowed truth. The basic criterion for the texts that will be published is that they effectuate such a theoretical short circuit. After reading a book in this series, the reader should not simply have learned something new: the point is, rather, to make him or her aware of another—disturbing—side of something he or she knew all the time.

Slavoj Žižek

INTRODUCTION

HABIT—THE UNHAPPY MEDIATOR

Like an irresistible tractor beam, almost all accounts of habit are drawn toward its mediating, adaptive, and stabilizing functions. In fact, habit is seen as the very embodiment of mediation, allowing us to take possession of our bodies and make them supple and skillful instruments through training and repetition. In enabling the body to function as a "middle term," habit allows us not only to cultivate our own bodily possibilities but also to adapt to, inhabit, and feel at home in our environment.[1] As Maurice Merleau-Ponty succinctly puts it, habit "has its abode … in the body as mediator of a world."[2] In doing so, habit mediates between the individual level of the body's accomplishment as a stable dispositional tendency and the supra-individual level of the social and symbolic fields of culture, customs, and institutions.[3]

This narrative of habit in and as mediation is frequently expressed either as the precondition of any bildungsroman of ethico-aesthetic formation, or, more commonly, the very embodiment of a *Bildung* of subjectivity. Such accounts often entail a more or less progressive, teleological, and developmental account of how we cultivate our *second natures*, which are produced through repetition and practice and which modify and shape corporeal dispositions that are not given but must be "self-posited" in and through habit.[4] Perhaps we might even call this a *Bindungsroman*, as it is predicated on the binding, repetitious, and universalizing qualities of habit that generate a unity and regularity that is essential to the edifying narratives by which we are encultured.

HABIT WITHOUT THE FLY-WHEEL

In contrast to habit's perennial role as a *happy mediator*, my theorization of habit emphasizes its excessive and disturbing qualities. Rather than assuming that habit is a way of expressing the ideal unity of dualities that perform their duet in habit's perennial tune of the well-tempered and mediated body, I wish to foreground a sense of habit that is constitutively unsettling and disruptive. I pursue a notion of habit that is emphatically not William James's proverbial "fly-wheel"—a mechanical device attached to a rotating shaft in order to regulate fluctuations in speed and force by evening out or dampening irregularities, sticking points, and excess friction, thus preventing it from spinning out of control. He highlights this metaphor in his most well-known definition of habit as society's most precious harmonizing and meliorating agent that trues us to our given dispositions and positions.[5] In my account, habit is more akin to a "cog-wheel rigidity"—a term that is used in Tom McCarthy's novel *Remainder*, a primary reference point in this book—that is constantly catching and overturning in abrupt fits and starts, reeling out of control, compulsively repeating, and beginning again and again (Rem, 220). *Subject Matter* explores a notion of habit that is of a piece with the destitution of subjectivity rather than its given role of founding, grounding, or stabilizing it.

This narrative of habit as an edification and stabilization of being is predicated on habit's role as a metaphysical mediator that overcomes a myriad of dualisms: nature and culture, body and mind, matter and spirit, object and subject, being and having, exterior and interior, passivity and activity, spontaneity and receptivity, resistance and permeability, transcendence and immanence, immediacy and mediation. In doing so, habit as a middle term affirms the continuity between extremes while serving as a method and technique for moving between them.[6]

Even aspects of "existence at its worst"—those dimensions of habit captured by terms such as automaticity, ossification, recalcitrance, inertia, thingness, mindless repetition, deadening, and indifference—have a dialectical part to play, as they are seen as temporary obstacles, deviations, regressions, malign inversions, or falls from habit *proper*, most often characterized by terms such as fluidity, pliability, suppleness, harmony, balance, and grace.[7] Depending on the account, when the "revolving door" of habit turns from activity to passivity, livening into deadening, suppleness into rigidity, fluidity into fixity, it can be corrected and homeopathically regulated via the mediating techniques of "bodily understanding" that are internal to habit itself, which recalibrates and balances out any unmeasured and excessive drift away from habit proper, or, through the intervention of a brief dose of conscious attention and understanding that would mind the gaps, thus dividing automaticity against itself.[8]

This subtle balancing act tends to avoid the extremes of habit that might be summarized as either a life bereft of habits or one completely dominated by them. The first extreme has three versions: (a) the modernist/revolutionary ideal not to have any habits at all, a condition perhaps best exemplified by Benjamin's "destructive character" committed to the erasure of all givens, and thus the perpetual eradication of its own determining conditions; (b) the more quotidian and grim version of this ideal articulated by Nietzsche and James as the hell of a life entirely without habits, requiring one to endlessly repeat the simplest of tasks like walking or brushing teeth, with neither the time nor the energy to change or innovate, let alone revolutionize; or, in a more traumatic vein, (c) Catherine Malabou's "new wounded," who are completely severed from their previous habits and ways of being by the brutality of an external accident. The other extreme is a life completely weighed down by habit, where one is immobilized and possibly buried by the accumulated inertia of habit—the addictions, bad habits, routines, and stereotypes that elaborate on the death-driven tendency of habit via its automatisms and ossifications as it "drift[s] towards the thing," to use Paul Ricoeur's evocative wording.[9] The fact that the very habits of life and living themselves are what bring on the repose of death is well-captured in Hegel's account of habit and perhaps most vividly personified by Kojève's "undialectical man," who stops "negating the given and negating himself as given," thus succumbing to the inertia and automaticity of what Hegel calls "processless habit."[10] Perhaps we might characterize this as a condition of absolute adaptation.

The modernist ethico-aesthetic rhythm of habit change is the privileged explanation and technique for counteracting the deadening aspects of habit through a perpetual process of making and breaking habits, thus ensuring it remains a constantly renewed source of vitality. This conception of modernist habit change is meant to ensure that the extremes of habit are turned before they can ever definitively keel to one side or collide. Here I am thinking of Nietzsche's preference for "brief habits" versus "enduring ones," Bergson's account of "oppos(ing) new habits to old ones unceasingly … thus dividing automatism against itself," or art's role in the sensuous defamiliarization of the anaesthetizing aspects of habit with a long aesthetico-political legacy stretching from Pater to Proust and from Shklovsky to Brecht. Habit seems to glide between extremes without ever slipping, falling, or getting mired in them except as deviant states from habit proper. To use Ravaisson's phrasing, habit is an "indivisible middle term" that ensures "contraries merge" rather than collide.[11] By this logic, and in a strange and counterintuitive way, the notion of fluidity, ease and habit change can operate as a normative principle of the body (politic) par excellence for ordering and governing that entrenches all manner of privilege, domination and pastoral power.[12]

Habit's mediating function is also crucial when negotiating important divisions and thresholds within particular bodies of philosophical thought. Hegel's account of habit is exemplary here. Habit (*Gewohnheit*), or "second nature" (*zweite Natur*), plays a crucial role in his speculative philosophy, negotiating all the important thresholds and transitions between nature and culture, body and soul, soul and spirit, subjective and objective spirit and, ultimately, absolute spirit.[13] In so doing, habit manifests itself at critical junctures in Hegel's *Philosophy of Nature*, *Philosophy of Mind*, *Phenomenology of Spirit*, and *Elements of the Philosophy of Right*.[14] In Hegel's most explicit account of habit, in section numbers §409 and §410 of the "Anthropology of Soul" in *Philosophy of Mind*, the third and last volume of his *Encyclopedia of the Philosophical Sciences*—as well as the detailed elaborations of these sections on habit in his *Lectures on the Philosophy of Spirit*, 1827–8—it is a way of healing the divisions, disruptions, fixations, and miring in "particularity" (*Besonderheit*) that is a feature of mental and bodily derangement and disease (*Verrücktheit* and *Krankheit*). Habit allows the "self-feeling soul" to break with its unmediated absorption in itself through habit in and as a "mechanism of self-feeling" (*Mechanismus des Selbstgefühls*).[15] Habit is the actualization of the soul as the mediation between body and spirit, enabling the body to be, as Hegel writes, "the middle term by which I come together with the external world as such."[16] It is hardly surprising that the conscious "I" makes its appearance at the very end of the account of habit in *Philosophy of Mind*, where the "actual soul," enabled by habit's mediation, is precipitously transfigured in and by a "consuming lightning flash" (*verzehrender Blitz*), into an "'I' as the self-related, individually determined universal," thus preparing the crucial groundwork for the section on the "Phenomenology of Spirit. Consciousness" that immediately follows it.[17] By the conclusion of the "Anthropology" section, man appears as the "incarnation of spirit."[18]

Simply put, habit is a crucial moment in the Hegelian axiom that the truth of immediacy lies in its sublation and mediation. Habit is a second, cultivated nature, posited by the soul, and thus is a mediated immediacy produced through repetition and practice that modifies and shapes corporeal dispositions. Habit accomplishes an "abstract universality" of embodiment that subsumes the body as an "immediately concrete thing," defined as a set of externally relating parts and thus enabling a "transcending of the immediate" that is "the arrival at the immediate."[19] Habit's simple self-relating unity, therefore, anticipates the speculative unity and movement of the concept and "concrete universality," laying the foundations and beginning to embody all the "higher order" aspects of spirit in its mediation of body and soul, particular and universal, substance and subject, and judgment and syllogism that, according to one reading, achieves its ultimate dialectical integration in the last section on "Absolute Knowing" in the *Phenomenology of Spirit*. Habit gives us the first awakening of the absolute as it emerges from abstract immediacy into a mediated immediacy that is accomplished through the sublation of mediation and from the parting and particularity of judgment as it begins to embody the syllogistic mediation of particular and universal.

Even the historiography of habit itself is touched by its own mediating terms, such that Félix Ravaisson's influential nineteenth-century treatise *Of Habit* is characterized as a *synthesis* of the ancient and modern senses of habit as "grace" (ease, facility, power) and "addiction" (machinic repetition), thus balancing the more positive accounts of habit in the Aristotelian/Hegelian tradition with more negative ones in Cartesian and Kantian ones.[20] This is not to mention the very words "mediation" (*Vermittlung*), "middle term"/"mediating middle" (*Mitte*), or "third term" (*Dritte*) that are prevalent in most philosophically oriented accounts of habit that draw on Hegel (almost every account of habit from the nineteenth century to the present) and his elaboration of these key Aristotelian terms of the logical syllogism.[21] Other more common words and terms for this mediating function that are used to characterize habit's grounding, adapting, balancing, and unifying functions—such as "ballast," "anchor," "lightning-rod," "veiling," "tempering," "facilitating," "settling," "sedimenting," or "ingraining"—reverberate through a diverse set of writers and philosophers up to the present.

My fundamental claim in this book is that habit is a repetitive operation that generates bodily, material, and psychic disruption that is not exceptional or necessarily pathological but is rather an often disavowed, quotidian familiarity that trips us up in everyday life more often than we would like to admit. I begin with the premise that habit is a disturbance in and of the environment as such, up to and including habit itself as the medium, milieu, and environment that is constitutive of the subject.[22] My account of the *too much* rather than *just right* logic of habit is fully attentive to its constitutive antagonisms, divisions, ruptures, voids, excesses, fixities, and drives. Contrary to claims that habit is an interiorization, pacification, and binding of unruly (first) nature, matter, and drives resulting in a second nature that creates the foundations for the continuity of consciousness produced by the "habitual ignoring of gaps," I claim that habit is precisely the instauration, elaboration, and exacerbation of these gaps.[23]

As such, habit is a constitutive unease or *desease* rather than an ease or facility. I shall employ the term "desease" throughout the book, employing an older Anglo-French etymology, literally meaning *ill-at-ease* rather than a disease or a pathological condition. If Freud once claimed that in order to arrive at the normal one must study the pathological with its "distortions and exaggerations," I am approaching habit in the spirit of Adorno's comment that "in psycho-analysis nothing is true except the exaggerations."[24] Here, I pursue the sense that conditions of habit at its "worst" are originary and not merely deviations from habit proper that is their presupposed normative measure. In addressing the unruly, disruptive, and unsettling nature of matter as it relates to bodily repetitions, this book elaborates a notion of habit that generates and is generated by unsettled material excess that is the very perturbation of subjectivity. My notion of habit runs counter to any "orthopedic" discourse of mediation that attempts to close, fill, veil, facilitate, bridge, or mind the gaps and infernal openings that habit's daemonic "compulsion to repeat" incessantly generates in order to sustain a well-tempered imago of habit.[25] As will become clear, psychoanalytic dimensions of repetition, such as the death drive, automaticity, circling, deviation, disruption, excess, and the function of missing, are also central to my account of habit.

FIXITY, FLUIDITY, AND SUPERFLUITY

The notion of fluidity is always coursing through any discussion of habit as its medium and telos. The presumed inculcation and accomplishment of habit as a second nature is often evidenced by an ease and grace that has overcome the recalcitrance and exteriority of matter. In the discourse on habit, the successful incorporation of habit is evidenced by a gesture that has shed all excess, inertia, time, energy, and complication, as if it had "unresistingly pervaded" corporeity through and through, thus stripping it of its inflexible foreignness.[26] The language and concept of fluidity that dominates discussions of habit proper overemphasizes its capacity to smooth over units into unity: to convert the external into the internal; the particular into the universal; accident into necessity; mechanical repetition into organic connection; fixity into flow. It tends to iron out the gaps and disturbances generated by habit through an emphasis on its ability to create continuity out of discontinuity. Habit's mediating function puts the emphasis on balance and adaptability to such an extent that automaticity, passivity, inertia, recalcitrance, routine, and thingness are seen solely as threats to habit proper and its ideal qualities of fluidity, pliability, and aliveness. They are considered pathological deviations from a presupposed state of balance, (punctuated) equilibrium, or homeostasis, and constitutive of all forms of intractability, bad habits, addictions, and resistance to change. Even when the inertial, mechanical, and material excesses of habit are featured, they are seen as a degradation or a regression measured by their deviation from the fluid quality of habit.[27]

Disparaging and subordinating automatism in such a way is common in theories of habit and is particularly strong in the French tradition—and also in certain strands of American Pragmatism—which spans Ravaisson, Bergson, Ricoeur, Merleau-Ponty, and Latour. Bruno Latour's claim that there is no "inertia" in habit proper but only in bad habits or addictions echoes Paul Ricoeur's claim that automatism cannot be understood in its own right but only by starting from flexible habit.[28] Issues of resistance, recalcitrance, rigidity, and exteriority, however, are not just disruptions of the smooth workings of habit proper or a sign of relapse or regression to states that habit has failed to cure or overcome; rather, they are constitutive of habit and are generated by its repetition compulsion. I am interested in the *Real* of habit that is produced by the extremes of its entanglement in particularity *and* its appropriation to universality through the "mindless mechanism" of automaticity. This entanglement in the imbalances between particularity and universality seizes and pulls habit apart, engendering the disruptions, gaps, and excesses that we tend to smooth over. An overemphasis on habit's veiling function stresses how these gaps are filled in or transimmanently bridged over, thus converting cut into continuity or, in its more deadening sense, how habit as a "heavy curtain," to use Proust's wording, dulls and dampens senses and drives.

A fluid and fully functioning habit supposedly sloughs off all disruptive, extraneous, and senseless matter so that it does not become a disturbance or drag in the engendering of a dynamic, meaningful, and connected life. These senseless and hermeneutically resistant material remainders are, however, at the very essence of habit, which we often disavow or downplay in order to emphasize a more comforting immersion in habit's effects of continuity. Habit often becomes entangled in and overwhelmed by the superfluity of matter rather than overcoming it and rendering it completely pervious and "without resistance and with ease."[29] Habit itself regularly generates modes of resistance that are the primary material to work with and from.[30] In and through habit, corporeity often remains intractable and belligerent rather than pliable and reliable, and any hylomorphic fantasy of dissolving excess matter, movement, energy, and parts into an ideal "plastic individuality" is perpetually sundered, by the desease of habit.[31]

Rather than habit as a nascent form of bodily self-positing, which produces a "second nature" through mediation, my account sees habit as more of a *de-positing*, such that we are mired in its strange materiality; habit remains—to twist some Hegelian terminology—an evacuating actuality or a "fragmentary and uncertain actuality" that resists its own privileged vocabulary of incorporating exteriority/otherness and rendering it soluble.[32] Habit insistently generates the indeterminacy and inconsistency that it is supposed to settle.[33] The material anaesthetics of habit that I am interested in is based on its *failure to mediate a world*, which persists in and as a stain of the strange, contingent, unruly, and indeterminate matter that it generates.

Habit's consistency is mealy at best, and these particulars are never adequately universalized into a coordinated, self-relational unity. I argue that the repetitions which define habit are often not successfully interiorized, incorporated, and bound into a unity that would provide a stable *conatus* for the subject. I use the term "per-severing" in this book to call attention to this mortifying and sundering death drive that is generated by habit's compulsion to repeat. Habit is often not our "second happier nature," as Agamben characterizes it in his account of habit as a form of possibility enacted by and through the free "use" of the body.[34] The true value of the apocryphal quotation—"Habit is a second nature! Habit is ten times nature"—that appears in James's account of habit is that it exponentially ups the stakes in habit's doubling down on nature's own weaknesses, perturbations, and excesses.[35] Habit as a second nature that supposedly engenders our stable ways of being out of the primordial discord of exteriority and division is often a hyperbolic elaboration on the derangement of *first nature* and an incessant repetition of the "prematurity of birth" and "motor incoordination" that is outlined in Lacan's "Mirror Stage."[36]

The key words in my reading of habit are often "not-there" in the very catchwords and sentences that emphasize the fluidity of habit. Take, for instance, Gaston Roupnel's poetic and pithy description of acquired habit in his book *Siloë* that is quoted in Bachelard's *Intuition of the Instant*: "through the effect of acquired habit ... the gestures ... shed their excessive dimensions and useless complication; they simplify and abridge themselves. Parasitic movements disappear."[37] What if we took seriously the full speculative implications of just one word in these two sentence—"abridge"? This word is often used to describe how the acquisition of habit saves time and energy by removing unnecessary resistance, closing the gap between parts, units, and stages of a movement or action, and thus facilitating ease, grace, and flow in the accomplishment of a unified action or movement.[38] But there are harsher connotations of the word "abridge" that invoke seizing, cutting out, and cutting off, not to mention the accumulative excess of all these "off-cuts" that overflow and generate senseless material signifiers that are often recalcitrant rather than facilitating. The very language used to account for habit often downplays or disavows its "phylolytic drive" and "desperate analysis," two phrases used by Rebecca Comay and Katrin Pahl to characterize the abstract negativity that cuts through Hegel's *Phenomenology of Spirit*.[39]

Perhaps we might pay closer attention to this language of imparting partialness that is of a piece with the words, sentences, and phrases used to develop accounts of habit that emphasize its fluidity, solubility, and stability. It is as if the language of habit calls for such short-circuiting, but then this language of parts and division is simply relegated to the nascent stages of habit formation, only to reappear as the return of the repressed in fully accomplished habit. For instance, take this key passage on second nature from Aristotle's *Nicomachean Ethics*, translated by Miles Burnyeat: "Those who have learned a subject for the first time connect together the propositions in an orderly way, but do not yet know them; for the propositions need to become second nature to them [δεῖ γὰρ συμφυῆναι]."[40] Burnyeat's translation is quite fitting, in many ways, for συμφυῆναι, whereas W. D. Ross translates it as "has to become part of themselves."[41] This wording is echoed in John Dewey's claim that habit is "intimately *a part* [my emphasis] of ourselves."[42] This parting needs more attention in our accounts of habit.[43]

I refuse to assume that habit, as a merging or intersection of conceptual pairs, smoothly conducts the traffic between them rather than short-circuiting and creating a potential crash site for all kinds of flows, whether they be corporeal, material, communicative, or economic. Habit does not simply shed its excessive dimensions of matter, time, energy, complication, and effort.

Instead, it often generates them as surplus matter, relentless deviation, and infinite per-severing rather than sublated moments, fluid mediations, and vital spontaneity. These surplus movements, steps, units, and forces are often interpreted as signs of pathology, as Merleau-Ponty makes clear in his account of the patient Johann Schneider's "morbid motility" in *Phenomenology of Perception*.[44] But this denegation of habit's more unruly dimensions starts to sound a bit like Hegel's "beautiful soul" in the *Phenomenology of Spirit*, "casting out onto the world the disorder that constitutes his being."[45]

A CRACK IN THE MIRROR, A RENT IN THE VEIL

The emphasis on mediation that is prevalent in discourses of habit is often beholden to and in the service of a comforting notion of habit as an "ideal unity"; a second nature emerging out of "primordial discord" and "motor un-coordination."[46] It is, to use Lacan's words from his account of the Mirror Stage, a "salutary imago" of bodily coordination, relative homeostasis, and the jubilation of imaginary mastery that downplays this scene's dramatization of the irreducible gaps, mal-coordination, and precipitation that are the destitution of this ideal unity. The "specular image" of habit remains mired in a primordial and precipitating discord that is forever marked by "motor impotence," "libidinal dynamism," "turbulent movements," and a "leaning-forward position" that is always on the threshold of collapse, not reflected back into restitutive acts of stabilization or orthopedic propping up. The habitual body is stained by and mired in all sorts of sticky matter, off-cuts, deciduous objects, disconnected limbs, and exoscopic body parts driven and generated by its repetition compulsions that erupt and interrupt rather than bind. In talking about habit's ideal unity, we are often taken in by the lure—the temptation—of this "gestalt" as a goal rather than a bait that precipitates us in ways that dramatize a "fragmented body" that is always an incomplete remainder with regard to its bodily coordination and its orthopedic composure.

In this book, habit is perpetually trying to engender itself but remains stuck in the "gravel-pits and marshes" that surround the fortress of the ego, as it fails to generate the orthopedic support and specular image of habit that would mediate between a Subject's *Innenwelt* and *Umwelt*. There is a tendency to generate fantasies of habit that more or less progressively move from a fragmented image of the body to fantasies of orthopedic totality without accounting for the persistence of those unstable grounds ("gravel-pits and marshes") that do not offer stable foundations or adequate building material for the construction of any fortified structures of the ego and its edifying narratives. An attentiveness to how habit is involved in the "shattering" of the "*Innenwelt* to *Umwelt* circle" manifests a much more disturbing account of habit's temporal and material precipitation and its effects.

In fact, the gestalt that Lacan raises in his account of the Mirror Stage in relation to the image of unity is not used in the usual sense referring to a perceptual/psychological/vital wholeness but rather as an exteriorized cut out shape, set up in front of us as a lure of one-sidedness, marked by repetition and fragmentation. It echoes Hegel's "shapes" (*Gestalten*) of knowing that are also characterized by a one-sidedness and resistence to "*inwardizing recollection*" (*die Er-Innerung*).[47] Indeed, the very word "gestalt" is repeated four times within the space of a few paragraphs in the short "Mirror Stage" article, as if to emphasize that repetition is the eruption of jouissance at the very heart of this imaginary unity and mastery. Like Adorno's perspicuous remarks about Hegel's *Phenomenology*, everything in the "Mirror Stage" is anathema to any traditional sense of gestalt theory in regard to part-whole and figure-ground relationships, and thus is inimical to any "tendency to harmony."[48]

If Lacan claims in *Seminar II* that "the Subject is no one. It is decomposed, in pieces," and only finds its unity in its own specular image, of what kind of unity do we speak?[49] Lacan's sentence resonates with an anxiety-ridden passage that appears in Paul Ricoeur's classic hermeneutico-phenomenological account of habit in *Freedom and Nature: The Voluntary and Involuntary*: "I am one only in a constantly repeated conquest of the renascent scission."[50] If the self wins itself ("I am one"), that looks more like a Sisyphean task involving a compulsive repetition that incessantly generates the per-severing rebirth of scission that never has time to heal and continues to breach in uncontrollable ways that are well in excess of any attempts to "one them over" into a reparative and stable image of bodily unity. I would argue that, through habit, the body is not just prone to regress or relapse into earlier stages of psychic/organic/material development or pathological states of instability, derangement, madness, addiction, and collapse (as many accounts suggest). There are many instances in which the habitual body is more or less than willing to take up arms (and many other body parts as well) against itself that are immanent and often more quotidian conditions of possession or paranormality, not to mention paranoid and persecutory delusions.

Although Lacan refers to the hyperbolic example of the interior panels of Hieronymus Bosch's *Garden of Earthly Delights* to invoke the extremes of these exoscopic representations of the "body in pieces" coming back to haunts us, we are, in fact, riveted to them by habit itself. It is not insignificant that Hegel's Behmian-inspired "Night of the I" from his Jena System Lectures is alluded to right before the account of habit in *Lectures on the Philosophy of Spirit*, 1827–8, and later on in the "Psychology" section of *Philosophy of Mind* as this "night-like mine or pit" (*diesen nächtlichen Schacht*).[51] I would argue that this mine or pit—an "inner precipice" to use Hegel's wording from the Preface to the *Phenomenology of Spirit*—persists, indeed is further elaborated, in his account of habit as the mechanism of self-feeling. (This Hegelian mine or pit (*Schacht*) renders another dimension to the metaphor of *drilling* in habit formation, that assumes that repetition sediments a resourceful habit rather than punctuates, ruptures, and fragments.) Habit often remains sunk into this unconscious and indeterminate realm of a "wealth of infinitely many representations, images"—a phantasmagoric condition in which disconnected body parts suddenly shoot up, only to suddenly vanish (*verschwinden*)—without the inner connectivity, universality of reflection, adequate determination, and possession promised by its repetitions.[52]

This phantasmagoria show resonates with Lacan's characterization of the drive as a "montage" that resists the "simple unity" that habit self-posits as a "universality [that] is brought forth, produced, and proceeds out of particular cases."[53] The role of repetition (*Wiederholung*) that is so crucial to all accounts of engendering a body of habit, is more like a "compulsion to repeat" (*Wiederholungszwang*)—a "repetition automatism" as Lacan sometimes refers to it—that is indicative of a drivenness that does not possess the satisfaction of the drive but rather is an overdrive that gears into habit's given role in binding the drives.[54] I am interested in the disruptive *Real* at the core of the symbolic and imaginary dimensions of our imago of habit as a form of bodily unity, mastery, and self-preservation that tends to dominate psychological, sociological, and phenomenological accounts of habit.

THE ANAESTHETICS OF HABIT

Drawing on both Hegelian and psychoanalytic coordinates, the term "anaesthetics" that appears in this book's title is meant to work *against* the given meaning of this word in ethico-aesthetic modernism that often pits aesthetic disruption against the anaesthetic (read deadening) dimensions of habit. It is meant—like the word anamorphosis—to call attention to aspects of habit and habit *formation* that resist and undermine the aesthetic mandate that informs most accounts of habit as an orthopaedic totality predicated on an organic and restitutive relationship of part to whole. Here, repetition, which plays such a crucial role in habit and aesthetics, is compulsive and divisive. These death-driven anaesthetic dimensions that are internal to habit simply cannot be mastered or equated to deadening.

My anaesthetics of habit concerns the resistances to mediation and fluid movement that are evidenced in Hegel's philosophy and certain lines of psychoanalytic thought and practice. More specifically, it draws on the "activity of separating" that is dramatically accounted for in Hegel's account of understanding (*Verstand*) in relation to reason (*Vernunft*) in the *Phenomenology of Spirit*. I would argue further that his account of habit in the *Philosophy of Mind*, and Lacan's dismantling of the basic coordinates of what he calls "transcendental aesthetics" in his *Seminar on Anxiety*—which I take as a treatise on habit that furthers the logic first explored in his account of the Mirror Stage—are both indicative of an activity of separating that disorients habit's given coordinates and coordination. Lacan's topological account of the non-relation between being and having is especially notable on this account.[55] Given the novel and film on which this book focuses, it is germane to note that Lacan specifically uses the terms *remnant* and *reste* ("remainder"/"residue") to refer to these deciduous "cut-offs"; these objects whose status escape the status of the object derived from the specular image.[56]

Lacan's anaesthetics is another instance of his return to Freud, and thus an elaboration of the latter's claim that psychoanalysis is precisely invested in the materials cast off by the other sciences: "the inconsiderable events which have been put aside by other sciences as being too unimportant—the dregs, one might say, of the world of phenomenon."[57] It is not, however, simply a matter of the unconscious dimensions of everyday life that other sciences do not take seriously—jokes, slips of the tongue, bungled actions—but rather the psychoanalytic insistence on a logic and technique of repetition, resistance, instability, failure, and meaninglessness that generate dregs in excess of the very analytic practices that dredge them up.

The anaesthetics of habit is also bound up with an ontology of waste—all the parts, units, and particularities that are generated by its compulsive repetitions that are often far in excess of its capacity to settle and sediment into solid ways of being. This anaesthetics is also fully in play in the movement and materiality of Hegel's speculative philosophy that can also be characterized in terms of a compulsion to repeat that generates cut-offs, parts, and dregs through its movement of the concept. If Hegel's "speculative sentence" (*spekulativer Satz*)—to which I shall return in chapter 1—is the paradigm of speculative movement as such, then it is important to note that *Satz* not only means a grammatical sentence or logical proposition but in common German usage also a jump or leap as well as dregs and grounds. What generates these grounds is the fact that Hegel's recursive figure of speculative movement, the "circle of circles" that "coils" and "winds" around itself, is just as much about abrupt jolts and cuts as fluidity and continuity, and its process of annulation produces all kinds of "off-cuts," static parts, fragments, and remainders that accumulate and bog down the "self-moving movement" of speculative thought as it is set in motion through an arrythmia of insistent halting.[58] As a result, the tempo and movement of the concept—and I would add habit—generates an odd kind of "static logic"—a term that is always used negatively to characterize the fixity of the subject that Hegel's speculative movement is meant to unfix and render fluid—that is habit's very echo chamber.[59] What I want to account for in my anaesthetics of habit is precisely the surplus matter, remainders, and repetitions that per-sever and precipitate like unsettled coffee grounds, and that never seem to settle down as the grounds for, or *arche* of, subjectivity. I want to take seriously and somewhat literally the idea that habit is "the residue of repetition" (Malabou), or, to use Tom McCarthy's wording, "the stain of being."[60] Of course, there is still a staging to this anaesthetics of habit, but it is more extreme, one-sided, topological, and perturbing than any discourse of habit's orthopaedic status can account for.

NO FOOTLIGHTS—ON STAGING THE SET-UP ERROR

For my purposes, a balanced and illuminating staging of the logic of habit as *breakdown* would be the ultimate distortion. I shall cast a much harsher light that will bring into stark relief all the rents, cracks, and fault lines that habit generates in its obstinance and inertia rather than a balanced, subtly modulated mise-en-scène of habit as a role model for plastic individuality. Fredric Jameson has encouraged us to think about Hegel's notion of positing (*Setzung*) not just in terms of conceptual and mental operations, such as presuppositions (*Voraussetzungen*), but also in the sense of theatrical settings or pro-filmic arrangements—of how such sets are set up, how props are propped up, how presuppositions are framed to produce their fictional effects. This immediately raises the question of exactly what kind of filmic set design and stagecraft is in question.

Jameson offers some rudimentary indication of how "certain depths are calculated, and an optical center also carefully provided, the laws of perspective invoked in order to strengthen the illusion to be achieved," and how the staging is illuminated by "lighting in foreground and background."[61] Although he never adheres to such staging himself, this dramaturgy sounds a bit too classical; an Albertian/Renaissance set up involving the measured regulation and distribution of bodies in one-point perspective as the precondition for a legible and dramatic content (*istoria*) to take place before the viewer's eye. Merleau-Ponty's invocation of theatrical staging in regard to habit describes this as a realm of darkness that would allow the performance of habit's gestalt figure/(back)ground structure to become salient.[62] In my account of habit, to quote Roland Barthes, "there are no footlights—this is an extreme theater. Whence the awkwardness—or, for some perverse types, the pleasure."[63] Whatever the case, this is emphatically not what Hegel might call a "theatre of happiness," which we would not even register, like habit proper operating behind the scenes in a "mute weaving of spirit."[64] In what follows, habit always manifests one of the chief characteristics of Hegel's "unhappy consciousness" (*das unglückliche Bewusstsein*) in that it remains "internally divided" (*in sich entzweite*), disrupted, and never adequately stabilized or restored by its own operations.[65]

Accordingly, my account of habit without the footlights embraces what Bruno Latour might call (pejoratively) a "set-up error," which results in a flawed staging or lighting in theatre. For Latour, this set-up error marks the fallibility of the moderns, who do not see the interconnectedness of things and thus tend to exaggerate one mode over and against another owing to the given lighting conditions that are artificially produced from a fixed onto-historical perspective. For my purposes, habit's fixation requires a hyperbolic narrowing down—a bit like the cinematic concept of "partial décor" that is utilized for the reenactments in the novel and film *Remainder*—in order to bring into full relief the fault lines, cracks, and stains created by habit's disturbing performance of anaesthetics (Rem, 120).[66]

In order to capture the lurid and "de-positing" aspects of habit in the following chapters, I shall embrace a good dose of "one-sidedness," "fixity," "isolation," "abstract negativity," and "picture-thinking"—precisely those qualities that Hegel warns us about, while simultaneously fixating on them, lest they wreak havoc on conceptual unity and internal connectivity, which are their purported sublation.[67] This Hegelian terminology will be worked through in the subsequent chapters, but perhaps it is worth noting that "abstract" in Hegelian terms means exclusive of its opposite, hence the one-sidedness, whereas "absolute" encompasses its opposite, and thus the latter is the ideal movement of speculative thought as it overcomes the static logic of the understanding and its sundering one-sidedness. Accordingly, my account of habit is fully invested in the anaesthetics of its static-generating logic and per-severing detachability, not to mention an attentiveness to the persistent invocation and repetition of the one-sided "figure of eight" in *Remainder*, and its correlates in Hegel's "circle of circles" and Lacan's "inner eight."

Habit without the footlights and the fly-wheel embodies all those conditions that exemplify "existence at its worst," and that are supposedly indicative of the abolition of freedom, such as automatism, rigidity, stuckness, resistance, and recalcitrance.[68] In this stark lighting, habit further strains existing accounts that acknowledge its tempered instability by characterizing it as a "weak generality" (Gilles Deleuze); "unity of essence and accident" (Catherine Malabou); "stable instability" (Tom Sparrow); "balanced off-balancedness" (Rebecca Gagan); "mastery of non-mastery" (Michael Taussig); or a "stabilized madness" (Ruda/Žižek).[69] Simply put, I want to push this per-severing logic of habit to its extreme implications.

HABIT, HEGEL, AND *REMAINDER*

The staging of habit's breakdown in this book features a short-circuiting encounter between Hegel's philosophy (of habit), psychoanalytic dimensions of repetition, Tom McCarthy's novel *Remainder*, first published by Metronome Press in 2005, and Omer Fast's feature-length film interpretation of the novel, also titled *Remainder* (2016). McCarthy and Fast are invested, to differing degrees, in all the issues that habit raises in relation to repetition, materiality, ontology, temporality, mediation, movement, persistence, mastery, transmission, pattern, disposition, virtuality, adaptability, inhabitation, failure, depositing, and death (not a comprehensive list by any means).[70] But McCarthy, at least, prefers to get at those issues through a trenchant critique of originality and authenticity—and through intellectual traditions that supposedly run counter to idealism in philosophy and idealist concepts of art. Thus, the terms "bad habit" and "second nature" appear only once in *Remainder*—and related terms for habit in a very select few other instances from his work (to which I will return)—however the notion of the "second-hand" is repeated throughout the text (Rem, 22, 24–26, 290). All I can say is that my way is through habit.

Remainder's obsession with the relationship between repetition and matter, subject and substance, fluidity and fixity, mediation and immediacy echoes—indeed amplifies and distorts—the odd materiality and strange temporality of Hegel's speculative movement in general and his account of habit in particular. In what follows, *Remainder*, psychoanalytic notions of repetition, and Hegel's philosophy of habit are not so much put into measured conversation with each other but rather form a turbulent echo chamber that results in a vertiginous overlapping and recoil that generates further repetitions, disturbances, and counterthrusts. Although my conception of habit is developed through such an enounter, it should be clear from the previous pages of this introduction that my aim is to develop a broader claim about the constitutively unsettling and disruptive aspects of habit.

At the beginning of *Remainder*, the unnamed narrator is involved in a terrible accident. He is hit by debris falling from the sky and subsequently loses most of his habitual actions that we take for granted. As a result, the movements in *Remainder*—grammatical, narrative, topological and bodily—are "repeating compulsively," "buffeting," "short-circuiting," and "jerking" back and forth (Rem, 9, 27, 44, 71, 102, 127, 180, 186). The narrator, who is called Tom in the film, is perpetually caught up in his own gestural tautology, as if his body is perpetually searching for itself in a coil of precipitation and delay, resulting in a constant state of bodily dispossession. He is pulled and torn between uncoordinated contractions that mark his spatiotemporal disconnection from people and things as matter and words spill forth, pool, and are drawn back into an abyss of ellipses, sentences that trail off, gestures and actions that fail to accomplish their goals, and the generation of "surplus matter" that is perpetually falling, spilling, and catching (Rem, 91). The narrator's condition never seems to improve or result in a stable disposition—a "being-at-home-with-oneself we call habit"—to use Hegel's ambivalently punctuated phrase.[71] Rather, he is set in motion as his body is stirred, perturbed, and buffeted by insistent remainders and grounds that are not soluble in the fluidity of a particular stance, action, grasp, or even a holding up. As such, *Remainder* is an unflinching exploration of a logic of habit and repetition that is about its unsettling of ontology, matter, and time rather than its stable ground.

After some moving descriptions of the narrator planning out his every step in order to achieve basic acts that we take for granted, like walking or picking up a carrot, he has a Proustian moment at a party in an acquaintance's apartment, triggered by a small crack in the plaster wall of a bathroom. This déjà vu moment invokes an intense feeling of an indeterminate space and time when he had a sense of seamlessness, fluidity, and "just being" that was not subject to the incessant detours, delays, and reroutings of "understanding" that he must now go through "after" the accident to undertake even the simplest of actions (Rem, 24, 61–73). In the wake of this defining "event," the narrator spends the money he receives as a settlement for the accident to "re-enact" his intense feeling of this "remembered building," in which his "movements had been fluent and unforced" (Rem, 64–67). He buys an apartment block (Madlyn Mansions) in the Brixton area of London, evicts the occupants, "half white and half West Indian," in a brutal act of further gentrification in order to reconstruct that space and inhabit it, and then hires "re-enactors" to repeat the scenes and conditions triggered by the déjà-vu moment that "spread outwards from the crack" (Rem, 66, 104).

As the novel proceeds, the narrator's compulsion to repeat intensifies to dizzying degrees, both within the apartment building and extending to many other scenes and events outside it. As his compulsions intensify, these repetitions and reenactments generate more anomalies, excesses, recalcitrant substances, and remainders that need to be taken up in further repetitions. After the final reenactment—a bank robbery that takes place in an actual bank (during working hours) thus attempting to merge the reenactment with the event—the narrator eventually tries to erase all remainders, including the annihilation of himself as an absolute remainder. In *Remainder*, the narrator's endless repetitions result in the utter destitution of subjectivity rather than its foundation and stabilization.

The word "speculation" is taken seriously by the narrator in *Remainder* who, like Hegel in his *Encyclopedia Logic* or Adorno in his *Lectures on Negative Dialectics*, ruminates on this "speculative word," including its non- or protophilosophical origins in terms of optics, wonder, finance, and as an exigency to press beyond the factual domain of the given (Rem, 46, 123–124, 157).[72] This is simply to say that speculation colors *Remainder* through and through, working its way into every aspect of the novel and the film, from its punctuation, grammar, sentence structure, and camera angles to its handling of matter, habit, gesture, movement, temporality, and finance. *Remainder* is a trenchant elaboration of the unsettling logic of Hegel's speculative sentence—the very paradigm of his speculative movement of spirit—that is characterized by its excessive overpunctuation, grammatical oddities, jarring recoils, incessant delays, precipitous leaps, abrupt jerking backing forth, buffeting, collapsing, spilling, and remaindering.[73]

Hegel's speculative sentence demands a speculative attitude to be set in motion, and repetition is at the heart of this way of reading. Like the protagonist's daemonic drive to repeat and reenact in *Remainder*, the movement of the Hegelian concept and the plotting of the dialectic—and I mean plotting in McCarthy's sense of "*discerning* … nodes and paths, tracing … bifurcations, switchbacks, junctions"—also occurs as a system of recursions, repetitions, and reenactments.[74] This is particularly true for habit, which is predicated on unifying a "great series of mediations" via repetition that is supposed to result in a self-posited immediacy that is the "simple bond of all these mediations."[75] In *Remainder*, however, the narrator's "compulsion to re-enact" generates so many units, pieces, gestures, steps, surplus matter, and deviations that he is perpetually stuck (Rem, 186). He can never generate a simple bond of mediated immediacy, despite all his dreams of fluidity and cutting out the gaps and detours that make him "completely second-hand" (Rem, 54). If habit is the conversion of the particular or contingent accident into a nominal universality that then becomes an internal necessity—the soul's body becoming "an accident brought into harmony with its substance"—then this trajectory never seems to be accomplished in the novel or film.[76] The narrator is never tempered or ortho-organized in ways that would internalize these incessantly repeated accidents into a stable form of life.

Thus, my reference to a short-circuiting encounter between *Remainder*, psychoanalytic notions of repetition, and Hegel's speculative philosophy is not meant as a loose metaphor. In fact, the very terms "short-circuited" and "circuit" are explicitly invoked throughout the novel, and resonate with other related words and terms, in ways that do justice to the temporal and material aspects of its topological implications, which can account for both infinite deviations, recoils, delays, and circlings *and* brutal cuts, gaps, and precipitous leaps (Rem, 27, 64, 102). These cuts and glitches are also a feature of Omer Fast's film and Dirk Dresselhaus's (Schneider TM) riveting and machinic musical score, which is another insistent and spectral instantiation of the static logic of repetition and habit in *Remainder*. This logic of cutting in, out, and off results in brutal coincidences of overflowing and emptying out that constitute the unsettling paroxysms of matter that habit generates through its repetitions.[77] *Remainder*'s per-severing account of the eternal "detour through understanding" is an important aspect of my rethinking of habit and a compelling way to reimagine the vexed role of understanding in relationship to habit and repetition—one that I undertake in chapter 2 via the crucial relationship between *Verstand* ("understanding") and *Vernunft* ("reason") in Hegel's speculative philosophy (Rem, 22–23, 152). My aim, however, is not simply to engage in a Hegelian reading of *Remainder* but rather to further emphasize the instabilities and "lines of 'fragilization" already inherent in Hegel's account of habit through my reading of the novel and film.[78]

Reading Tom McCarthy's novel alongside Omer Fast's film has been important for my account of habit. To use a striking image from the novel, this pairing is like a ball repeatedly kicked against a wall, such that the distance between the wall and the kicker manifests as a cracking reverberation that establishes both a "delay" and a "near-overlap" with its "source," thus disturbing the ability to clearly distinguish between cause and effect (Rem, 142). After an initial and intense exchange of ideas between McCarthy and Fast, the film was developed independently with Fast's own vision, such that they supplement each other in provocative ways. These supplements include the fifty-pence coin passed back and forth between the actors in the film, which further explores the issues of surplus and senseless matter along with finance capital, which resists smooth circulation and is never made entirely soluble in any currency that may be fluidly exchanged. Fast's film also features a young boy who appears to Tom during his déjà vu moment in the bathroom at Madlyn Mansions and who reappears whenever Tom feels fluid and "everything is right"—what the narrator characterizes as "just being" (Rem film, 39:00:04; Rem, 24). This boy usually appears out of focus and blurred, registering the gaps and divisions in the ontology of habit, as well its impersonal and indeterminate aspects, rather than functioning as a simple visual analogy for a distorted vision or memory.

Fast also intensifies the novel's obsession with death, firearms, and forensic procedures by including a film noir-like murder plot, thus recalling Hegel's claim in the *Phenomenology of Spirit* that all conceptual understanding is equivalent to a murder. This point is directly made by McCarthy and Simon Critchley in relationship to Hegel and language in their earlier collaborative work as the International Necronautical Society, a project about the vehicles and crafts for staging and inhabiting death through the repetition and reenactment of motifs and moments from the historical avant-garde.[79] Habit always invokes death, murder, and violence at its own hands—as Hegel makes clear—just as any death-driven compulsion to repeat does not stabilize the subject but is always a matter of its vacillation and self-divestiture. Habit's cadence, tempo, and material existence in *Remainder* is more akin to a faulty catching mechanism that wrenches the self from itself rather than to a stabilization of oneself.

I have already drawn attention to Fredric Jameson's interpretation of Hegel's "positing" in terms of "theatrical settings or pro-filmic arrangements." If there is a *cinematic* form of picture-thinking in Hegel's philosophy—a connection that Adorno astutely calls attention to—then perhaps it is more like an unruly or failed cinema, whose movement might be characterized as a reeling mechanism—the filmic version of a Hegelian "circle of circles," the circling movement of the psychoanalytic drive, or what *Remainder* terms "looping back" in the form of a "figure of eight" (Rem, 137, 226, 268). This mechanism is perpetually catching, overturning, twisting, cutting out, getting stuck between frames, and spooling in unruly and entangling recoils. It is either reeling too fast or too slow (or both simultaneously) to convert those individual cells/frames/pictures into a fluid cinematic movement. This reeling tempo is at stake in both Hegel and *Remainder* and manifests in the perpetual detours, delays, and speeding up that the narrator/Tom demands of himself and the reenactors. To get a feel for this tempo, we need to superimpose Adorno's observation that the reader of the *Phenomenology of Spirit* is required "to develop an intellectual slow-motion procedure," and Catherine Clément's suggestion that "we might engage in a speeded-up reading of the dialectic, the way a cartoon film could show it," as if a "mad filmmaker" had decided to bring *Science of Logic* to the screen.[80] This jerky tempo—an insistent feature in *Remainder*—recalls Rebecca Comay's evocative characterization of Hegel's speculative sentence as "driving with the brake and gas pedal at the same time."[81]

The constant tarrying with all the parts, pieces, and picture-thinking in Hegel's movement of the concept contributes to the sluggishness and inertia of the *Phenomenology of Spirit*, just as the sheer accumulation of matter—and the inscriptional techniques that render its proliferation in the novel and film—overwhelms the narrator. Habit's sundering actions generate ever more surplus matter and an increasing demand for new acts of *rend(er)ing* that bury the narrator in endless chains of remediation. The perpetual delays, detours, tarrying, and falling behind in *Remainder* also require precipitous acts of acceleration, such that these two movements never catch up and thus the habitual body never quite "catches on" (to resort to a phenomenological vocabulary often invoked in discussions of habit). Rather, it is perpetually entangling itself in a recoil of precipitation and delay. The compulsion to repeat in Hegel and *Remainder* generates a multitude of cuts that produce ever more "surplus matter" that is never adequately bound, sublated, or digested into a unified action or absolute gesture of grasping itself (Rem, 91). This repetition automatism calls attention to the quasi-automatic character of the movement of spirit in Hegel's *Phenomenology*—a point that is emphasized in his characterizations of habit as a mechanism of self-feeling or a spiritual mechanism—and to a persevering reeling movement that intimately connects habit to the novel, film, and the filmic dimensions of the *Phenomenology of Spirit*.[82]

A LOGIC OF BREAKDOWN

Perhaps the word "breakdown" best captures this dual sense of habit's sundering and collapse.[83] The logic of breakdown is at work in the relentless subdivisions and multiple repetitions that are primary features of the reenactments in *Remainder*. Such an understanding of habit echoes with some recent accounts of the *Phenomenology of Spirit* that argue that it is much more of an anti-bildungsroman than a bildungsroman, characterized by anxiety, despair, failure, brokenness, and delay. This is due in no small part to the sheer accumulation of all the shapes of consciousness, way stations, and deviations that the speculative movement generates and that are well beyond spirit's capacity to absorb, incorporate, or transmit.[84]

The discomposure and breakdown that I am trying to engage with receives its most devastating articulation in Hegel's Preface to the *Phenomenology of Spirit*: "Spirit only wins its truth by finding its feet in its absolute disruption."[85] This is echoed in an earlier and deceptively gentler Wittgensteinian-sounding aphorism derived from Hegel's aptly titled "Wastebook," dating from the Jena period: "The questions which philosophy does not answer are answered in that they should not be so posed."[86] In fact, the very terms "breakdown" and "breaking down" are important in Hegel's vocabulary (see next chapter) and this logic of breakdown, I argue, is central to the subject matter of habit itself.

The anxiety-ridden nature of habit is predicated on a drive to make and unmake in vertiginous ways that do not balance out. In fact, habit is more akin to an unbearable contradiction that resists mediation. In the following chapters, I shall explore habit's affinity with Hegelian notions of understanding, judgment, infection, vanishing, kenosis, magic, non-actuality, derangement, anxiety, abstract negativity, one-sidedness, rigidity, externality, and staining. These notions highlight the temporal and material resistances to mediation that are generated by mediation's detours but which are never dialectically unified or interiorized such that the sublation of mediation by mediation into the simple unity and immediacy of habit is never achieved. I focus on extreme states of stuckness, recalcitrance, and resistance to movement, fluidity, and change thus paying attention to the specific *anaesthetic* qualities that habit as breakdown generates—all those grindings, catchings, shreddings, frictions, static, bits, parts, glitches, poolings, and viscosities that stain *Remainder* through and through. The anaesthetics of habit might indicate the grounds by which we are driven to breakdown, thus allowing us to see how we are mediated out of existence by the ways we are taken hold of—by ourselves and others—so we can begin to imagine how to not only break down but also out. (Of course, this requires us to think differently about what "out" would mean here.)[87]

SUBJECT MATTER AND HABIT

The term "subject matter" (*die Sache selbst*) in the title of this book is incessantly repeated in Hegel's writings.[88] There is no precise, stable, or consistent translation of *die Sache selbst* into English, nor is there one meaning of this phrase in Hegel's philosophy. H. S. Harris calls attention to this polysemy in his introduction to a collective translation of chapter 6 of the *Phenomenology of Spirit*, where the term appears frequently, as it does in the Preface and other key sections in the *Phenomenology*. Fredric Jameson characterizes the phrase as an "untranslatable German expression" although, like many others, he recognizes the imperative of that untranslatability and offers a few translations of it himself: "the point," "the main issue," "the main thing," "the matter at hand," "the heart of the matter." Rocío Zambrana adds quite a few more: "the thing itself," "the real thing," "matters themselves," "the subject matter," "the thing that matters," and "reality."[89] Terry Pinkard's new translation of the *Phenomenology of Spirit* identifies a few more translations not mentioned above—"the point of it all" and "what is at stake"—and adds a new one into the mix, which he favors throughout: "the crux of the matter," which I shall return to in my discussion of the topology of the figure eight movement that is a striking feature of *Remainder* and its plotting.[90]

For my purposes, "subject matter" is taken as a felicitous term to describe the explications of subject and substance in Hegel's speculative philosophy and the strange matter that habit generates in its grounding of the subject. The notion of a subject emerging from substance is in many ways at the core of Hegel's philosophy and is best captured in an important and oft-cited sentence from the Preface to the *Phenomenology of Spirit*: "everything hangs on grasping and expressing the true not just as *substance* but just as much as *subject*."[91] This passage is sometimes read as damning evidence of Hegel's identity thinking that is predicated on a notion of the subject as an absolute master of a process of going outside itself and coming home to itself; a way—in which habit plays a crucial role—of overcoming alienation and otherness. This most clichéd and extreme version of Hegel is well-known: he is a completely closed and circular thinker whose philosophical idealism is, in essence, a narcissistic system that swallows, subsumes, and sublates all difference, otherness, fixity, and resistance as mere moments in spirit's incessant forward and upward movement of self-identity. From this perspective, Hegelian philosophy is an idealism that purges all difference, (base) materiality, and exteriority as they are *aufgehoben* in the relentless teleological and totalizing movement of speculative thinking. One of the primary places where this rhythm is played out is in habit and its legacy of second nature that mediates our relationship between subject and object, interior and exterior, allowing us to become at home in the world.[92]

My reading of the relationship between subject and substance in habit does not see it as evidence of identity thinking but rather of a *kenotic* relationship that puts pressure on any sense of habit as a second nature that would mediate the exteriority and recalcitrance of matter in and as fluidity. Hegel's major discussion of habit in the *Philosophy of Mind* is concerned with soul, which is a "stage" that occurs when spirit is still bound to its unruly natural grounds, and thus habit never simply self-posits itself in ways that adequately stabilize this exteriority of matter and drives. Rather, habit is a further elaboration and generation of those disturbances, and thus it fails to restore the unity of subject and predicate that Hegel claims it does in taking possession of the body, enabling it to become an "ideal subjective substantiality" of its corporeity instead of its mere substance.[93]

Subjective spirit often fails to accomplish the unity of particular and universal by reducing the particulars to a mere feature of its being through the effects of habit, resulting in the latter's manifestation as a "nominal universality" in a singular and actual body.[94] Habit generates the production of an odd and unruly subject matter due to it being caught between the extremes of its entanglement in particularity and its seizure by universality via automatism. Thus, habit never emerges from its perturbed ground within which the I precipitously makes its appearance, first as a kind of proto- or pre-Fichtean (weak) willing in the description of habit as a self-positing, or at the end of the account of habit in the *Philosophy of Mind* when the "I" appears like a lightning flash that transfigures soul into a more spirit-like substance. In my account, habit is never able to adequately stabilize and coordinate the unruly relationship between subject and substance, and thus it is not simply the first stable manifestation of a coherent self. I want to account for how the subject matter of habit "actualizes" (*verwirklicht*) as a persistent, "non-actual" (*unwirkliche*) desease rather than an ease.

Remainder is a compelling account of the unruly materiality that habit generates through its repetitions and reenactments. Habit remains a "crux of the matter": an irresolvable difficulty, an oddly immaterial resistance, and a vertiginous crossing that comes to its breaking point in *Remainder* via the topology of the figure eight and its fixation at the intersection of its circle of circles (see chapter 4). Just as the anthropologist Claude Lévi-Strauss remains the central inspiration for the main protagonist in McCarthy's subsequent novel *Satin Island*, for my purposes Hegel's speculative anthropology of habit—which pushes at the limit of any anthropology—is at the crux of the matter in *Remainder*.[95]

This conception of subject as substance and substance as subject challenges any presumed stabilizing function of habit as a *hexis* that emerges from second nature. The relationship of subject to substance in *Remainder* is not one of appropriation, incorporation, and interiorization, but rather the mutual disruption, absolving, and *kenosis* of the "sub" in both subject and substance that produces habit in and as a strange subject matter. Any substance that habit calls forth—not to mention the potential but hardly necessary subjectivities emerging from such subject matter—is perpetually sub-emerging from a materiality that is constitutively cracked self-sundering, drilling, and emptying.

KENOSIS AND THE STAINED SOUL OF HABIT

Remainder's process of generating surplus matter and its precipitous emptying out is best described by the Greek word *kenosis*, translated by Hegel as *Entäußerung* in the *Phenomenology of Spirit*. *Entäußerung* and its variants are ubiquitous in Hegel's writings, and have been translated into English as "exteriorization," "externalization," "relinquishing," "self-emptying," "objectifying," "realizing," or "alienating." I prefer to work toward an interpretation of this concept that emphasizes it in terms of overflowing, spilling out, and staining.[96] *Entäußerung* or *entäußern* and its variants appear twenty-eight times in the culminating short section on "Absolute Knowing," in which Hegel's philosophy has been interpreted to be at the summit of its totalizing, interiorizing, and enclosing tendencies. Thus, this section has often been the focus for readings of Hegel as a vulgarly teleological thinker of digested and accomplished knowledge without remainder or difference. But it is precisely in this culminating section in which spirit is at its fullest expression where this emptying out of subject and substance is fully dramatized, resulting in an exteriority that spills out and stains. My emphasis on these dimensions in *Remainder* resonate with these and other passages in Hegel, such as the sections on the beautiful soul in the *Phenomenology of Spirit*, in which issues of spilling out, staining, and vanishing are addressed. Thus, kenosis is not the incarnation and unity of the finite and infinite, or the full spiritualization of matter, but rather where spirit is "divested of itself"—to use an alternate translation of *veräußerten* that Pinkard offers in a footnote instead of the standard "alienation."[97]

The modes of kenosis in *Remainder* that I explore involve the excessive generation of matter through repetition and its simultaneous voiding and spilling out that begin to address the strange materiality of habit that does not provide any stable, consistent subject matter. Kenosis is key to the anaesthetics of habit's strange subject matter that cannot be equated with alienation and subsequent acts of interiorization. Through incessant acts of kenosis, habit voids itself by spilling out, staining, and getting stuck on these sedimentations, thus demonstrating how it is an act of *remaindering*. This self-emptying and depositing sense of the subject as substance is the photographic negative of the language of self-engendering and self-positing that Hegel mobilizes in his account of habit. *Remainder*'s trenchant exploration of habit as a profound failure to mediate is marked by a simultaneous logic of overflowing and emptying out that is generated by its repetitions.

I am particularly interested in the excess matter generated by kenosis and its techniques, that wrench not only the body away from itself, but also matter from its own consistency, thus causing it to spill, overflow, and pool. Often this is due to the body being seized rather than any tempered possession of it. At times, these contractions are so abrupt that they can manifest as disconnection—from our own bodies, gestures, actions, or words, or from other people and the environment—and my account is attentive to this kenotic anaesthetics of the "cut-off" and "cast-off."[98] These repetition and reenactment compulsions generate excess matter *and* empty the body of meaning rather than cultivating it in the Merleau-Pontyean sense of the body as "a grouping of lived-through meanings which moves toward its equilibrium."[99] The constant vanishing and reappearing of this unruly kenotic excess produces the "un-matter" in *Remainder* that is central to the unsettling logic of habit as breakdown that I pursue throughout the book (Rem, 171).

(CHAPTER) BREAKDOWN

Remainder begins with a terrible accident. In chapter 1, I explore this inaugural scene in close detail. The unnamed narrator of the novel—named Tom in Fast's film—is hit by "something falling from the sky. Technology. Parts, bits," and subsequently loses most of the habitual actions that we take for granted (Rem, 3). The accident creates "a white slate," "a black hole," or a "crater" from which the novel takes its inaugural and compulsive repetitions that are carried through in the numerous reenactments that are its primary feature (Rem, 3). The indeterminate *cause* of the accident suggests that this traumatic event does not simply come from the outside. What we are witnessing in this opening scene is also the grounding (down), unsettling, and foundering of the subject through the autodislocating and pulverizing effects of habit and its repetitions. The subject arrives in and as a failure to consolidate, owing to the recoil of the body from itself as it registers its own expiration in and through habit. Throughout the novel and film, the narrator/Tom's accident is incessantly repeated and reenacted—not simply because once traumatized we are prone to being retraumatized, although this is surely true—but rather because this "re-" is inaugural and the inherent traumaticity of habit as our emergence into subjectivity is never simply over and done with. After the bits and pieces crash through the glass atrium in the film—and after a significant temporal delay and suspension between the falling debris and its impact—Tom is "hit." He is flattened out on the pavement and barely identifiable within the heap of aggregate debris. This remarkable opening scene in the film elaborates a sentence that occurs very early on in the novel: "I have vague images, half-impressions: of being, or having been—or, more precisely, being *about* to be—hit" (Rem, 3).

I argue that this sentence should be read as a speculative sentence—as should the novel as a whole—which is the paradigm of Hegel's speculative movement of spirit as articulated in the Preface to the *Phenomenology*. If a standard predicative sentence consists of the externality of the relations of subject and predicate such that the substantive subject independently and passively supports the *accidents* of its contents (predicates), then a speculative sentence enunciates a more disturbing entanglement of subject and predicate, in which reading, repetition, and habit play a crucial role. The disruptive and disturbing aspects of habit are further elaborated in terms of the anxiety-ridden relationship of being and having that is crucial to all accounts of habit and to the speculative sentence.

The speculative sentence is precisely where the coinciding of subject and substance is relentlessly overpunctuated and ground down, and where it founders in a repetitive recoiling and self-division that is pursued down to the level of the sentence, word, grammar, and punctuation mark in *Remainder*. Here I put forth a different interpretation of Hegel's notion of the "fixed subject" and its "static logic" in relation to habit's logic of breakdown that is attentive to its modes of de-positing, division, detour, delay, and collapse. This breakdown is linked to habit as a material, ontological and temporal form of the death drive and dead time. Habit and its repetitions in *Remainder* are compulsive rather than measured and thus do not engender stability. Habit as the "not yet self" (Hegel) that is caught up in its repetitions, divisions, and endless circling imparts the body with a strange temporality such that it never quite catches up to itself or catches on and is often at the brink of collapse. The final section of the chapter circles back to the inaugural accident through McCarthy's account of Sophie Ristelhueber's *Fait #60* from his storyline for an exhibition of seven works of art from the "la Caixa" Collection, *Empty House of the Stare*, that in many ways not only reenacts and repeats the opening scene of *Remainder* but also a striking paragraph from the *Phenomenology* on crashing and collapse that I highlight in its relationship to habit as breakdown.

In chapter 2, I explore how habit in Hegel and *Remainder* generates parts and excess matter rather than incorporating them into a fluid and unified action. In Hegel's anthropology, habit is supposed to repair and restore the fluidity of the body that has been blocked by the fixity and fixations generated by bodily disease and mental derangement. But rather than repair bodily fluidity, habit actually doubles down on the issue of fixity and disease—or as I shall be calling it, desease—as it fails to mediate the immediacy and immersion in particularity that is a feature of Hegel's account of mental and physical derangement. After the accident, the narrator in *Remainder* is forced to make an eternal "detour through understanding," and all his reenactments are meant to "cut out the detour" so he can be immersed in and be at one with his actions. However, all the reenactments that he performs never overcome this detour to achieve the goal of fluidity, as his experiences create ever more detours, delays, repetitions, and excess matter. The narrator repeatedly breaks each sequence of a reenactment down to its constituent parts, not in order to fix the problem but rather to proliferate and "relish" all the way stations that supposedly comprise habit as a unified way of being (Rem, 161–162).

I explore this contradiction at the heart of *Remainder* via Hegel's speculative account of the relationship between understanding (*Verstand*) and reason (*Vernunft*). *Verstand* is a hyperanalytic mode of thinking and finite cognition that is characterized by dividing, isolating, distancing, abstracting, parting, atomizing, anatomizing, dissecting, and, in its more frenzied and brutal Dionysian manifestations, by a tearing apart and dismembering. In contrast to these analytic divisions and abrupt separations, speculative reason is the ability to see the fluid/organic interconnectedness and plastic exposition of these dead parts as dialectical moments in the "self-moving movement" of the life of spirit. But the plotting of *Remainder* shows us that the narrator's supposed ideal of inhabitation without remainder or detour is an impossibility because understanding's power of mortification—its capacity to cut out, cut off, and separate, and its consequent generation of circuitous detours, repetitions, incorrigible deviations, incessant delays, and material excess—is internal to habit itself and thus cannot be outplayed. It is precisely the incisive and mortifying aspects of understanding in habit that generate a sundered body rather than a lived body that is at peace with the given unifying and mediating functions of habit. The cunning nature of understanding in *Remainder* forces us to revisit and revise the given phenomenological accounts of habit and bodily understanding. Throughout this chapter I am attentive to the persevering quality of habit in Hegel and *Remainder* that manifest in an obsession with all modes of cutting, spilling and staining, that range from an automaticity in overdrive to forensic procedures to the short-circuiting aesthetics of the infinite judgment.

In chapter 3, I further explore the anaesthetics of the narrator's bodily anxiety as it registers an overproximity of the habitual body rocked by its own eruptive bond. It is a further exploration of the habitual body that is buffeted by its own perturbations, a condition predicated on the fact that habit does not settle or sediment all the particular steps, units, excess, and senseless matter that it is supposed to gather and canalize in a smooth, continuous, and unified way. Habit rivets us to our bodies, relentlessly exposing us to its temporal and material disruptions. The narrator's last clear memory before the accident is "being buffeted by wind" twenty or so minutes before he was hit by the falling debris (Rem, 7). This "buffeting" scene is repeated throughout the novel and film whenever the narrator has a feeling of being at one with and seamlessly immersed in his actions.

At first glance, these moments seem to be where the narrator is touched by the grace of habit such that the dead weight of externality and otherness has been quickened with spirit (*begeistet*).[100] But the words used to describe these moments, such as "buffeted," "static," and "tingling" are speculative and hold unbearable tensions within them. These turbulences vibrate the body and unsettle any immersion and fluidity as the narrator is impinged by surplus excitations and drives generated by repetitions that are in excess of any binding and incorporation. This condition hardly results in a comforting and stable disposition, or the fluidity of "being at-home-with-oneself in habit," but rather it is more akin to being suspended within the body's inability to settle into its acts and inclinations. This chapter offers a counterscenario to accounts of habit that overemphasize it as a process of bodily sedimentation and ingraining that disavows the corporeal inconsistency that habit generates.

In the second part of the chapter, I focus on the obsession with the grasping "second-hand" in *Remainder*, Hegel, and Freud. In so doing, I show how the concept of habit gets caught up in its own excess materiality such that it is no longer able to get a grasp on itself and its ability to handle its own otherness. The concept (*Begriff*) is crucial for Hegel's speculative philosophy, as is, by extension, conceptually comprehending thinking (*das begreifende Denken*). *Begriff* can be translated as both "concept" and "grasp or grip," and the verb *begreifen* incorporates *greifen*, which means "to grasp" or "to seize." These speculative resonances are of a piece with Hegel's philosophy of the hand that is addressed in his *Science of Logic*, *Encyclopedia Logic*, *Philosophy of Nature*, *Philosophy of Mind*, and *Elements of the Philosophy of Right*. There is rarely any sustained or detailed attempt to explore the anaesthetic dimensions of these terms as they manifest themselves in the grasping hand in Hegel *and* with an attentiveness to specific literary, visual, and artistic manifestations (the same does not hold true for the importance of the hand in Deleuze or Heidegger).[101]

I put Hegel's concept of grasping and his philosophy of the hand in conversation with Freud's notion of *bungled action* (*Vergreifen*), and the insistent, per-severing "second-hand" in *Remainder*, paying close attention to the prefix *ver-* that is ubiquitous in Freud and Hegel's terminology—for example, in *Verstand* (understanding) and *Vernunft* (reason) that I explore in chapter 2—and which means both "carrying through" and "deviation from." These scenes of the hand make clear that habit is a part-body that never really unifies due to its non-actuality that disrupts any (virtually) coordinating body image. The chapter concludes with a detour through an act of picture-thinking that actualizes the odd material, spatial, and temporal qualities of habit's subject matter. It focuses on Jules Bastien-Lepage's painting *Jeanne d'Arc* (1879), featured in Ben Lerner's novel 10:04, where the future saint's left hand creates a "glitch in the pictorial matrix" that resists unified bodily incorporation and pictorial unity thus attesting to habit as an unbearable contradiction rather than a "firm holding together."

In the concluding chapter, I circle back (again) and work through some of the major terms and issues that are central to my account of habit and repetition. I further explore the unsettling matter that habit generates through the topological "figure of eight" that is repeatedly invoked in *Remainder*. *Remainder*'s obsession with the figure eight is hardly surprising given McCarthy's specific understanding of plot and narrative that is not driven by psychological depth or content but rather geometry and topology. In *Remainder*, the figure eight's incessant, one-sided overturning through its circuits of repetition generates the strange subject matter of habit as an evacuating non-actuality that McCarthy characterizes as "un-matter," a "material negative," or the Real of matter. Like the materiality generated in psychoanalysis, the matter that habit always returns us to is shot through with negativity, gaps, senseless signifiers, virtuality, and spectrality. I put these aspects of *Remainder* into conversation with Hegel's account of the soul in (second) nature as a "universal immaterialism," his "circle of circles," and Lacan's "inner eight." The repetitious and looping movements in *Remainder* perpetually drive open the closed loop of habit by doubling, crossing, and twisting it, thus creating cuts and openings *within* its absolute immanence and self-closure from which matter is generated and emptied out in a kenotic insistence that prevents the subject matter of habit from settling or ingraining as a solid ground or foundation. In *Remainder* this topology is often deadly and more like an accident site than an arc of action, movement, or gesture that one might fluidly inhabit. Simply put, it is a *disinhabiting ring*.

Perhaps the oddities of matter are at their most disturbing in *Remainder* when massive amounts of matter magically vanish and vaporize, only to gush forth and overflow with even more insistence. *Remainder* is a trenchant intensification of the vocabulary of *Verschwinden* in Hegel's speculative philosophy; that is to say, it is a vanishing of the vanishing of the vanishing ... that manifests as a kenotic drive that resists incorporation and mediation. This is a notion of kenosis that does not come to an end but rather keeps on opening and spilling beyond the end like that of *Remainder*, in which the "end" is thrown back to arrive at the beginning of an accident, breakdown, and collapse that has always already happened and has yet to happen. In a hyperbolic logic of the not yet arriving at the beginning, the repetition of all these "turning backs" in *Remainder* throws us back to the beginning again so that we might free the ending from its routine framework. We do so not by exiting habit—or avoiding the extreme implications of the autopilot of automaticity at the heart of habit—but by collapsing into its logic of breakdown so that we might break down differently into the unbearabilities that catch us up.

1

FALLING STUFF

FALLING STUFF AND THE DESTITUTION OF SUBJECTIVITY

Remainder begins with the non recollection of a terrible accident (Rem, 3). The unnamed narrator of the novel—named Tom in Omer Fast's film—was hit by "something falling from the sky. Technology. Parts, bits" (Rem, 3). He subsequently loses most of the fluid and habitual actions that one normally takes for granted (figures 1.1 and 1.2). A catastrophe literally befalls him, but we are never given the source of these broken parts and bits, and thus we can never locate the determinate cause of the disaster on which the novel is premised: "Just got hit by a falling ... falling stuff, you know" (Rem, 32). The indeterminate cause of the accident suggests that this inaugural trauma does not simply come from the outside. In the sentence above, the ellipsis points punctuate the indeterminacy of the cause and object of the narrator's fall into a stuttering tautology of two gerund-like participles that generate an indeterminacy within the flow of time through an "incessant immanence" that is "eternally arriving."[1] As a consequence, we should not assume that this fall is caused by some predetermined object or that the narrator's condition is a fall *from* any preexisting state of plasticity. His collapse is neither solely caused by some external source, nor is it a fall from a previous state of balance or bodily unity.

The parts and bits that fall from the sky at the start of the novel are not simply debris that have broken off and fallen from a determinate and wholly identified technological object. They do not necessarily issue from an airplane that has crashed, a building crane that has toppled over, or an orbiting satellite. Rather, these parts and bits are unhinged and subtracted from any preestablished contextual coordinates. *Remainder* is therefore not simply an exemplary case of the loss of habitual action as a result of a traumatic accident from the outside. Nor is it a complicated bildungsroman of the partial or total recovery of a previously "plastic" body that has been disturbed by a brutal and contingent external accident, necessitating the subsequent travails of "reparative plasticity" or, in a more destructive sense, an exemplary account of the "new

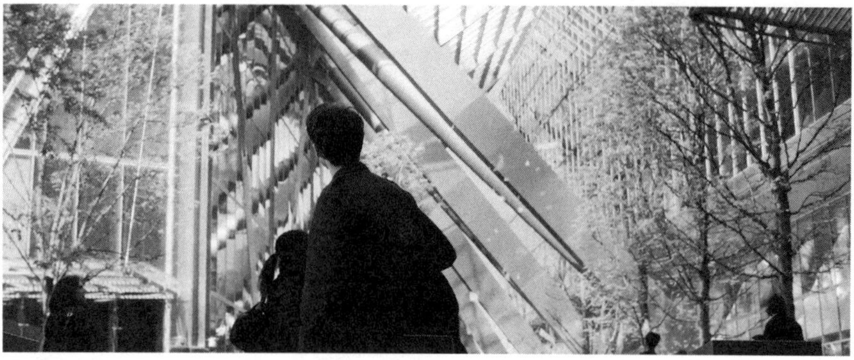

FIGURE 1.1
Shards of glass descending like snowflakes. Film still from Omer Fast's *Remainder*. © Omer Fast.

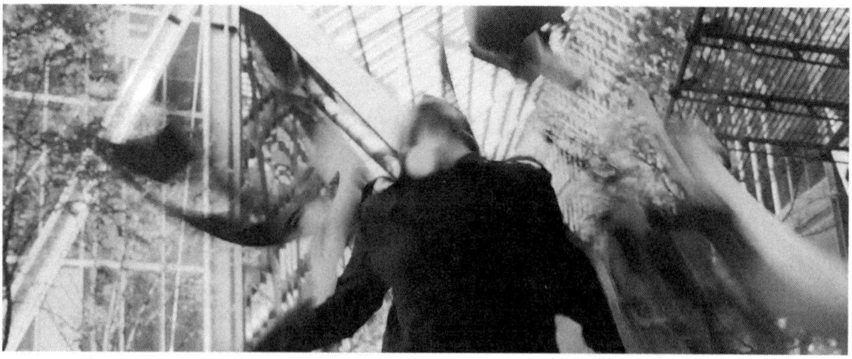

FIGURE 1.2
Tom being hit by "something" falling from the sky. Film still from Omer Fast's *Remainder*. © Omer Fast.

wounded," who survive their ordeal brutally sundered and erased from their prior form of subjectivity that is characterized by "disruption of habits" and the "tragic loss of life skills" and marked by an emotional coldness and indifference. *Remainder* is not merely a genre of "neurofiction," although it is no doubt tempting to read *Remainder* as fundamentally about the "omnipresent possibility ... of undergoing and surviving a senseless, random, unforeseeable neuro-trauma eventuating in an ontogenetically unprecedented post-traumatic subjectivity," to use Adrian Johnston's useful description of Malabou's account of destructive plasticity.[2] Despite the exceptional traumatic accident that befalls the narrator at the start of the novel/film, *Remainder* shows that habit is a fundamentally uncanny and extimate desease at the heart of the subject. It is a repetitive operation generative of material, temporal, and psychic disruption that is not exceptional but is rather an often disavowed, quotidian familiarity that trips us up more often than we would like to admit. The narrator is not unusual, as his friend Greg points out, but rather "just more usual than everyone else," a point with which he concurs and universalizes: "Other people really were like me; they just didn't know they were" (Rem, 24, 28).

The accident in *Remainder* creates a "black hole" or "crater," from which the novel takes its inaugural and compulsive repetitions (Rem, 3). It is important to note that the accident that blows a crater in the narrator—and in the very act of narration—is also a crater blown within matter itself—an irruption that is both an overflowing and a hollowing out—and thus, in a repetition of a repetition, we have a crater emerging from a crater.[3] This double convulsion and dislocation inaugurates the novel's repetitions that persistently spew forth the myriad sticky and viscous substances in, and by which, the subject is caught up. The subject as "crater" is simultaneously spilling forth excess matter and voiding himself; the site of a perpetual self-emptying that is truly kenotic (see chapter 4). In doing so, the *sub* in *substance* and *subject* never accomplishes an adequate balance between the drive for preservation and exposure to the outside in order to generate habit as a necessary accident.

If, as Bachelard writes, "the individual is essentially nothing but a sum of accidents and, what is more, that sum is itself accidental,"[4] then we need to see that sum not as the correct answer to an addition of one thing to another, but rather more as a heap of externality with no internal binding agent. The habitual subject remains tethered to substance's own self-alienation; a matter in which it remains mired and which never stops overflowing its limits throughout the novel and film. "Tripped … up again" and again by matter, the subject in *Remainder* emerges as a buckled material and temporal relief of fractures, cracks, and overflowing craters that are in excess of any closure, grounding, or foundation (Rem, 282).

In an early statement of the International Necronautical Society, McCarthy and Simon Critchley insist that "thinking begins with a disaster—or, more precisely, with the forgotten origin of a trauma that clefts the self in twain and in whose ripples all subsequent thinking must find its counters."[5] In many ways, their claim is not only a rudimentary definition of the Lacanian Real; it is also, from my perspective, a good definition of habit itself as an "inner impediment" (Hegel) or a "nascent alienation" (Ricoeur) that cleaves the self rather than an orthopedic procedure that fills, veils, or ignores its own gaps. In *Remainder*, repetition is an incessantly dividing, fragmenting, and evacuating actuality that perturbs and buffets the body, inaugurating all manner of collapse and breakdown. If the "propensity to repeat" is generated by traumatic rupture and interruption, as McCarthy notes, the effect of that repetition is not necessarily stabilizing and unifying, as many accounts of habit would have it, in emphasizing how we are "appropriated to universality" by repetition, thus establishing our first stable form of self as "simple self-relating unity."[6] Instead, we might ask, does repetition itself in fact generate the rupture? For it is precisely the nature of habit to forget its origin and pass out of time—due to its automatic repetitions (the way it is appropriated to universality)—and become "more and more impersonal, more and more foreign" in a way that can remain within us as delay, automaticity, inertia, intransitivity, thingness, and inner otherness.[7]

Habit shares a strange not yet ontology with the psychoanalytic drive in its compulsion to repeat, its circular movement, and its odd atemporal temporality. This results in a suspension of time that curves and circles back, such that beginning and ending endlessly loop in ways that disrupt any given notions of before and after, cause and effect, inside and outside, or behind and in front. *Remainder*'s opening scenes give a different inflection to the Hegelian term "turning back" (*Rückkehr*); Tom is perpetually flattened, lying prone and barely visible within a heap of debris as per the first scene.[8] The accident is not simply a falling *from* a given antecedent condition or, concomitantly, a fall *onto* something else. Rather, the condition of falling is originary, in the sense that Hegel stresses in what he calls the "speculative nature of philosophical beginning," which we might characterize as the time of the "not yet": "That which begins, as yet *is* not ... But further, that which begins already *is*, but *is* also just as much *not* yet."[9] Hegel falters in his own beginning, as Adorno perspicuously notes, because his philosophy "wants to express itself as a process, in permanent *status nascendi*."[10] If habit as a second nature is supposed to *engender* our stable ways of being out of the primordial discord of exteriority and division, in *Remainder*, by contrast, there is a compulsive repetition of the prematurity of birth in and through habit that Hegel characterizes as the "not yet self" (*noch nicht Ich*) in the *Philosophy of Mind*.[11]

This anxiety of beginning registers as an inertia that impedes forward movement, connectivity, communication, and adaptation. Like consciousness in the *Phenomenology of Spirit*, the narrator in *Remainder* arrives still-to-be-born and thus is always beginning again and again, never seeming to learn his lessons by heart. The subject arrives in, and as, a failure to consolidate, owing to the recoil of the body from itself as it registers its own expiration in and through habit. *Remainder* exposes us to a constitutively excessive and deranged sense of repetition that is the unstable ground for the traumatic emergence of an ill-at-ease subjectivity. If trauma is not primarily something that affects the already constituted subject but is rather the explosion of subjectivity itself, then I argue that habit is central to this destitution, poignantly captured in *Remainder*'s opening scene.[12] The subject arrives as an unbearable falling and spilling outside of itself.[13]

Although the narrator's accidentilization is incessantly repeated and reenacted throughout the novel and film, that is not simply because once traumatized we are prone to being "re-traumatized" but rather because this "re-" is inaugural and the inherent trauma of emerging into subjectivity is never finished. To put it in McCarthy's own Lacanian articulation of the relationships between accident, trauma, materiality, and the real, the accident is "a radical and disastrous eruption *within* the always-and-irremediably inauthentic; a traumatic real; a real that's linked to repetition."[14] The real is an entity's own excessive materiality that "overflows all boundaries damming in the thing's—and everything's—identity, and thus threatens ontology itself."[15] The "surplus matter" and "un-matter" perpetually referred to in *Remainder* are generated by the repetitions and reenactments that perpetually threaten ontology itself (Rem, 91, 171). *Remainder* unflinchingly pursues the implications of habit's logic of disturbance to its hyperbolic ends in and as a death-driven threat to ontology itself, up to and including the murderous matter of (self-) destruction.

REPETITION, HABIT, AND THE SPECULATIVE SENTENCE

In the film's remarkable opening scene, we hear, but do not see, the glass from the atrium shattering; this is followed by a long temporal suspension as the shards of glass float gently down like snowflakes. Then, abruptly, we hear and see the brutal impact as Tom crumples to the pavement, having been hit by "technology ... parts, bits," and barely identifiable within the heap of fallen debris (figures 1.1, 1.2, and 1.3).

This scene elaborates a fragment of a sentence that occurs early on in the novel: "I have vague images, half-impressions: of being, or having been—or, more precisely, being *about* to be—hit; ..." (Rem, 3). The sentence is engorged

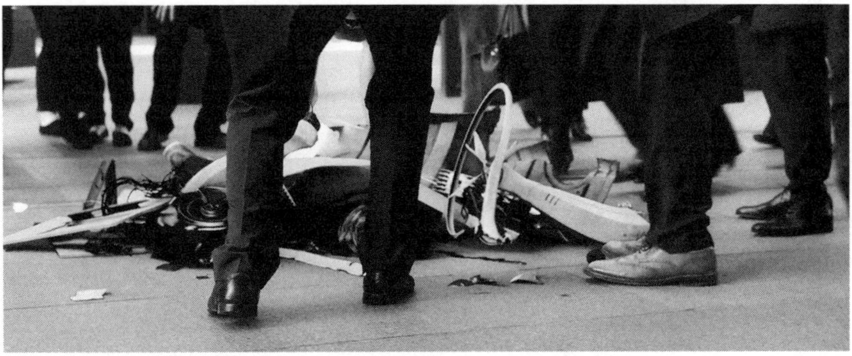

FIGURE 1.3
Tom buried under the fallen debris. Film still from Omer Fast's *Remainder*. © Omer Fast.

with alternatives (or), hesitations (commas), qualified compounds (hyphens), haste, abbreviation, contraction, resistance (dashes), and emphatic, suspended acts of falling (italics).[16] The present tense of the "I have" is infinitely delayed, and detoured through a dense tangle of "being" (the present participle), "having been" (the perfect participle—a combination of present and past participle), and the "being *about* to be—hit" (an adverbial clause).[17] The adverbial clause "being *about* to be—hit" suggests the verge of something being done now, with a sense of immediacy. But it can also suggest that the event is still in the future, and this clause is further divided and delayed by the italics and an em dash that leave the stranded remainder of the "hit" cut off from its "subject," and so also from its role as a transitive construction—to be hit by ... *something*—thus rendering it intransitive.[18]

In this sentence, the present tense is neither a stable, unified, and synchronous now, nor a point of transition from the past to the future, nor a perpetual suspension within the presence of the present. Rather, it is more akin to a spasmodic short-circuiting or a vertiginous turning point that spins and contracts in unruly tempos, engendering a sentence materialized and tensed with shards of present, past, and future.[19] The sentence is the generative cause and result of its always already having been "hit"—accidentalized, if not murdered—as it piles up as an excessive heap of fractured and barely coordinated temporal contractions, such that there is no stable before or after the accident, as it is the accident itself which inaugurates temporalization. The narrator is a "defile in time. ... A kink" (Rem, 252). The odd way that Tom, about to be hit by the falling debris at the very start of the film, holds his mobile phone between his fingers suggests that he has already been accidentalized before being hit by the external debris (figure 1.4). Throughout the film, this originary scene of accidentalization is repeated in myriad slapstick situations in

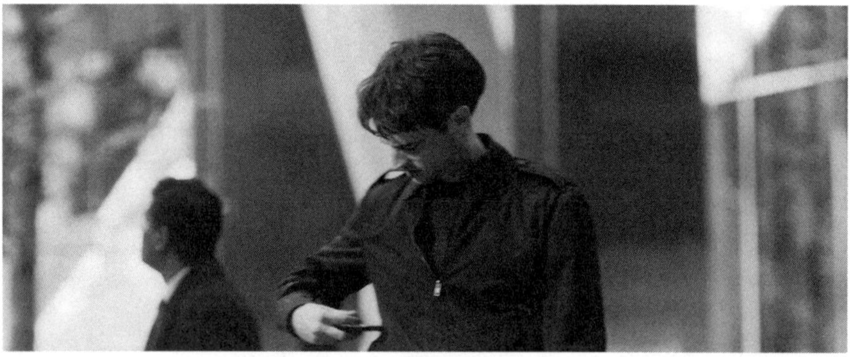

FIGURE 1.4
Tom gripping his phone "before" being hit. Film still from Omer Fast's *Remainder*. © Omer Fast.

which Tom is perpetually being hit or knocked down and "about to be hit." In this condition, the narrator is not just knocked down, but rather rendered in a deponent state of "passibility" beyond the very coordinates of before and after, activity and passivity, protension and retension, life and death.[20]

The "being *about* to be—hit" sentence contracts into the accusative object of an action precipitated by the grammatical structure of the sentence itself, as its overpunctuation pulverizes the subject rather than putting the dot on any sovereign "I" that would confidently navigate it from beginning to end. Although the "I" in this sentence—which does not appear in a sentence further on that elaborates the opening page of the novel ("Just got hit by a falling ... falling stuff, you know.")—already appears to be established and actively narrating the event, the sentence enacts a shattering that is never fully stabilized through the subject's active position (Rem, 32). The accident is not simply the cause of the "I"'s present condition, or something that happens to a grammatically stable subject in control of narrating the event, but rather it is an effect of the ongoing "hits" afforded by the indifferent grammar of the sentence.

The resistances of this sentence are indicative of the temporal paradoxes of relating something about subject formation that is logically prior to the "I"'s narrative capacity, as it is constitutive of that very capacity.[21] In this sentence, the subject encounters the hit as its own substance rather than simply receiving it as an external accident that is inflicted upon it. The narrator is "what the accident had left" (Rem, 4). Or, in Hegel's words, "the antecedent *comes to be* only by being *left behind*."[22] This sentence in *Remainder* is one in which grammatical form itself is an obstacle to grammatical flow. The sentence recoils, and its forward movement is halted, suspended, and reversed as it becomes stuck on its own recursions, impediments, and divisions.

More specifically, *Remainder*'s opening sentences should be read like a speculative sentence, the paradigm of Hegel's speculative movement of spirit that is most forcefully articulated in the Preface to the *Phenomenology of Spirit*.[23] *Remainder*'s anaesthetic is a trenchant continuation of the logic of the speculative sentence in both spirit and letter, as the novel and film are characterized by overpunctuation, grammatical oddities, jarring recoils, interminable delays, precipitous leaps, abrupt jerking back and forth, all manner of cutting off, collapsing, staining, spilling, buffeting, and remaindering. If a standard predicative sentence consists of the externality of the relations of subject and predicate such that the substantive subject independently and passively supports the accidents of its contents (predicates), the speculative sentence disrupts this stable set-up. Hegel uses the proposition "*God is Being*" as an example of this in the Preface.[24] "*God is Being*" can be read in normal logical/predicative terms as a principle of identity, such that the predicate *being* is applied to the subject *God*, or it can be read speculatively, such that "it is not a motionless subject (*ruhendes Subjekt*) tranquilly supporting the accidents; rather, it is the self-moving concept which takes its determinations back into itself."[25] In speculative reading, the content is no longer the predicate of the subject but is rather its substance, and the subject has passed over into the predicate, and thinking loses the fixed objective basis that it had in the subject. As a result, the normal flow of predication is impeded: "the motionless subject itself breaks down [*geht zugrunde*]" and begins to "totter" (*schwankt*).[26] The disruptive and disturbing relationship between subject and substance in the speculative sentence, in which destitution and failure are always in play, has important implications for the unsettling anaesthetics of habit I pursue.

Hegel makes it clear that the speculative sentence is differentiated from any other type of sentence not by its (philosophical) content but rather by the way in which the reader comports themselves in relation to it.[27] In other words, the speculative sentence demands a "speculative attitude" to be set in motion, and *repetition* is at the heart of this way of reading.[28] A speculative reading requires the sentence to be read at least twice to register the recoil and strangeness that disrupts given ways of predication. As Hegel notes this "unfamiliar impediment" (*diesem ungewohnten Hemmen*) of the speculative sentence—which sets up an interference between given and speculative ways of predication—gives rise to the specific reproach of unintelligibility leveled at "philosophical literature" that "so much has to be read over and over again before it can be understood."[29] If we need to read a speculative sentence again and again, it is not only because the sentence creates disruptions within the forward movement and *flow* of normal predication through resistance, counterthrust, and arrhythmia but also because such a reading generates those very disruptions and disturbances. In other words, we do not stand "above" this movement but rather we are moved and driven by and through it.[30] It is important to note that Hegel's logic of the speculative sentence is infected to the core with the abstract and sundering dimensions of understanding and judgment and, in my interpretation, habit participates in that disruption of and resistance to speculative unity.[31]

It is often not sufficiently stressed how central the issue of habit is to the speculative sentence. It is precisely in the sections on the speculative sentence in the Preface that the terms "habitual" (*gewöhnlich*) and "habit" (*Gewohnheit*)—and variants such as *gewohnten* and *ungewohnten*—are featured.[32] In fact, the terms *gewöhnlichen* and *gewohnten* appear in the same sentence—translated by Pinkard as "usual" and "customary" and by Miller as "usual" for both—in the section about having to read the speculative sentence again and again (§63): "The philosophical proposition [*der philosophische Satz*], because it is a proposition, evokes the common opinion about the usual relationship [*des gewöhnlichen Verhältnisses*] between subject and predicate and the customary procedure [*des gewohnten Verhaltens*] of knowing. This procedure and common opinion about such a procedure destroys its philosophical content. Common opinion then learns from experience that it means something other than what it took itself to have meant, and this correction of its opinion compels knowing to come back to the proposition and now grasp it [*zu fassen*] in some other way."[33] On the face of it, it is hardly surprising that the term "habitual" appears in this sentence, as speculative thinking "does not stop at what is given," and thus its repetition suggests the disruption of the given notions of the logical proposition indicated by the terms "usual" (*gewöhnlich*) and "customary" (*gewohnt*).[34] But it is precisely this crucial reference to habit that receives the least attention in scholarship on Hegel's speculative sentence, in the sense that it is most often acknowledged in a given way.

The intimation is that the repetition of "habitual" calls attention to the fact that the traditional ways of thinking about the relationship between subject and predicate are incapable of doing justice to the complex movement between subject and substance, essence and accident, that Hegel wants to highlight in his speculative philosophy, and that a speculative reading dislodges and disrupts our "fixed" habits of grasping predication that prevent speculative movement.[35] Thus, the speculative sentence unsettles the static logic of usual predicative statements and its fixed subject (*festes Subjekt*). But this reading does not really go far enough. The entire sentence is marked by disruption, fragmentation, and collapse that is generated *by* habit, and thus our comportment to it cannot simply be thematized and subsumed as a disruption of our habits of thinking *about* those issues. It is not simply a matter of disrupting the habitual relationship of subject and predicate or, more generally, disrupting habitual ways of thinking, predicating, or acting, but rather this disruption is internal to habit and enabled by its very logic.

What I am trying to account for is how habit as an internal impediment generates the kinds of collapse, disruption, recoil, repetition, and overpunctuation that are driven through the speculative sentence. The relationship between subject and predicate also plays an important role in Hegel's discussion of habit as a crucial moment in the anticipation of the unity of the concept and the life of the mediating middle: "habit is the subject and being is the predicate … and both have their stability (*Halt*) in habit so that the subject is no longer dominated by drives [*Triebe*]."[36] But habit does not master those unruly drives but rather generates them; it never manages to restore the unity of subject and predicate that would allow habit to take possession of the body in and as the "'ideal,' subjective substantiality" of its corporeity.[37] As such, habit does not result in the "plastic individuality" that it supposedly generates, nor does it adequately foster the "goal of plasticity" that the speculative sentence is meant to elicit.[38] The speculative sentence in Hegel and *Remainder* articulates how we are set in motion by habit and how the static generating logic of habit is punctuated such that particularity is suspended and remains as the unsettling of fluidity and ease.

SATZ AT THE HEART OF *SETZEN* AND THE FAILURE TO INGRAIN

In the speculative sentence, the movement of predication is reversed and is no longer an accidental attribute of the subject that it is attached to, but a feature of it, such that the two recoil upon each other. Words and phrases such as "impediment," "counter-punch," "counter-stroke," and "thrown back" repeat and pile up in the space of a very few pages in the relevant sections of the Preface to the *Phenomenology* as Hegel describes how the speculative sentence produces a blockage and recoil in which the forward movement and flow of predication is halted and reversed, as it becomes stuck on its own excesses, obstinacy, inertia, and resistance.[39] The speculative sentence is precisely where the co-imbrication of subject and substance is articulated, and their relentless and repetitive recoiling and self-division is pursued down to the level of the sentence, word, and punctuation mark.

The very word *Satz* in the phrase *spekulativer Satz* not only means (grammatical) sentence or (logical) proposition, but also in common German usage denotes a "jump" or "leap" as well as "dregs" or "grounds."[40] In the speculative sentence, as Werner Hamacher notes, the "hypostasis" of the securely presupposed subject of knowing, the subject of reading, and the reified subject of the grammatical proposition collapse.[41] The originary meaning of "hypostasis" is "sediment"—referring to the solid remainder that settles at the bottom of a fluid, and, in its current medical definition, indicates a condition that impedes circulation. In its philosophical meaning, this sedimentation and settling is translated as the underlying reality, the solid foundation or substance, as opposed to accidents or attributes that lack substance. Thus, "hypostasis," a word used to express the fundamental ontological concept of existence, is a process in which being is reified and given consistency.[42] The speculative sentence, however, stirs up this sediment and never lets it settle. It undermines the securely supposed and fixed subject, thus taking seriously habit's grounding—in the sense of an unsettling action of generating sediment—that emphasizes perturbation and inconsistency rather than stability and consistency. The speculative sentence in *Remainder* granularizes the subject rather than establishing a unity and universality through habit's inaugural acts of self-positing.

It is striking that, in Hegel's account of habit in the *Philosophy of Mind* and his *Lectures on the Philosophy of Spirit*, the terms "posited," "posited by me," and "self-positing" are repeated like an uncontrollable tic that seizes the text. In a single page of the *Lectures on the Philosophy of Spirit* that inaugurates the discussion of habit, directly after the last section on self-feeling, those terms are repeated at least seven times, like a depositing stain.[43] These sections on habit read more like an anxiety-ridden repetition compulsion that brings the velleity, inertia, and de-positing aspects of habit to light, rather than consolidating it through repetition. If habit is a "universality of reflection," a "posited universality," in which that universality is "brought forth, produced and proceeds out of particular cases," this does not seem to be accomplished in the very act of writing habit.[44] In his critique of the overemphasis on the Fichtean dimensions of Hegelian positing—where habit is often articulated as an "unconscious positing" that buries primal willing further into corporeity—Adorno is attuned to the de-positing always bearing down on the movement of Hegel's thought and that results in a "shattering [of] that self-positing."[45]

If habit is the primal scene of a self-positing that gives shape to a subject that can mediate its substance by internalizing and negating abstract immediacy and externality, then *Remainder* makes it clear that this process is shot through with a de-positing that is an excessive and ongoing sedimenting, staining, ungrounding, and recoiling of that substance within the act of positing, well beyond any measured or balanced rhythm between internalization and externalization that is central to overly culturological interpretations of *Bildung*. Habit is the "residue of repetition," a "stain of being," that is cast adrift within an overflowing and excess of matter generated by its own compulsion to repeat. The "subject is a residuum," as Deleuze writes in *A Thousand Plateaus*.[46] But this is true in the Hegelian sense in which the subject's foundering is produced by the substance's self-alienation in and through habit's resistance to mediation.[47]

In fact, the narrator in *Remainder* is fascinated by the word "residual" and explores it in all its dimensions—mathematics, physics, law, grammar, chemistry—toward the end of the novel, when he is preparing for the final bank heist reenactment, and where he contemplates the need to "eliminate" and "vaporize" the material traces of all the reenactments—including himself and all the other reenactors—to cover up their crime and prevent communication of it leaking out (Rem, 268–274). But the narrator's status as residual persists, and is further dashed, as Naz taps "R-e-s-i-d-u-a-l" into his mobile to look up its implications. Here, the atomization of the word is not so much in the service of semantic meaning—cutting up the letters as an alienating and analytic moment in and as a necessary step in order to gather them together in "mechanical memory" as a precursor to "free thinking"—but, rather, an act of "punctuation that causes thought to stumble."[48] The process of analytic separation, ideally intended as preparation for the abridgments of mechanical habit and memory that would allow the word to sharpen, simplify, and quicken with meaning, now overflows into senseless material signifiers that are recalcitrant rather than facilitating. One might think of these dashes as a thousand little immanent counterstrikes that punctuate and disturb the precipitous appearance of the "I" described as a lightning flash that transfigures the "actual soul" that has been prepared by habit's "subterranean weaving of spirt" into a more spirit-like substance. In habit and the speculative sentence, the arrival of the "I" is developmentally delayed by its own unruly sedimentation owing to the temporal, spatial, and material instability of its precipitated subject matter.

THE FIXED SUBJECT

In the Preface to the *Phenomenology*, Hegel refers to the motionless and fixed subject (*festes Subjekt*) that itself breaks down (*geht zugrunde*) in the movement generated by the rhythm of the speculative sentence and, in doing so, breaks down the presupposed "enduring ground" of the subject.[49] But this breakdown is not just a matter of loosening fixity by incessant acts of analysis so that it becomes fluid. Rather, this breakdown—bordering on collapse—is internal to the subject matter of habit itself, as it is to obsessional neurosis and anxiety in Freud and Lacan, which are characterized by relentless acts of anatomization, undoing, redoing, and recursion.[50] Thus, I am arguing for another sense of what Hegel pejoratively calls a "fixed subject" that is not "the hypostasis of the securely supposed subject of knowing" but rather one that is perpetually brought to a grinding halt(ing) in and through habit.[51] Such a fixed subject articulates the surplus de-positing, sedimentation, and remaindering in the word "hypostasis" that refuses to decant its meaning in and as a consolidated, consistent, and stable state of those precipitates.

Mediation in Hegel's speculative philosophy is never a middle element between extremes, as Adorno aptly noted, as it takes place in the extremes itself, meaning that mediation is always brought to its breaking point.[52] Once these extremes are brought to a point of breakdown, the subject is overwhelmed by its own self-generated dregs. Rebecca Comay vividly captures the tempo and rhythm of speculative reading attuned to a sentence that is always spinning its wheels—frenetically overturning its grounds—and that brings speculative movement to a grinding halt: "To read every sentence as a speculative sentence is like driving with both the brake and the accelerator pedals down at once. To think philosophically is to dash again and again against the same wall, digging the same hole, skipping and turning like a stuck record, forever repeating."[53] Likewise, in *Remainder*, the narrator participates in conversations that cycle over "the same ground again and again," and has the most trivial of incidents "'played and replayed like a stuck record … residual'" (Rem, 38, 236). In so doing, habit and its writing often countermand Hegel's "method of truth," in which the comprehending of the "subject matter," although "analytic," is equally "synthetic."[54]

In terms of habit, we should not take this inertia and compulsion to repeat merely on the level of a machinic tonus that seizes the narrator's body in *Remainder*. More than this, the fixed subject engages with a certain aesthetico-logic of plotting (taken in McCarthy's sense) and breakdown that repetitively overpunctuates its own interruptions in a hyperbolic "scanding" that makes generous use of punctuation marks such as the dash, with all its connotations of precipitous speeding up, separating, and perpetually impeding what it is

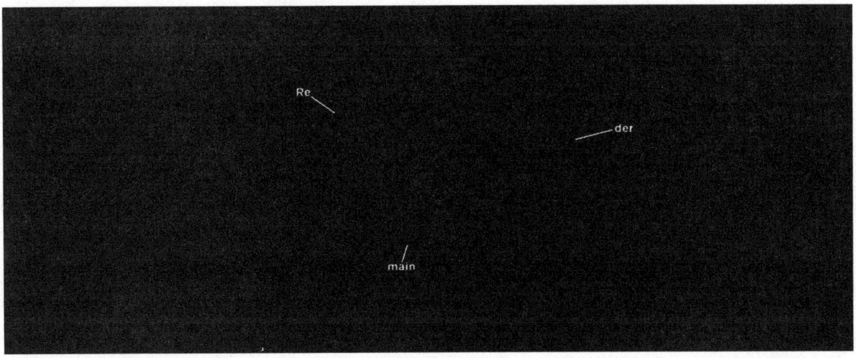

FIGURE 1.5
Re—main—der, opening credits. Film still from Omer Fast's *Remainder*. © Omer Fast.

connecting. In fact, the shortest speculative sentence in the novel, "I—*am*—*real*," is doubly dashed as the flow of the sentence imparts in the collapsing co-incision of subject and predicate (Rem, 177). The narrator's repeated attempts "to be real—to become fluent, natural, to cut out the detour ... that makes us all second-hand and second-rate" are countermanded by the crack of the real: the constitutive self-division, recoil, and collapse of subject and substance that is a feature of the speculative sentence (Rem, 264). Even the word "Remainder" in the opening credits of the film—"re-main-der"—disaggregates, just as the narrator literally "gags" on the "-l-" in "Settlement" ("*Set-l-ment*") in the early pages of the novel (Rem, 4) (figure 1.5). The settlement here alludes simultaneously to that word's legal dimensions, the narrator's monetary recompense for the accident, and his inability to engender any kind of phenomenological bodily sedimentation. Even when he tries to let the feeling induced by the crack in the wall "settle down" in him, he cannot but again upset himself (Rem, 4, 68). Nor is the reader granted any "settlement," as the very word is repeated six times within one paragraph with different weighting and grammatical emphasis (Rem, 4).

The settlement never converts into an ease, fluidity, or stable ground; it never makes the narrator "better, whole, complete," nor does it put him "back on [his] feet" (Rem, 5). In the final reenactment of the bank heist toward the end of the novel, the narrator describes a bank robber reenactor stumbling: "The carpet was flat. I saw his foot feel for the kink, and feel more, staying behind, while the rest of him moved on. The rest of him moved so far on that eventually it yanked the foot up in the air behind it" (Rem, 290) (figure 1.6). In the film, the bank robber is impossibly suspended in the air as pound notes fall out of a bag and levitate beside him, like the shards of glass at the beginning of the film, before falling in an entangled heap (figure 1.7). McCarthy's wording, and Fast's filmic account of it, strikingly resonate with the language Katrin Pahl

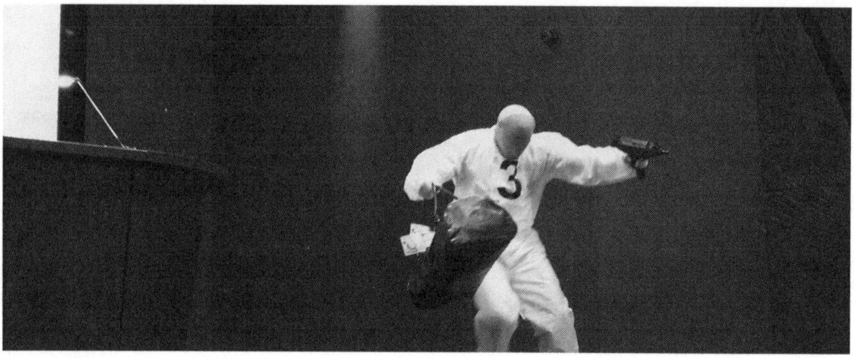

FIGURE 1.6
Bank robber reenactor tripped up by the "ghost kink" in the carpet. Film still from Omer Fast's *Remainder*. © Omer Fast.

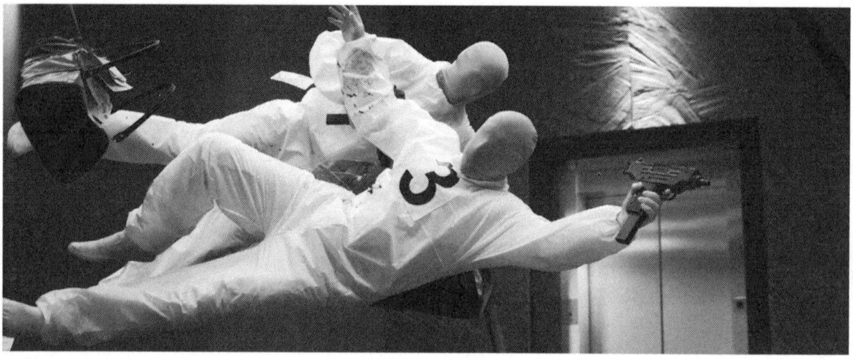

FIGURE 1.7
Bank robber reenactors suspended in the air after colliding into each other. Film still from Omer Fast's *Remainder*. © Omer Fast.

uses to describe the disturbing rhythm of Hegel's speculative sentence in terms of "losing one's footing" and being "tossed in the air," by which the reader is left hanging at the end of the speculative proposition "with one foot in the air," as the subject gets entangled in the predicate.[55] The upending of the reader of the speculative sentence is also felicitously corroborated by Terry Pinkard's slightly odd translation of one of the most famous lines from the Preface to the *Phenomenology*: "Spirit only wins its truth by *finding its feet* [my emphasis] in its absolute disruption."[56] In the relentless logic of breakdown in the speculative sentence, the promise that the narrator's settlement would put him "back on [his] feet" could only mean to resurrect him as perpetually tripped up and driven to the ground, always already finding his feet in absolute disruption (Rem, 5, 282).

Remainder is a trenchant continuation of the logic of the speculative sentence in its excessive and odd modes of punctuation, repetition, and reenactment. The counterthrusts, delays, recoils, dashes, hits, and collapses that we encounter in the speculative sentence at the "mechanical" level of its speculative grammar are compulsively repeated throughout *Remainder*.[57] The narrator's movements are characterized by overshooting, doubling back, jerking back and forth, and short-circuiting (Rem, 27, 71, 102). This punctuated trajectory is a feature of all the reenactments in the novel and film, such as the pianist reenactor whose "music ran, snagged and looped back on itself, first slowing down then speeding up," or when Tom instructs the "liver lady" to "freeze—reverse—stop—forward—frieze" (Rem, 142; Rem film, 51:45). Like *Remainder*'s daemonic drive to repeat and reenact, the movement of the Hegelian concept is also tripped up by its "plotting," a word which McCarthy describes in terms of "discerning ... nodes and paths, tracing ... bifurcations, switchbacks, junctions."[58] This results in a recursive remediation—"a replay and a replay of the replay"—that is a feature of Hegelian dialectics and *Remainder's* hyperbolic reenactments, repetitions, and feedback loops.[59]

In *Remainder*, the narrator cannot accomplish an immediate "adroitness in execution" in spite of the series of elaborate mediations via repetition; there is no self that is "the simple bond of these mediations."[60] As such, he twists and divides himself in an and as a "unreconciled immediacy" and an "alienated mediation."[61] The narrator's repetition compulsion—his drive to relentlessly repeat and reenact—generates so many units, pieces, parts, gestures, steps, deviations, and surplus matter that he entrenches himself in the fragments and fragmentation of his own acts of mediation. For all his dreams of being seamless, fluent, and natural by cutting out his "eternal detour," he remains constitutively and "completely second-hand" (Rem, 67, 23, 54).

In *Remainder*, habit never seems to accomplish what Bruno Latour calls its "smoothing over" or "veiling" function, by which it adjusts "the junction points *without splices* and without any *visible* breaks in continuity."[62] Rather habit is "less concerned with the join, less tempered."[63] For the narrator, there is no cure for cutting out the detour, as that detour is precisely what the narrator's second-handedness as second nature perpetually enacts. Precisely when he wants to cut out the detour, he is hit again by what Hegel calls a "counterpunch" (*Gegenstoss*) of yet another catastrophic "hit," overflowing substance that blows back, or deviation that resists fluid and forward movement, and is played over and over again like a stuck record.[64] The repetitious "drilling" at the level of the form and content of the novel, film, and the narrator's reenactments creates holes and gaps that drain meaning, in the same way that overpunctuation evacuates the writing of its flow of signification in favor of the obtrusiveness of the signifier. Instead of repetition serving as a preparatory act of ingraining the subject in and through the secondary automaticity of habit for mechanical memory, it becomes a prolonged and relentless recursion through the recoiling of the speculative sentence. The reader/viewer is ground down into the signifiers and materiality of words that are dredged up by these repetitions and that resist the flow of meaning.[65]

Words in *Remainder* are often reduced to senseless signifiers and letters that never reach the point of being digested in terms of rote, mechanical learning as a necessary step for interiorization and the foundations for meaningful communication.[66] The incessant atomization and subdivision of words and sentences into infinitely small units in *Remainder* is Joycean in its logic and persevering insistence. Each letter, in turn, closes off and becomes the launching point for further detours to look up other words in a hyperbolic drive to deviate.[67] This machinic process is aided and abetted by the grammatical dash—a literal "flat lining." During the tire repair shop reenactment, the narrator instructs the reenactors to speak their lines—repeating a conversation ten pages earlier—in disinterested and monotonous voices, all deadpan and neutral: "'*You've—got—a—dent*.'" There was a pause before the driver answered: "'*I—know—that—that's—not—why—I'm—here*'" (Rem, 177).

This process is also Beckettian in the precise sense relayed by Billie Whitelaw, one of the playwright's favorite actresses, who recalls him conducting her like a "metronome," reenacting the character Winnie's lines for her in the deadpan way he is trying to invoke: "Let me see if I can get it right—[*flat monotone*] 'A-no-ther hap-py day.'"[68] Throughout the novel, there is a tautologous and paratactic re-repetition of the same consonants, words, phrases, sentences, and conversations, with slight transpositions. In a narrative condition reminiscent of a psychoanalytic scenario, we hear the echoing of analyst and analysand plotting patterns and translations of homophonic alliterations, repetition of consonants, epistrophic excesses, and endless chains of synonyms and allosemes that clog up the text.[69] *Remainder* is replete with double consonant words such as "settlement," often in the form of phatic "waste scraps" like "heyy!," or onomatopoetic words such as "Tssked," in which repetition erupts *within* individual words.[70]

Remainder is a prime example of what Lacan calls "fixion"—a text flush with the real—in which the jouissance of the letter and its agglutination of consonants choke its meaning.[71] Lacan's notion of *lalangue*—translated as *llanguage* by Bruce Fink—a neologism created from the word *lallation*—which refers to the sounds emitted by a newborn before they can articulate them as speech—emphasizes the senseless materiality of the signifier. With the definite article *la* placed where we would expect a space in written language, the promise that a noun will follow is not fulfilled, and "thus the *predicative* [my emphasis] function of a grammar is thereby disabled," as David Metzger perspicuously notes, thus furthering the unsettling work of the speculative sentence.[72] This kind of stuckness is a persistent feature of *Remainder* and registers as a glitchiness that promises an impossible beginning that never arrives.

"UNHAPPY TRISTRAM!"

In terms equally applicable to *Remainder*, McCarthy describes Laurence Sterne's *Tristram Shandy*, as "the most glitch-ridden book imaginable—it's *all* glitch."[73] McCarthy further characterizes it as an act of "ontic devilry": a book entirely comprised of "digressions—interruptions, divagations and departures, side-tracks and reroutings and just plain delays."[74] As McCarthy and Peter Szendy note, this is often attributable to the excessive use of the dash, which takes over as a relentless, overpunctuating grammatical machine. *Remainder* is, like-wise, replete with dashes, which precipitously launch us forward and boomerang us back in a kinking and jerking motion (Rem, 71, 226).

Owing to *Tristram Shandy*'s many detours and delays, McCarthy notes, the titular main character is not born until two-thirds of the way into the novel, like the narrator in *Remainder*, who never seems to get past arriving at the beginning in the still-to-be-born condition of the second-hand. In *Remainder*, these glitches—sonic, bodily, electronic, digital, economic—bring us into contact with an exteriority, thingness, rigidity, and automaticity that cut into the relationship of being and having. At the ontic level, this "devilry" is not exceptional; "he [Tristram] is in fact simply *more* normal than everybody else," as McCarthy writes, just as Greg informs the narrator in *Remainder* that he is not unusual but rather, "just more usual than everyone else" (Rem, 24).[75] When Naz inquires how the first run-through of the Madlyn Mansions went, including all its inevitable glitches, he responds: "'It went ... well, it went ...' I started. I didn't know what to tell him" (Rem, 152). Later, having considered all the failures and uncontrollable deviations and mediations that could not be cut out, the narrator responds to Naz's query in the following way: "'It was ... It was a beginning,' I told Naz. 'A beginning?' he repeated. 'Yes,' I said. 'A very good beginning'" (Rem, 152).

Hegel's dialectic, which has been likened to a gigantic "processing machine" that reduces, abbreviates, condenses, and abstracts, is also a "hyper-system" that overloads and generates breakdowns through its endless remediations and deviations that generate all the particulars, picture-thinking, way stations, and remainders that it never masters.[76] It is thus hardly surprising, then, that McCarthy invokes Hegel in his discussion of *Tristram Shandy*: "Here, Sterne seems to anticipate Hegel's Total System—and its collapse. Rather than lead in a straight upward line toward pure spirit, the path Tristram envisages for thought and history (or history-as-thought and thought-as-history) twists round in a Viconian *ricorso*, as progress gives way to repetition."[77] But the novel's coiling movement, which generates repetition and surplus matter, is, to my mind, more suggestive of the movement of the Hegelian concept than it is a perspicuous critique of Hegel via Vico's *ricorso*.

Echoing McCarthy's summary phrase, "it's *all* glitch," Frank Ruda and Rebecca Comay write that "the *Phenomenology* itself amounts to nothing but a gigantic dash" that punctuates Hegel's speculative philosophy through and through.[78] Like the narrator in *Remainder*, spirit in the *Phenomenology* never seems to learn its lessons by heart, requiring them to be repeated and reenacted again and again, thus problematizing any upward movement of progress in both texts. The circular and recursive movement of the speculative sentence is not indicative that any fluid unity of the particular and universal, subject and predicate, has been achieved, but instead enacts their perpetual recoiling and collapse. In *Remainder*, repetition's circuit "has the pattern of an eight" that thoroughly unsettles its subject matter and cuts into itself like an annulating machine that piles up units, pieces, grammatical fragments, and accidents; the very stuff of habit's glitchy subject matter.

The traumatic structure of habit—alluded to in its repetition at the heart of Hegel's account of the speculative sentence in the *Phenomenology*—contributes to the perpetual vanishing of a vanishing subject characterized by sundering and collapse. The ontic devilry at work in *Remainder*'s speculative sentence is attributable to its compulsion to repeat—a compulsion Freud aptly characterizes as "daemonic"—that drags us back to the sundering effects of the object-cause of the trauma that it keeps circling around and getting tripped up by. Peter Sloterdijk captures this constitutive precipitation and belatedness in characterizing habit as our "innermost not-yet," echoing Hegel's notion of habit as the "not yet self."[79] This not yet subject is perpetually launched forward and thrown back in a curvature that we might characterize as a figure eight that is the plotting of a repetitious short-circuiting that cuts incessant gaps in the fluidity of speculative movement.

The speculative sentence in *Remainder*—and the temporal formation of the subject—is fractured prior to the possibility of any cohesion. Speculative-like sentences in *Remainder* perpetually collapse like a bridge that abruptly ends in the middle; rather than coinciding as a unity of extremes, it caves in (see section on the infinite judgment in the following chapter). Through the anaesthetics of the speculative sentence, the reader is driven to reenact the fact that the prehistory of the subject in and as habit, never stops happening. The sundering effects of habit shatters the subject's emergence into a perpetual delay at the level of the body, grammar, language, and speech. *Remainder*'s speculative writing elaborates the material and temporal oddities of habit that, as Ricoeur notes, "resists my effort to conceive it in the first person."[80]

The not yet temporality of this anticipatory subject is not carried by the "I" in McCarthy's speculative sentence, and, therefore, "the subject cannot simply be identified with the speaker or the personal pronoun in a sentence."[81]

Here, the "I have" spoken by the narrator never seems to grasp or stabilize its "being," and the "subject" is perpetually suspended within the logic and force of a "hit" in a sentence that declines into an unruly heap of temporal fragments under the autogenerated antagonism of an impersonal grammatical machine. It is in this precise sense that the speculative sentence is driven by a time of simultaneous precipitation and delay that disrupts the forward flow of predication and whose rigidity and resistance is never rendered sufficiently plastic in its figuration and movement.

HABIT, ANXIETY, AND THE OVERPROXIMITY OF BEING AND HAVING

Remainder's speculative sentences implicate and undermine two of the basic, interrelated definitions of habit: the relationship of having to being, and the conversion of the particular or contingent accident into a nominal universality and an internal necessity. The logic of habit in and through the speculative sentence disarticulates the possibility of any balance, equilibrium, or homeostasis in regard to having and being, accident and necessity. The ability to have or carry being—to form a way of being—is one of the definitions of habit as stable *hexis* (*hexis* and *habitus*, the Latin and Greek nominatives for habit, are derived from the verbs *echein* and *habeo*, meaning to have or to hold). But in my account of habit, there is no "indissoluble cohesion" or "perfect circularity" between being and having in habit, but rather an infinite absolving and anxiety.[82]

Hegel directly addresses the relationship of being to having in the *Science of Logic*, to critique the misguided notion that "I *have* the concept, just as I also have a coat, complexion, and other external properties."[83] Having in relation to being is not meant to be taken in the "ordinary ways of speaking" as an external property or accident attributed to a thing or subject.[84] Habit is a way of being that is me, rather than a property or thing that I externally possess. In other words, habit is a "mine" that is "me" in the speculative sense that it is internally posited. But this having in relationship to being always bears a nascent and internal alienation that can never be "is-ed" away.[85] In contrast to Latour's claim that "without habit, we would never have dealings with essences, but always with discontinuities," such that the "world would be unbearable," in *Remainder* it is the operations of habit itself that generate that unbearable condition.[86] Thus, habit is not just a matter of our bearability—a stable way of carrying our being—but rather the breakdown of bearability and our being-carried-away.

Lacan captures the anxiety-ridden relationship between being and having in the form of a question: "Can you bear the life that you have?"[87] In his *Seminar on Anxiety*—an unacknowledged treatise on habit in relationship to anxiety and the destitution of the subject, which should be read as the psychoanalytic companion to Émile Benveniste's classic essay, "'Être' et 'avoir' dans leurs fonctions linguistiques"—he characterizes it as a "relation of being *not without having*."[88] Habit here is akin to a state of bodily anxiety; a perturbing and disruptive overproximity that is always too close, too intense, and too much to bear, rather than mediating a way of having our being. Indeed, habit rivets us to that anxiety, as it is precisely a condition engendered by our own embodiment, so that the "I am" and the "I have" are brought (too) close to each other in ways that prevent their perfect circularity. The relationship between being and having bears the status of a non-relationship—more like an unsettling one-sided mobius-like topology than a measured dialectic of interiorization and exteriorization mediated by habit.[89]

The surplus excitations and agitations generated by habit's repetition compulsion are constantly at stake in our embodiment, and habit is often not a settling of accounts with them, let alone a self-defense against these drives. Habit's repetitions can seize and contract us in an intransitivity beyond any transitive action to which phrases such as "contracting a habit," "taking possession of our body," or "getting a hold of oneself" allude. As Benveniste notes, "having" is a "stative" (*statique*) verb with a stubbornly exterior relation to identity, and habit often seizes corporeity in ways that are much less willful and poised than its self-positing would suggest.[90]

Perhaps the term "set in motion" (*Bewegtheit*) captures this sense of an intransitive transitivity that registers as the buffeting, jerking, and glitching of the part-body of habit "being set adrift." *Bewegtheit* is the past participle of *Bewegen*, an important term for Heidegger that speaks to a fundamental passivity—our "movedness"—with regard to how we are thrown into the world. It is also an important term for Hegel in terms of the "movement" (*Bewegung*) of the concept and the speculative sentence. The sense of passivity, or more accurately, a driven intransitivity, is crucial for any account of the speculative sentence, despite Hegel's critique of the subject that passively receives its predicates in the speculative sentence. In this respect, *Bewegtheit* exceeds Heidegger's use of the term as a mode of temporalizing the ecstasies of past, present, and future. In my account of habit, being set adrift suggests the effects of unruly drives that buffet and set us off course by what Lacan calls the "gust effect" that I will elaborate on in the following chapter.

Habit generates a meaninglessness material contingency and inconsistency in the body that disrupts its totality from within. This might account for the anxiety registered in phenomenologico-hermeneutical accounts of habit's ineradicable automaticity and its "passion to become a thing."[91] I am therefore attuned to habit as a "nascent alienation," a source of ongoing distress as a result of its persistence as "a thing-like opacity and otherness" within us.[92] My reading of habit therefore runs contrary to phenomenological accounts of habitual embodiment, which emphasize the lived body and its accomplished proprioception. Owing to habit's unbearability, being never fully takes (its) place. As *Remainder* demonstrates, although we might be stuck in or to place, we do not easily adapt to our environment or comfortably inhabit our milieu, whether that be the body or any of its privileged objective correlates, such as the imago of architecture as one of those quadratures of the ego that would offer us an orthopedic therapeutics for our bodily inhabitation, coordination, and unity. Without the presuppositions of stable grounds and the cultural glue established by habit, we cannot assume that it generates any cohesive *building* material, nor any smooth conversion from *Bindung* to *Bildung*; from habit (*Gewohnheit*) to inhabit (*bewohnen*); from bodily disposition to the realm of ethico-cultural position or substance (*Sittlichkeit*). In *Remainder*, the ability to have or carry being is countermanded and suspended, resulting in an incapacity to grasp and stabilize time as it unravels in an unruly amalgam of temporal contractions that short-circuits and stains the very body or sentence that tries to compose itself. The arrhythmia of the speculative sentence is the grammar of impeded movement that manifests how the static logic of habit is imparted.

HABIT'S DEATH DRIVE AND DEAD TIME

Due to the accident, the narrator in *Remainder* is rendered in a state of living rigor mortis, in which his jerky movements, odd gestures, and stiffness are seemingly set against the fluidity of habitual action that we count on for all our daily tasks, such as eating, gripping, walking, driving, and speaking, not to mention dwelling and inhabiting. After the accident, Tom is taken to the hospital and hooked up to bits and pieces of medical technology, which keep him alive; we learn that he is "not dead, clinically speaking" (Rem film, 03:07:14). While the narrator's lawyer is on the phone discussing the inability of his client to break the settlement agreement, by exclaiming, "my client is a vegetable," Tom's friend Greg, another lawyer in the firm, quickly raises a sign that reads: "He's awake!!" (Rem film, 03:07:14) (figure 1.8). Tom might have been buried alive, but he has not flatlined.

In the hospital, the narrator lays "abject, supine," trussed up to "all sorts of tubes and wires pumping one thing into my body and sucking another out" (Rem, 4). These medical devices "pulse" the protagonist as they impart a machinic tempo to his vegeto-thalassic existence: "electronic metronomes and bellows making this speed up and that slow down, their beeping and rasping playing me, running through my useless flesh and organs like seawater through a sponge" (Rem, 4). (I will return to the repeating figure of the sponge in the next chapter.) The machinic tonus of short-circuiting movements continue to seize, possess, and play him, as Tom's bodily gestures and asynchronous movements pull him apart such that he never quite manages to compose himself in any balanced way (figures 2.19 and 2.20). Despite

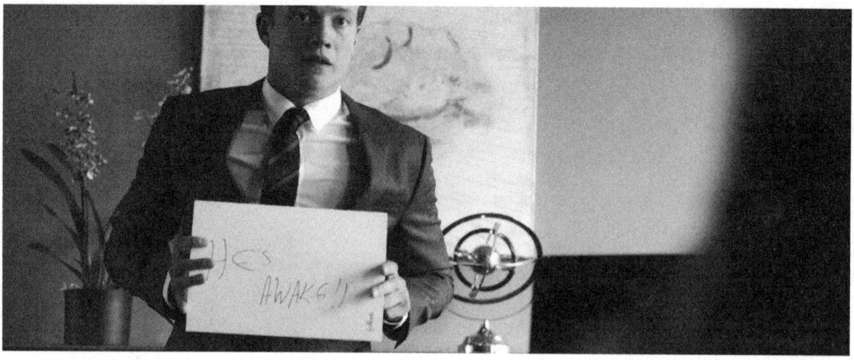

FIGURE 1.8
"He's awake!!" Film still from Omer Fast's *Remainder*. © Omer Fast.

the narrator's eventual resurrection from his flattened, "prone" state after the accident, to a "supine" one in the hospital, to his eventual vertical inclination when he leaves the hospital, he is never rendered upright and stable. In fact, he is perpetually knocked down throughout the novel and film, such that his exteriority is in contact with other myriad material surfaces in a persistent repetition of the opening scene, where he is of a piece with bits and pieces of material debris that have no origin or gathering point.

These inaugural scenes of the accident in the novel and film offer us a bodily existence that is seized at the point where the thresholds of passivity, automaticity, and inertia rack it as a force of death in life. Subsequently, repetition in *Remainder* displays more of the features of imbalance that we associate with the notion of the death drive owing to its compulsive machinic dimensions. The reenactments take on a desperate and uncanny "life" of their own, both locking the narrator into the circuit of his own obsessions and wrenching him out of his given bodily coordinates and connectivities.

In *Remainder*, habit is a material and temporal form of death drive in life.[93] It is a form of life that does not "shrink from death," as Hegel writes in one of the most well-known sentences in the Preface, but rather "endures it and maintains itself in it," thus demonstrating a certain capacity to incorporate death and to repeat it.[94] Hegel links habit directly with death in *Philosophy of Nature*, *Philosophy of Mind*, and *Elements of the Philosophy of Right*.[95] As Hegel notes, "it is habit of living which brings on death, or, if quite abstract, is death itself."[96] The same point is made by McCarthy, albeit without referring to habit as such: "Our very bodies are no more than vehicles carrying us ineluctably toward death. We are all necronauts, always, already."[97] Habit is the drivenness of this "vehicle" that drives us toward death, not just as the telos of life, but as a fundamental death-drive in life.

If spirit must discover a death that is proper to spirit, a "second death," then habit might be that second death, just as it is a "second nature" that is a nature appropriate to Spirit.[98] It is not just a matter of a death-dealing inertia and passivity that habit threatens at its limits, but a death drive that effects a detour within repetition itself that unhinges us and offers alternate paths to death that disrupt time, matter, and the body in unruly ways. As McCarthy has written, his main concern is repetition rather than progress, and that repetition is a matter of how to "die in new, imaginative ways."[99] Habit's repetition compulsion drives us to immanent forms of breakdown that potentially offers new forms of living through our unlived bodies that speaks to the imperative, and impossibility of, as McCarthy writes, "inhabiting death."[100] In disturbing ways, it is often the case that in *Remainder* the narrator's inertia and fixity, which refuses to be "quickened with spirit," is when he seems to be the most alive.

If, as Hegel writes, habit is where the body establishes its mediation of subject and predicate, so that the subject is no longer dominated by drives, in *Remainder* subject and predicate tend to fall outside each other, which is another definition of death that Hegel accounts for in his *Encyclopedia Logic*.[101] Instead of habit as the development of a relatively stable conatus through interiorized and idealized repetitions resulting in a mode of self-preservation that adjusts the organism in balance with its internal and external environment, the narrator's "strange conatus" is more akin to a per-severing death drive.[102] The repetitions in *Remainder* are not bound or sublated into a stable habit but rather perpetually get stuck and impale the protagonist on the viscosities of matter generated in and by the wake of habit.

"Drift," the English translation for Lacan's French translation of Freud's psychoanalytic drive (*Trieb*) as *dérive* is suggestive, as it captures the fact that repetition automaticity deposits excessive debris and detritus in its wake as it incessantly circles around. These sticky grounds—which are also simultaneously voided—do not offer any stable launching point for the meaningful subjectification of time as a flow of retentions and protentions; rather, they spill out, coagulate, and bloat the present with other potentialities. What results is a recalcitrant intransitivity that pulls all spatiotemporal movement back into the virtual potentialities of time and matter that are not reducible to their given identities, coordinates, or plot lines. This opens up what Deleuze has called a "dead time" within the time of the accident: "This dead time does not come after what happens; it coexists with the instant or time of the accident, but as the immensity of the empty time in which we see it as still to come and as having already happened."[103] In *Cinema 2: The Time Image*, Deleuze provides a further articulation of "dead time" that strikingly resonates with the opening scene and sentence in *Remainder*: "An accident is about to happen, it happens, it has happened; but equally it is at the same time that it will take place, has already taken place and is in the process of taking place; so that, before taking place, it has not taken place, and, taking place, will not take place ... etc."[104] It is precisely this dead time that opens up the odd modes of temporality, movement, and materiality that are then elaborated throughout the novel and film, resonating with the "immanent not-yet" of habit.

"KERR-THUNKK!"/"THUMP! KADUMP!"

In a scene that, in many ways, reenacts and repeats the opening lines of *Remainder*, McCarthy launches his "plotting" of a story line/exhibition for an exhibition of seven works of art from "la Caixa" collection in Lisbon, titled *Empty House of the Stare* (2019–2020), through a brief three-page encounter with Sophie Ristelhueber's *Fait #60* (figure 1.9).[105] He calls attention to the fact that this enigmatic and "humanoid" machine face has been "violently dismantled," "spilled," "splatted," and "smashed against a desert floor." A couple of lines later, he writes that it appears as if "the thing had got so drunk it tripped

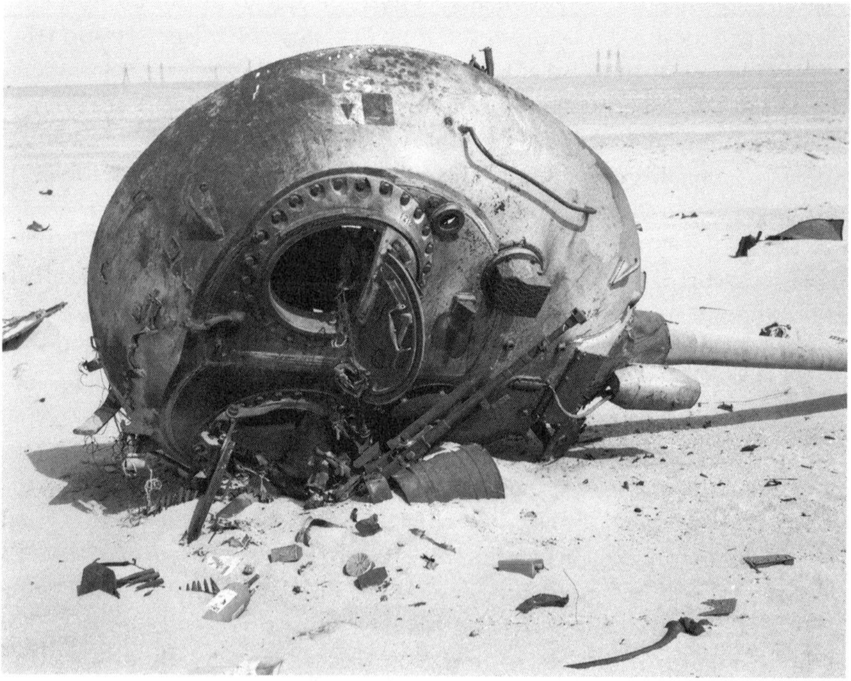

FIGURE 1.9
Sophie Ristelhueber, *Fait #60*, 1992. Color photograph, silver print mounted on aluminum. © Sophie Ristelhueber.

over and smashed itself," in some sort of Bacchanalian revel. Significantly, he notes that this is not just a technological disaster, but also a more general ontological and metaphysical collapse, in which reality is "starting to crumple in on itself, to implode," thus suggesting that this disturbance is in the order of the traumatic real. At this point, McCarthy precisely refers to this enigmatic object as a "*thing*," suggesting that its traumiticity exists well in excess of any given context, connectivity, or numbering of a "fact" or "done deed" among a large inventory of others, including all the other photographs in Ristelhueber's compelling photographic series depicting the battle-scarred landscape of Kuwait following the end of the Gulf War.

This short section on *Fait #60* is given the odd title of "Kerr-thunkk!/ ¡Catacroc!" in the bilingual English and Spanish publication, invoking the thing's fall through the onomatopoeic language of comic strip speech balloons—perhaps drawing on Hergé's Adventures of Tintin bande dessinée album series, which was the subject of McCarthy's first nonfiction book. As fate would have it, it also resonates with Hegel's strikingly similar language in the *Phenomenology of Spirit*—in this case, the rather cartoon-like language of "Bautz! Baradautz!" to use the original German—that appears at the end of §545 in the text.[106] These words, derived from Goethe's 1805 translation of Diderot's *Rameau's Nephew*, render the French word *patatras!* that Terry Pinkard translates from Hegel's German version as "thump! kadump!" and A. V. Miller as "bang! crash!"[107]

In the *Phenomenology*, this passage gives dramatic play to the temporality of precipitation and delay that characterizes a new form of consciousness, Enlightenment rationality, the arrival of which is likened to a "pervading infection" (*durchdringende Ansteckung*) that has already spread widely and permeated every "organ of spiritual life" before one is even aware of what has happened. And then, all of a sudden, this new form of consciousness gives the old idol of (religious) superstition "a shove with the elbow, and thump! kadump! the idol is lying on the floor."[108] In this section, we get one of the strongest articulations of (Enlightenment) rationality—and, later, absolute knowing—as an "irresistible airborne contagion."[109] This language of infection gives play to a precipitous immediacy that does its work of mediation behind one's back in a "cunning of temporality" that appears to bypass the complex process of mediation and transformation, before, "suddenly," the idol has precipitously fallen. The corporeal, political, and spiritual body is always trying to catch up to what has always already happened to it as a *fait accompli* or "done deed," to use McCarthy's characterization of Ristelhueber's *Fait #60*, thus marking a preposterous beginning that is "a by-product of its own aftermath"; the aftereffect of its own object-cause.[110]

But this precipitousness never completely hollows out the unaware idol. "The mute weaving of spirit" that Hegel returns to at various points in the

Phenomenology is indicative of the slow repetitive work of preparation that precedes and prepares the groundwork behind the scenes that can result in entanglement and tripping up just as much as any new condition; just as an infection, if it does not permeate through and through, is not the precursor to health—like an all-consuming fever before it breaks, in Hegel's account—and can inflame and get stuck in particularity, rather than sublating the bodily and political organs into moments of a universality. Likewise, the virtuality of habit that permeates the corporeal body with universality often gets entangled in particularity, contrary to Hegel's manifest claim that if an activity has become a habit with us, "then our self has so completely mastered all the relevant details, has so *infected them with its universality*, that they are no longer present to us as single details, and we keep in view only their universal aspect."[111] But habit is often a "seizure of corporeity"—Hegel specifically uses this kind of wording in his discussion of habit's taking possession of the body in the *Philosophy of Mind* and the act of eating and drinking in the *Philosophy of Nature*—that is not a mastery of self-possession, but a violent wrenching and dismantling that disrupts the body's unity and appropriation to universality.[112]

McCarthy's description of *Fait #60* stresses the violent dismantling of the unity of this "apparatus" or "assembly" into an intricacy of mechanical parts—hatches, wires, pinions, ratches, pins—that are so broken and shattered that they cannot even be named, let alone repaired, or even metaphorically/metonymically likened to a face, or an eye from that face, ripped from a larger technological, national, and political body. Rather, this "thing" persists as an anamorphic gaze that disrupts its given contextual coordinates and inserts a stain in the picture that is born of this deciduous part-object. Its arrival is simultaneously too late and too early, and thus in perpetual delay and drag, indicative of a general logic of "trascining" in *Remainder*, in which the real literally drags its disturbing thing around stuck to its very object-cause that can never be fixed, but only perpetually detached, or its stain incessantly spread.[113]

Like the opening scene in *Remainder*, Ristelhueber's *Fait #60* is literally a "done deed" in the sense that this thing has not simply fallen from some determinate world that it has separated itself from—an apparatus that perhaps functioned as a "high-mast floodlight" or as a sophisticated surveillance "camera" integral to a given political, technical, and energy network, which we might surmise was put to work in order to illuminate or surveil a specific stretch of geography located in the Kuwait desert for military operations during the Iraq War. The photograph is in excess of these coordinates. Hence McCarthy calls it a "*thing*, some kind of thing that does what it does (did what it did)," just as the narrator's accident "involved something falling from the sky. Technology. Parts, bits." (Rem, 3).[114] This thing is not just a matter of technology—just as habit is not merely a technique, skill, or routine (which is not to say that it is *other* than this)—but rather raises fundamental questions about ontology, materiality, and temporality. Although prepared through a long process of politico-technical assemblage and skill, like habit, this thing's effects are still precipitous and shattering.

Habit's material and spatiotemporal actualization is often disruptive, unhinged, and a potentially dangerous malfunctioning rather than a bloodless and peaceful diffusion of spirit in any corporeal or political body. What is important here is that this falling is already "cut off" and in an overripe state indicative of the *status nascendi* of beginning in Hegel's *Science of Logic*: "The ripest maturity, the highest stage, that anything can attain is the one at which its fall begins."[115] Of course, this "ripest" moment is also "overripe" *and* originary and not a fall from something determined and specific. If spirit begins in subjective spirit as habit, it remains there as a lapse (*Abfall*) and a "fallenness" (*Verfallenheit*) of spirit from itself.[116] It is a literal "lapse" of spirit in the genitive sense, that is to say, a gap, glitch, fall, and blunder in any progressive account of the appearance of the subject as a willing, conscious, forward-moving proposition predicated on the stabilizing function of habit. Second nature is an entanglement and deviation within the very coordination it is supposed to set upright and stabilize.

If habit is an originary techne or prosthesis that supposedly transforms the recalcitrant *Körper* into a supple *Leib*—to use the Fichtean-derived language that is embodied in more phenomenologically driven accounts of habit—then habit in *Remainder* arrives in, and as, a broken and violently dismantled mechanism, with its parts splayed across the ground like Tom's body, collapsed as a disconnected heap strewn among the mechanical parts of this ontological accident site (figure 1.3).

2

PER-SEVERING HABIT AND THE DESEASE OF THE FLUID BODY

After the inaugural accident in *Remainder*, Tom/the narrator must consciously consider everything he does, mentally moving through every step and watching himself do it before he can attempt even the simplest action. He has lost his "kinaesthetic fluidity" as a result of the accident and therefore must think about and regard each movement in order to perform even basic actions, such as eating or walking.[1]

If Bergson claims that habit (rather than memory) is the ability to undertake an action without calling up its representation—or, in a more aggressive formulation to which I shall return and complicate, repetitive action drives out representation—that fluidity is unavailable to the narrator, or to the case study patient Schneider in Merleau-Ponty's *Phenomenology of Perception* due to his brain injury.[2] Merleau-Ponty characterizes Schneider's movements as a "morbid motility," owing to his hesitations, deviations, and impediments to fluid movement.[3] Likewise, the narrator in *Remainder* must look at what he is doing while he is doing it and construct and rehearse detailed written or mental lists of each individual step constituting the sequence of actions required for a simple task like eating. He lists how many steps it takes to accomplish basic movements, and he must pay attention to and *understand* "each footstep, how the knees bend, how to swing my arms" (Rem, 14).

His post-accident "rerouting" physiotherapy is based on visualizing these sequential steps "in his head" before doing them. For instance, when he is asked to visualize all the movements involved in picking up a carrot as a preparation for actually doing so, he identifies twenty-seven movements. He counts seventy-five movements required to take a single step when walking (Rem, 19–22). These exaggeratedly precise, analytic, and quantitative accounts of the grueling mechanics involved in every step, unit, or sequence of movement are particularly detailed in the novel's incipit. There, the narrator is seeking to regain his lost sense of habitual fluidity and ease as part of his regime of "reparative plasticity" that promises to cut new tracks—to breach new neural pathways over the terrain of the "old tracks"—to remedy his neurological damage (Rem, 19).[4] But this breaching—the facilitation of smooth and fluid neural pathways—is haunted by another sense of breaching: a brutal rupture or gap, in addition to overflowing and superfluity, resulting from this excessive force.

Throughout the novel and the film, Tom is perpetually accidentalized—either being hit or about to be hit—leaving him perpetually suspended in what is commonly called the learning phase of habit formation. As I suggested in the previous chapter, he is always already arriving at the beginning and a condition of one still-to-be-born in and through habit. His ongoing accidentalization fixates us on and in the grounding conditions by which habits are established, thus undermining the progressive narrative (bildungsroman) that typically accompanies stories of its training (*Ausbildung*), molding, and formation (*Bildung*). In *Remainder* the "intractable" and "rigid" body never becomes a pliant and skillful instrument through training and repetition.[5]

The narrator's need to attend to each action before doing it, being perpetually stuck and driven to incessantly repeat steps, units, and gestures in his reenactments, is not simply an indication of the ongoing and lingering effects of irreparable damage to his brain such that he must perpetually think about and relearn actions that were previously unconscious and habitual. In fact, his rerouting training reveals how the process of "cutting new tracks" is bound to our general knowledge of neural plasticity in everyday habit acquisition and the process of forming any new habit whatsoever. They inform and are informed by each other, as Dewey makes clear: "an old habit, a fixed groove if one wishes to exaggerate, gets in the way of the process of forming a new habit while the tendency to form a new one cuts across some old habit."[6] It is precisely at the level of the *mechanics* of habit—exemplified in the "moments" of its acquisition and sedimentation—that the ineradicable production of gaps, cuts, parts, excess matter, and representations that are meant to be overcome are generated and most perspicuous. But I want to be clear: although the moments of habit acquisition and sedimentation might be where the instability of habit is most perspicuous, the per-severing logic of habit is always potentially miring us in this condition.

RATTLING OFF—ON CHAINS AND STREAMS

In his *Principles of Psychology*, William James vividly describes the learning phase of habit formation with an unruly amalgam of metaphors, which show how habit diminishes the necessity for conscious attention, reduces the gaps between sequences, adapts means and ends, and converts fixity into fluidity. "If an act requires for its execution a chain, A B C D E F G, etc., of successive nervous events," James writes, "then in the first performances of the action the conscious will must choose each of these events ... but habit soon brings it about that each event calls up its own appropriate successor ... until at last the whole chain, A, B, C, D, E, F, G, rattles itself off as soon as A occurs, just as if A and the rest of the chain were fused into a continuous stream."[7] Darwin, in his *On the Origin of Species*, calls attention to this flow in habit, observing that "one action follows another by *a sort of rhythm*."[8] In habit formation, the repetition of actions leads to fluidity: by being breached, a pathway becomes more fluid and canalized, enabling swifter and easier flow along its route as it is increasingly innervated. This conversion of a chain of individual links into a continuous stream is also described as integral to habit formation by Merleau-Ponty, who claims that the habitual subject "does not weld together individual movements" but rather moves fluidly within them.[9] Hegel points out that, when something has become a habit, "our self has so completely mastered all the relevant details, has so infected them with its universality (*sie so sehr mit seiner Allgemeinheit angesteckt*), that they are no longer present to us as single details and we keep in view only their universal aspect."[10]

Habit's ability to simplify a sequence of movements such that their execution is immediate and fluid, despite comprising a series of intermediaries, is identified by Hegel with the qualities of "adroitness" and "dexterity" (*Geschicklichkeit*). *Geschicklichkeit* indicates that a habit has been acquired and hardened into a stable and repeatable act.[11] In the contemporary neurocognitive psychology and biology of habit formation, this grouping of individual acts is often called "(motor) chunking."[12] Although McCarthy is clearly aware of contemporary articulations of neuroplasticity in *Remainder*, he often emphasizes more "analog" dimensions, persistently invoking numerical, mechanical, and electro-hydraulic metaphors. As N. Katherine Hayles rightly notes, the references to neuroscience in *Remainder* are mostly implicit.[13]

A ubiquitous example used to illustrate the accomplishment of adroitness and dexterity in habit is learning to play music, particularly the piano. The learning process and act of playing the piano are discussed in many commentaries on habit: from Hegel, Bergson, Merleau-Ponty, and Bachelard to Herbert Head and Alexander Luria, from William James and Samuel Butler, to Freud and Daniel Schreber, to name just a few. Unsurprisingly, a pianist also features prominently in the Madlyn Mansions reenactments in both the novel and film, although its source is undoubtedly a more feedback-driven model such as the pianist from Hergé's *The Castafiore Emerald* (figure 2.1).[14] In learning to play the piano, we might need to pay attention to the placement and movement of each finger, but an accomplished piano player need not notice each discrete step as their fingers glide across the keyboard.[15] In Hegel's specific phraseology, with such an aptitude, "the corporeity [is] rendered completely pervious (*durchgängig*), made into an instrument, so that when the conception (e.g. a series of musical notes) is in me, then without resistance and with ease

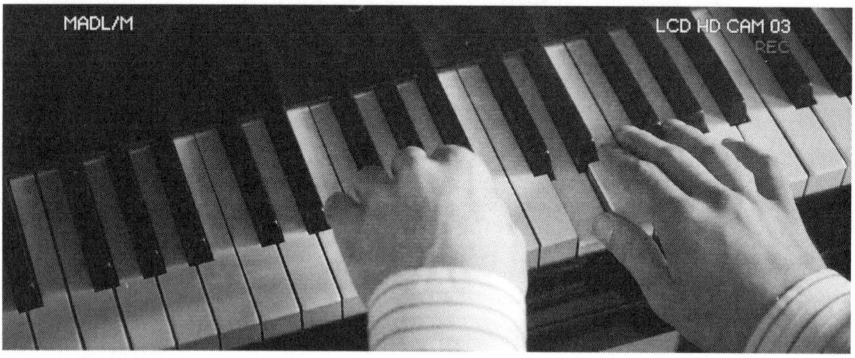

FIGURE 2.1
Pianist reenactor at Madlyn Mansions. Film still from Omer Fast's *Remainder*. © Omer Fast.

(*widerstandslos und flüssig der Körper*) the body gives them correct utterance."[16] Petry translates this *flüssig* more literally: "the body will express them correctly in a ready and fluent manner."[17] In *Lectures on the Philosophy of Spirit*, a similar statement makes clear how habit is a mediated immediacy that is rendered as an immediate mediacy: "The series (*die Reihen*) of movements are simplified (*vereinfacht*) in my self-feeling and the adroitness in execution (*Geschicklichkeit im Exekutieren*) is completely immediate (*ganz Unmittelbares*) in spite of the great series of mediations (e.g., playing according to notes). The self is the simple bond of all these mediations (*das Selbst ist das einfache Band aller dieser Vermittlungen*)."[18] Habit is acquired through repetition, which produces an indifference that abstracts us from our immersion in particulars—despite being generated through them—such that the individual is appropriated to universality and becomes unstuck from particularity.[19] In this narrative of habit formation, the sequences, parts, and units that constitute actions overcome their mutual externality in the indwelling totality of habit. As an ideality that pervades corporeity, the body becomes pliable, fluid, and at ease. Let's call it habit's version of *The Well-Tempered Clavier*. In the next chapter, I shall return to a more ill-tempered and unruly version of detached hands and fingers.

FIXITY AND FLUIDITY

Throughout the discourse on habit, the ideal marker of the successful incorporation and inculcation of a habit is the overcoming of resistance, blockage, and stuckness and the concomitant achievement of fluidity, fluency, and ease. The logic of overcoming fixity by fluidity courses through any discussion of habit as its medium and *telos*. Habit, at its best, seems to function as a cure, therapy, or conversion mechanism for transforming external into internal, mechanism into organism, unit into unity, particular into universal, fixity into flow. For Hegel, it is precisely *Flüssigkeit* (fluidity) that characterizes a healthy organism in his *Philosophy of Nature*, and the proper functioning of habit in the anthropology section of the *Philosophy of Mind*, whereas *Festigkeit* (fixity) characterizes the diseased mind and body. This is hardly surprising, as the difficult task of speculative philosophy is "to set fixed thoughts into fluid motion" (*die festen Gedanken in Flüssigkeit zu bringen*), as he famously writes in the Preface to the *Phenomenology of Spirit*.[20] Throughout Hegel's philosophy, *Flüssigkeit* is dialectically related to *Festigkeit* in and as "organic unity" and the "life of the whole."[21]

As noted in *Philosophy of Nature*, the individual organism "finds itself in a state of *disease* (*Krankheit*) when one of its systems or organs, *stimulated* into conflict with the inorganic power, establishes itself (*festsetz*) in isolation and persists (*beharrt*) in its particular activity against the activity of the whole, the fluidity (*Flüssigkeit*) and all-pervading process (*hindurchgehender Prozeß*) of which is thus obstructed (*gehemmt*)."[22] A similar passage in *Elements of the Philosophy of Right* makes explicit the full political implications of this line of thought: "The *idealism* which constitutes sovereignty is the same determination as that according to which the so-called *parts* (*Teile*) of an animal organism are not parts, but members (*Glieder*) or organic moments whose isolation and separate existence constitute disease (*Krankheit*)."[23] The healthy, sovereign body has overcome the division (*Urteil*) of the body stuck in and on its own dissociation into inorganic parts. Thus, mental and physical health is a state in which all the organs are fluid in the universal, such that resistance and fixation are overcome. Habit is a bodily form of mediation that, in acts of speculative alchemy-cum-homeopathy, converts chains, links, and parts into members of a well-integrated organism, and, ultimately, into fluid acts permeated by spirit. It is precisely through habit that we are meant to overcome a deranged, diseased, and disturbed corporeity.

"THIS BEING-AT-HOME-WITH-ONESELF WE CALL HABIT"

Habit is the "sign" and accomplishment of a state of bodily health resulting in a "firm holding oneself together (*das feste Zusammenhalten in sich selbst*), so that I do not become disunited in myself (*nicht entzweit in mir werde*)."[24] Hegel calls this the "hardening" (*Abhärtung*) of habit, not simply in the sense of steeling oneself against sensation, drive, or need, to avoid being immersed in and dominated by them, but precisely as means of holding oneself together in and as a unity. Thus, habit as hardening consists in "not giving into disunion, cleavage (*Entzweiung*), but holding to the abstraction of the self and persevering (*verharren*) in oneself."[25] I will continually return to this relationship between habit and persevering—or, as I prefer to impart Hegel's use of this Aristotelian–Stoic–Spinozan concept, per-severing. It is clear that habit's privileged work is the conversion of *Festen* as "fixity" in the particular at the expense of the universal—the manifestation of disease and disunity—to the *Abhärtung* ("hardening") that enables a *festes Zusammenhalten*, a "firm holding together," thus accomplishing the speculative integration of the particular and universal in and as fluidity.

Hegel characterizes such integration as "this being-at-home-with-oneself we call habit" (*dies Beisichselbersein nennen wir die Gewohnheit*).[26] This phrase, over-hyphenated in the English translation, is a leitmotif that is repeated throughout Hegel's writings in subtle variations. It serves to articulate how an emerging subject is predicated on a mediating activity that balances between particularity and universality, thus overcoming alterity by turning back, reflecting, and incorporating what is outside itself as an inner mediation, instead of becoming stuck on it as a finite impediment.[27] Significantly, the account of habit in the *Philosophy of Mind*, beginning in section §409, directly follows §408's discussion of madness, which is discussed as a disease (*Verrücktheit*) of "self-feeling." As many scholars have noted, Hegel clearly states at the beginning of §410Z that habit—or, as he calls it the mechanism of self-feeling (*Mechanismus des Selbstgefühls*)—is a cure for the disorder, derangement, division, disruption, and blockage (*Knoten*) of self-feeling that he characterizes as a "not-being-at-home-with-oneself."[28] So, madness, derangement, or disorder—the most prevalent English translations for Hegel's *Verrücktheit*—is the self's getting caught up in the one-sided particularity of a "fixed idea" (*feste Vorstellung*), leading this particular determination to become a fixation not subordinated to the simple organic totality of the whole.[29]

Habit, then, is precisely how self-feeling becomes a totality immersed in and generated from particulars but simultaneously indifferent to them, in the sense that I *have* these particulars as my "universal mode of being." Or, as John McCumber puts it, habit is where *me* becomes *mine*.[30] Habit does not simply dispense with particulars. Rather, through habit, particulars are sublated or converted from parts to members, from fixed determinations to moments. A habitual gesture or action, therefore, is optimally characterized as a balanced co-imbrication of spirit and matter, being and having; it is a mode of bodily proximity and self-feeling with minimal hindrance, gap, or recalcitrance.[31]

Habit as a "route to recovery," to use Malabou's felicitous wording in *The Future of Hegel*, is neatly encapsulated in a well-known passage from Alain's commentary on the *Philosophy of Mind*: "When freedom comes it is in the sphere of habit. ... Here the body is no longer a foreign being, reacting belligerently against me; rather, it is pervaded by soul and has become soul's instrument and means; yet at the same time, in habit the corporeal self is understood as it truly is; body is rendered something mobile and fluid, able to express directly the inner movement of thought without needing to involve thereby the role of consciousness or reflection."[32] Michael Ondaatje's poem "Her House" draws together many of the implications of Hegel's sense of habit: "On certain evenings, when I have not bothered to put on the lights, I hit my knees on low bookcases where they should not be. But you shift your hip easily, habitually, around them as you pass by carrying laundry or books. When you can move through a house blindfolded it belongs to you. You are moving like blood calmly within your body."[33] In this vivid example of gendered and domestic inhabitation, all exteriority, excess materiality, gaps, and junction points are smoothed over; the body glides through the material world with minimal resistance, hitches, snags, or coagulations, like blood circulating through the body.

Likewise, the narrator in *Remainder* desperately wants to inhabit his beautiful memory of the place in which his déjà vu of habit and inhabitation is fluid and seamless. But his longing is also clearly a deranged absorption (*Insichsversunkensein*) that sinks him into particularity and fixation as he persistently reenacts moments to the point of his own destitution.[34] In a scene that is an uncanny echo of Ondaatje's poem, the narrator tries to repeat a particularly graceful movement that he remembers occurring in his apartment: "how I'd turned half sideways as I'd passed the kitchen unit's waist-high edge—turned sideways and then deftly back again in one continuous movement, letting my shirt brush the woodwork" (Rem, 66). But he is never able to get this movement quite right in the sense that habit is supposed to "round off the edges of the phenomena that it covers," as Vilém Flusser writes, "so that I no longer run into them but make use of them unconsciously."[35]

In Hegel, the language of rounding off is meant to indicate that an individual is a "single rounded totality," rather than a mere composite or aggregate.[36] This rounding off is a "turning point" (*Wendungspunkt*), where being returns to itself at the extreme point of its absolute negativity as something "in and for itself (*an und für sich sein*)," an expression that the translator of Hegel's *Elements of the Philosophy of Right* renders as "to have being in and for itself," which is an almost textbook definition of habit.[37] But, in *Remainder*, the narrator's turning is always an overturning that results in all manner of twisting, wrenching, snagging, and tumefying that disrupts any fluid and continuous movement. The narrator's gestures are never sufficiently deft to let his shirt lightly brush the woodwork, "almost imperceptibly, like a matador's cape tickling a bull's horns": it either snags on the corner, drags across its edge, or doesn't make contact at all (Rem, 140–141).[38]

If a style of place is something our bodies "catch on to by moving with it" as Tom Sparrow suggests—drawing on Husserlian terminology that is primarily relayed through Merleau-Ponty, and commonly used to describe habit as an adroit bodily understanding: "it is the body which 'catches' (*kapiert*) and 'comprehends' movement"—it takes on a very different valence in *Remainder*.[39] The narrator is suffused with anxiety about his own cohesive stuff—how he hangs together or fits into the larger picture of how things are connected—because

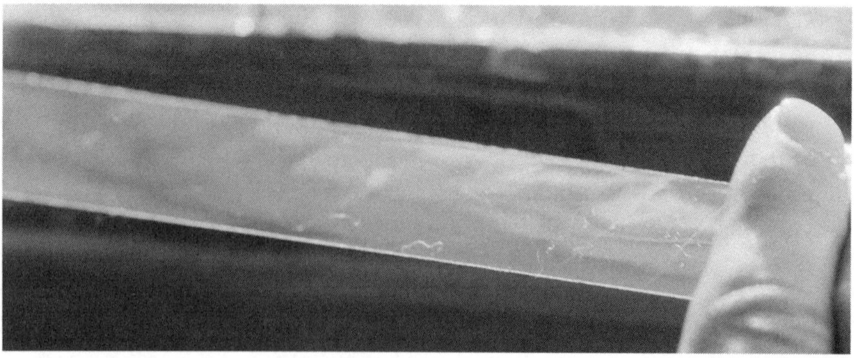

FIGURE 2.2
Tom holding a piece of tape. Film still from Omer Fast's *Remainder*. © Omer Fast.

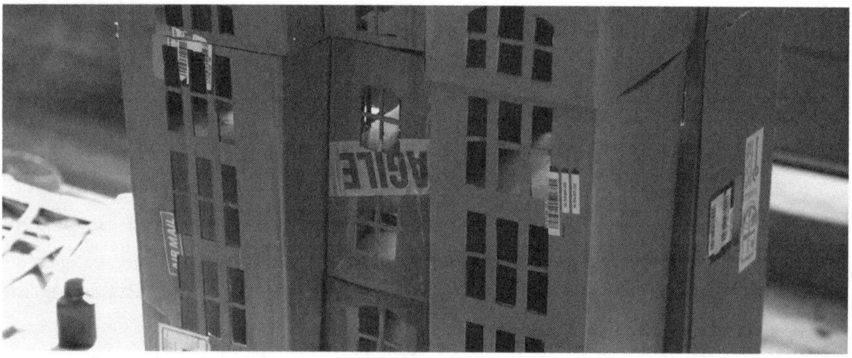

FIGURE 2.3
Cardboard model of Madlyn Mansions marked fragile. Film still from Omer Fast's *Remainder*. © Omer Fast.

of his own excessive tackiness and glitchiness (figure 2.2). The narrator's sense of exposure—which he exacerbates in and as overexposure rather than ameliorates—is due to the fact that he carries around his upheaval and displacement that is stuck to him.[40] He is stained by his internal out-of-jointness and thus he remains perpetually ill-adapted and unfit. In a brief meditation on prefab homes, the narrator is intrigued that all the pieces fit so neatly together: "'And they all slot in just like that?' I asked her. 'Without a hitch?'" (Rem, 35). But the narrator himself is not so well-designed—indeed, his edification is more akin to the montage-like model of Madlyn Mansions marked "fragile" that Tom constructs and then destroys in a "fury of destruction" (*Furie des Verschwindens*) that is characteristic of Hegelian abstract negativity or psychoanalytic acting out (figures 2.3 and 2.4).[41]

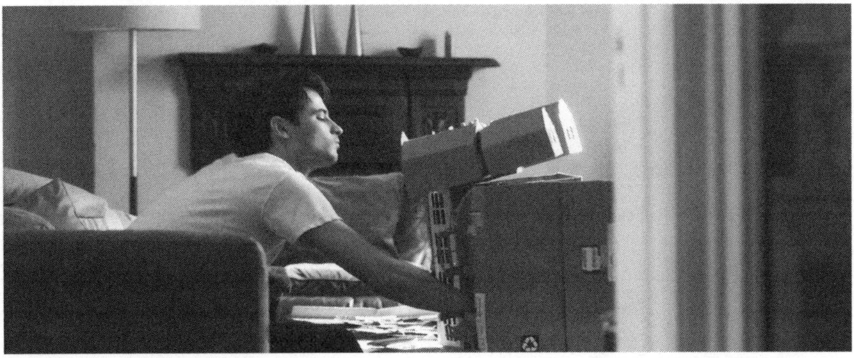

FIGURE 2.4
Tom smashing the cardboard model of Madlyn Mansions. Film still from Omer Fast's *Remainder*. © Omer Fast.

Like a joint that starts and stops, ratchet-like through a range of motion—a characteristic of "cog-wheel rigidity"—he is prone to "catch" (Rem, 220).[42] The narrator runs through his difficult matador-like maneuver again and again, "at half-speed, quarter-speed, almost no speed at all, working out how each muscle had to act, each ball and socket turn." After two days of practicing these movements, he has "three separate bruises on [his] side" from the many attempts to brush by this kitchen edge (Rem, 66, 140–141, 161). His tumefied body is the corporeal register of the bungled actions that far outnumber the few times that it worked (Rem, 161). Rather than fluidly circulating like blood in the body, he is "stigmatized"—a word which, in its Latin origins, means to prick or punctuate, but also to mark with an imprint, to cause contusions and cover with bruises— by the bull's-horn-cum-kitchen-edge.[43] As a result, he is "inflamed," all sluggish rather than fluid blood.[44] And out of joint, like his description of the tiny splinter of bone that remained after his kneecap was shattered in the accident and that "floated around beside the ball, redundant, surplus to requirements; sometimes it got jammed between the ball and its socket and messed up the whole joint, locking it, inflaming nerves and muscles" (Rem, 8).

BRUISED, BLOODIED, AND STAINED

If blood is a privileged metaphor for how the body fully digests and dissolves all otherness into an inner unity in Hegel's speculative philosophy, then when blood spills and coagulates into "globules" (*Kügelchen*) rather than fluidly circulating, we are brutally exposed to the outside.[45] In *Remainder*, blood is not the absolute paradigm of fluidity and universal solubility of subject and substance in Hegel's *Philosophy of Nature*, or Ondaatje's "Her House."[46] In the novel,

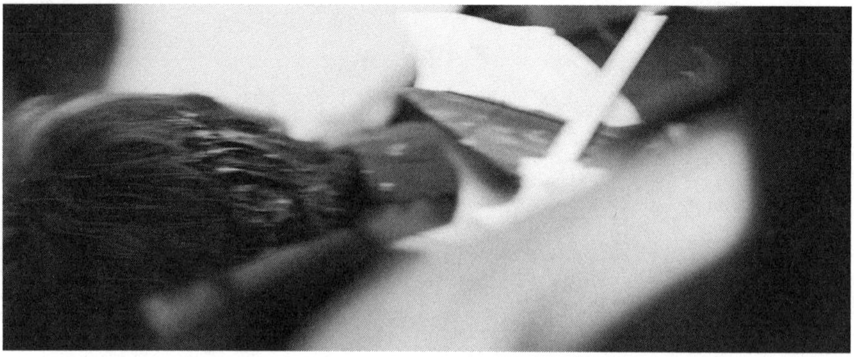

FIGURE 2.5
The back of Tom's bloodied head. Film still from Omer Fast's *Remainder*. © Omer Fast.

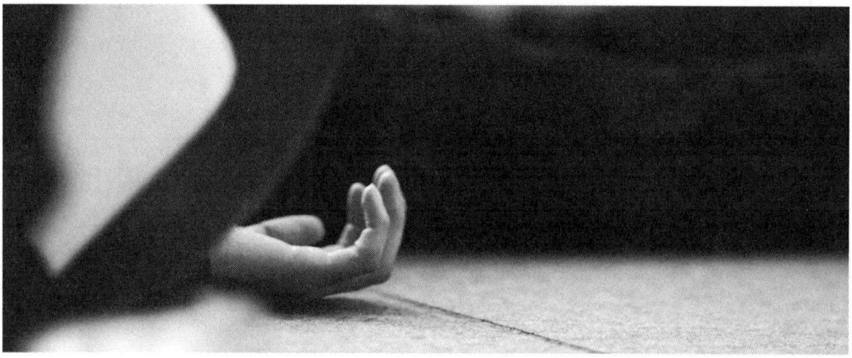

FIGURE 2.6
Tom's left hand appearing isolated and disconnected from his body under the heap of debris after the accident. Film still from Omer Fast's *Remainder*. © Omer Fast.

the narrator never moves like blood, calmly within his own body. Nor does blood circulate fluidly within his organism in the film—it is perpetually clotting, bruising, bleeding out, pooling, and staining.

Let's return to the film's opening scene. After the sudden and precipitous impact of the debris falling from the sky—preceded by the impossibly graceful shards of glass that descend in slow motion, like gently falling snowflakes—the camera pans into a close-up of the back of Tom's bloodied head, matted with sticky, dark, reddish-brown blood that coagulates with tufts of hair, protruding from the heap of debris that covers his body (figures 1.1, 1.3, and 2.5). This is followed by an out of focus panning shot that comes to a stop on the other side of the heap in a close-up of Tom's equally disembodied, twisted, and upturned left hand (figure 2.6).[47] Next, we see a

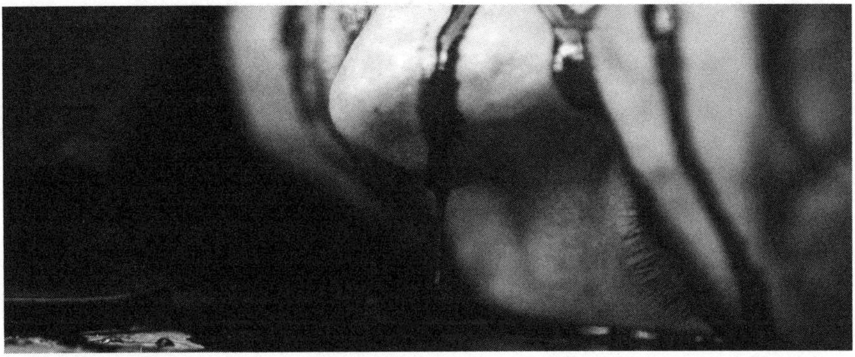

FIGURE 2.7
Detail of blood dripping from Tom's nose, while he is buried under the pile of debris after the accident. Film still from Omer Fast's *Remainder*. © Omer Fast.

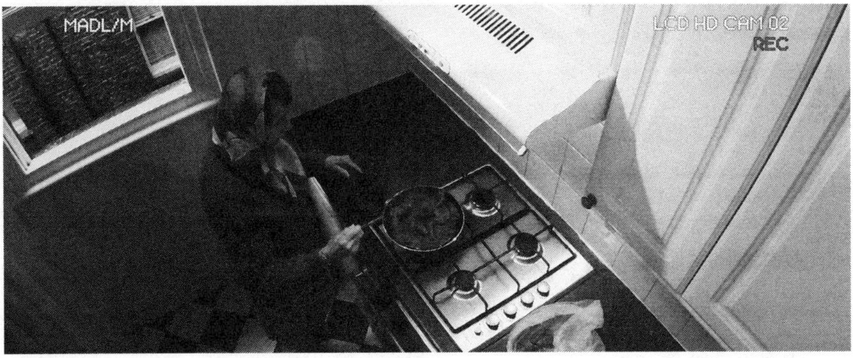

FIGURE 2.8
Liver lady reenactment (globules of congealed fat clogging up the ventilation system at Madlyn Mansions). Film still from Omer Fast's *Remainder*. © Omer Fast.

close-up of his sneaker-shod foot, quickly followed by a lingering shot of the bright-red, hypersaturated, glistening blood that sluggishly pools on Tom's nose, and then drips slowly onto the pavement in viscous globules (figure 2.7). These globules of blood are reminiscent of the congealed and clogging fat that accumulate during the liver lady's reenactments, eventually causing an embolism in the ventilation system and a bradycardic rhythm to her reenactments (figure 2.8). The camera then cuts to Tom's bloodied right hand, positioned palm-down, such that his lifeless fingers touch the blood-stained pavement and his mobile phone (figure 2.9). It is only at this point that the camera pulls out and we see a more distant overview of the scene, with Tom's bloodied face still visible between the legs of one of the bystanders encircling the disaster (figure 1.3). This inaugural moment of spilled blood echoes

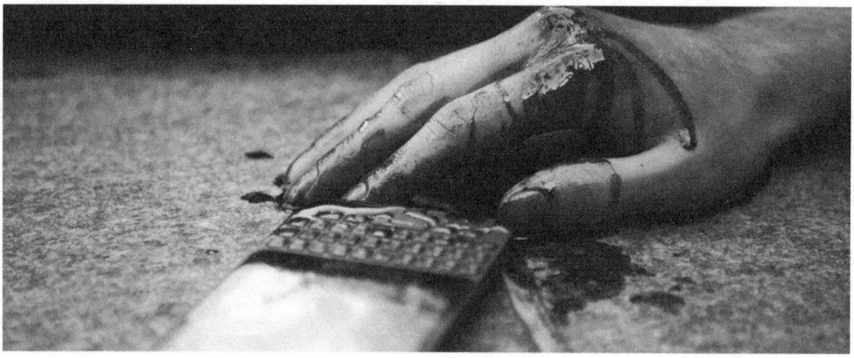

FIGURE 2.9
Tom's blooded right hand. Film still from Omer Fast's *Remainder*. © Omer Fast.

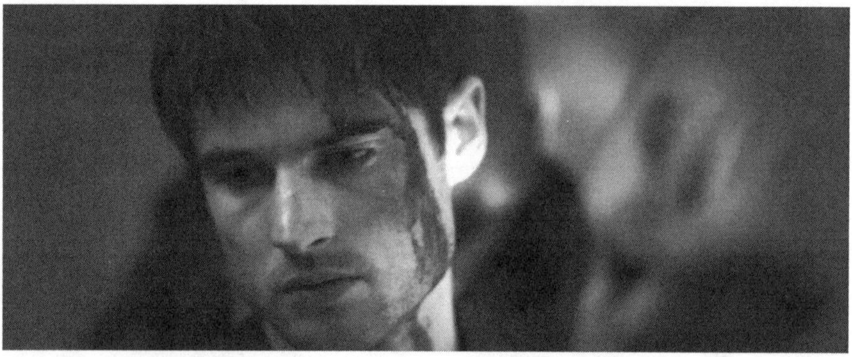

FIGURE 2.10
Tom caked with dried blood arriving at the party on Plato Road. Film still from Omer Fast's *Remainder*. © Omer Fast.

throughout the film as Tom is bloodied and battered by fists, tables, tasers, and his own bodily perturbations and imbalances as he is perpetually knocked down, tripped up, or collapsing. After he is punched in the face by a digeridoo player in a Tube station, he gathers himself and drags his stain along with him on his journey to a party on Plato Road where he will have his déjà vu moment of Madlyn Mansions in the bathroom. He arrives still caked in blood (figure 2.10).

EXPUNGING THE BEAUTIFUL SOUL (PORIFERA)

These bloody stains of the real stick to Tom and, try as he might, he can never wash them away. Tom enters the bathroom at the party, where he has his déjà vu of Madlyn Mansions that is triggered by a "crack." Even after attempting

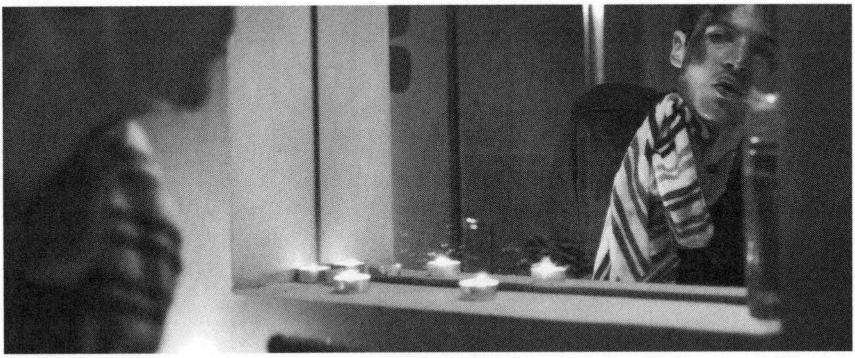

FIGURE 2.11
Tom in the bathroom at Plato Road trying to wash off the blood stains. Film still from Omer Fast's *Remainder*. © Omer Fast.

to clean himself up and wash away the blood at the urging of his friend Greg who is deejaying at the party, the residues of blood still stain him through and through (figure 2.11). The narrator's ideal of inhabitation without excess exteriority, detour, or remainder—recalling Hegel's concept of the beautiful soul that "lives with the anxiety that it will stain the splendor of its innerness" through its entanglement with the material world—is always producing residues, stains and spillage, even when he is attempting to wipe and wash them away.[48]

As noted in the previous chapter, immediately after his accident, the narrator is trussed up to "electrical metronomes and bellows" pumping one thing into his body and sucking another out as they run through his "useless flesh like seawater through a sponge" (Rem, 4). This comparison doesn't merely describe the narrator as a passive, lifeless sponge—or a living vegetable, as he is pejoratively referred to by his lawyer early in the film—it also conveys the passibility of his sponge-like state, which persists throughout the novel and film. The metaphor of the sponge is ubiquitous not only in *Remainder* but also throughout McCarthy's oeuvre as a primary figure for a notion of being, thinking, and writing that does not "blot" up matter in concepts, a notion that in his earlier work with the International Necronautical Society is directly associated with Hegelian dialectics (needless to say, I disagree with this interpretation of Hegelian idealism).[49]

As such, the sponge refers to the materiality and permeability of an uncontainable writing that spills through and stains the page, or as an odd sort of switching station for all manner of material and information circuiting through its channels. I would like to push this metaphor in a more Hegelian/psychoanalytic direction. Hegel directly refers to "pores" (*Poren*) in a discussion

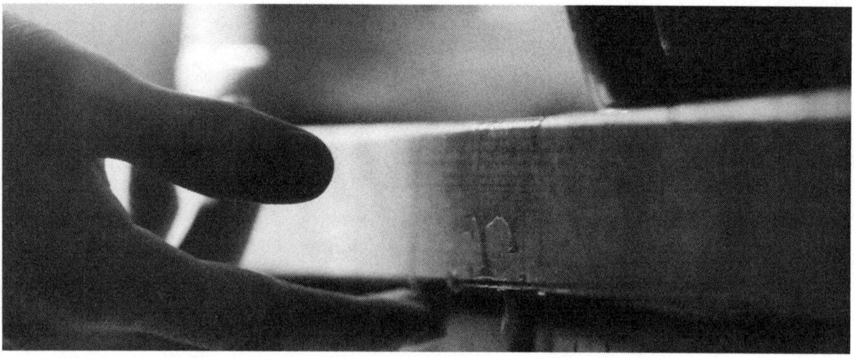

FIGURE 2.12
Spilled milk pooling and dripping from the kitchen counter. Film still from Omer Fast's *Remainder*. © Omer Fast.

of elasticity in *Philosophy of Nature* in order to criticize a conception of these holes as the negative moments of matter in the sense of their being present "*where matter is not*"—thus bolstering a sense of matter as only "affirmative"—and not as the negative of matter itself, i.e., "negation ... posited *in* matter."[50] The narrator's subject matter shares traits with the phylum *Porifera*, the literal term meaning "pore bearer," in that he is full of holes, such that his permeability is always at the limits of oversaturation, overflowing, and emptying out, and thus he does not simply absorb matter or wipe it away.[51] As I shall discuss further in reference to *kenosis* as an emptying or spilling out—and the nature of "un-matter" and immaterial matter in McCarthy (and Hegel)—it is clear that the narrator's leakiness is of a piece with a subject matter that is not only a pore bearer, but also, and concomitantly, a *poor bearer*. In *Remainder*, habit's fundamental role in establishing the very foundations of bearability is riven by his repetition automatism that is further punctuated by Schneider TM's machinic soundtrack that suffuses many scenes with its overwhelming acousmatic and sonic insistence. None of this repetitious drilling drums any stabilizing "kinetic melodies" into the body.[52] Rather, it seems to relentlessly punctuate, contributing to his status as an oversaturated and evacuating actuality.[53]

A striking scene early in the film shows Tom preparing coffee in his kitchen soon after returning home from the hospital. He begins to pour milk into a coffee cup, but it quickly overflows, spilling over the edge of the kitchen counter in an image reminiscent of the blood dripping from his nose at the start of the film (figure 2.12). As Tom brushes his finger gently across the rivulets of dripping milk, the camera cuts to his finger, which is dotted with granules of coffee grounds (figure 2.13). As Tom crosses the threshold from kitchen to living room, he abruptly trips, spilling the milk and himself all over the floor.

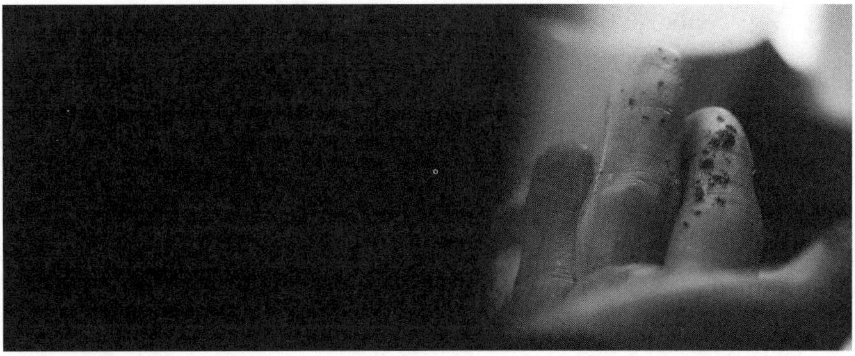

FIGURE 2.13
Tom's sticky finger dotted with coffee grounds. Film still from Omer Fast's *Remainder*. © Omer Fast.

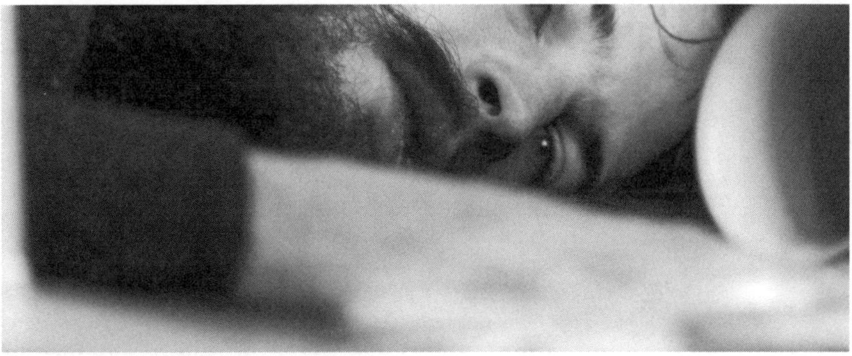

FIGURE 2.14
Tom, fallen to the floor, sliding his hand through spilled milk. Film still from Omer Fast's *Remainder*. © Omer Fast.

In a striking shot, he slides his hand through the pooling milk, and the camera's transition from sharp to soft focus makes it appear as though the hand is dissolving into the liquid (figure 2.14). But that dissolving is abruptly severed as the absorptive image cuts to another scene. We see the coffee cup tipped over, its circular rim directly adjacent to Tom's head on the floor, as the liquid spreads out and around the rims of these dual "craters" of matter that are simultaneously overflowing and emptying out (figure 2.15). When Tom tries to get up, he hits his head on a coffee table and collapses back again into the pooling liquid. We are then offered an anamorphic gaze from the perspective of the stain itself, so to speak, as we see a blurred image of a disaggregated still life of stranded objects, through the underside of an opaque glass table (figure 2.16).[54] Although the narrator is always trying to secure an

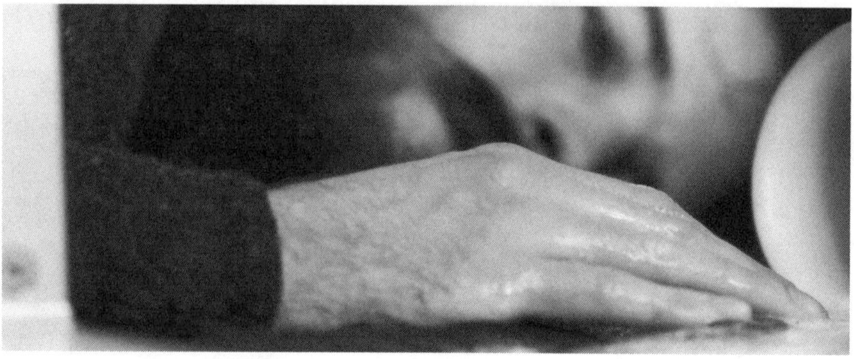

FIGURE 2.15
Circular rim of a cup and Tom's adjacent head. Film still from Omer Fast's *Remainder*. © Omer Fast.

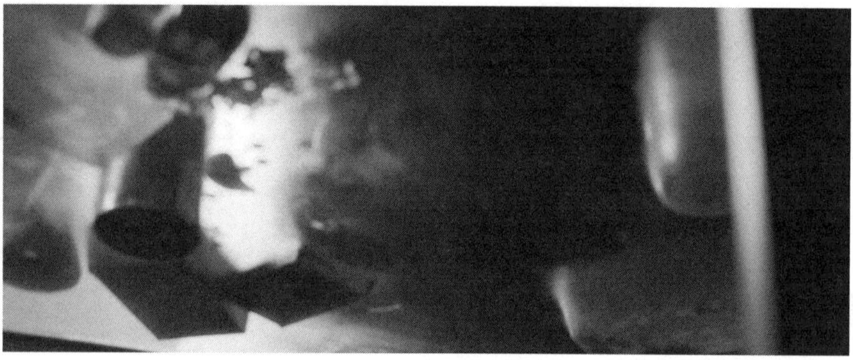

FIGURE 2.16
Objects on top of a glass table seen from the perspective of the stain. Film still from Omer Fast's *Remainder*. © Omer Fast.

elevated viewpoint to survey and ground his position and patterning within the world, he is bound to fail as he perpetually collapses into his own stain of being.

At no point do these scenes achieve any balance in the dialectic between the beautiful and stained soul of habit; the staining always overrides the sponging up of any matter. When the narrator notices that a "patch of oil" has formed beneath an engine being repaired by the motorbike enthusiast during the Madlyn Mansions reenactments, he insists that the patch be left as it is; he doesn't want it to "get wiped out" so he can capture it later on, sketching or taking frottage-like impressions of it and then making photocopies of those sketches (Rem, 150–151, 160). The narrator preserves it but also winds

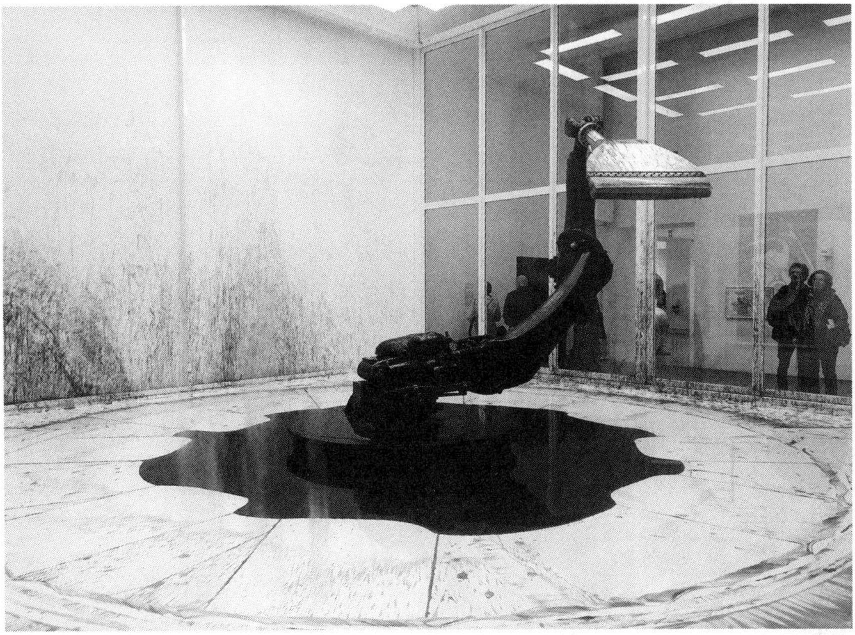

FIGURE 2.17
Sun Yuan and Peng Yu, *Can't Help Myself*, 2016. Kuka industrial robot, stainless steel and rubber, cellulose ether in colored water, lighting grid with Cognex visual-recognition sensors, and polycarbonate wall with aluminum frame. © Sun Yuan and Peng Yu.

up extending it in further acts of staining and cascading acts of rendering. The last two days before the first reenactment at Madlyn Mansions are devoted to what the narrator calls "'sweep'-days" to remove errors, inconsistencies, and omissions (Rem, 132). It is clear, however, that this process spreads further miscommunication, error, and misunderstanding, as fixing one thing offsets another, including the word "sweep" itself (Rem, 132–133). The narrator's compulsion to repeat, materialize, and exteriorize—to stain, remainder, and spill out—is never balanced out by his attempts to absorb, wipe clean, and digest.

The only other example that I have come across that is equal in pitch to the driven, uncontainable, and machinic logic of "expunging" the beautiful soul in *Remainder* is Sun Yuan and Peng Yu's disarming installation *Can't Help Myself* (2016). In it, a robotic arm brandishing a giant brush or squeegee labors to clean up the gallons of blood-red liquid that seem to spill from some Sisyphean wound it attempts to stem, like the narrator returning again and again to the crack from which his déjà vu sense of fluent being and movement in

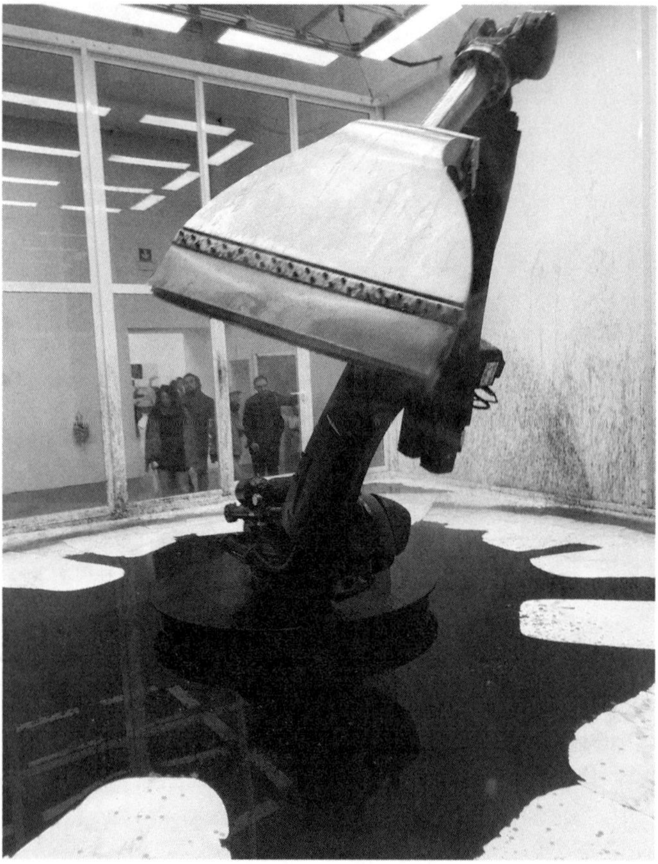

FIGURE 2.18
Sun Yuan and Peng Yu, detail, *Can't Help Myself*, 2016. Kuka industrial robot, stainless steel and rubber, cellulose ether in colored water, lighting grid with Cognex visual-recognition sensors, and polycarbonate wall with aluminum frame. © Sun Yuan and Peng Yu.

Madlyn Mansions spills out from and spreads (Rem, 66–67) (figure 2.17). The mechanism's desperate, algorithm-driven efforts only create more of a mess: its sweeping movements spatter and spread the oozing liquid all over the pristine white floor and the transparent glass box containing it (figure 2.18). The title of the piece suggests that the machinic repetitions of this arm are attempts to heal wounds that it is inflicting on itself. The anxiety that pervades the work signals the impasse between its formalization—the algorithm that drives the movements—and the impotence of the arm's particular physical acts. Its attempts to contain the blood-red liquid give viscous materiality to habit as the stain of being and residue of repetition.

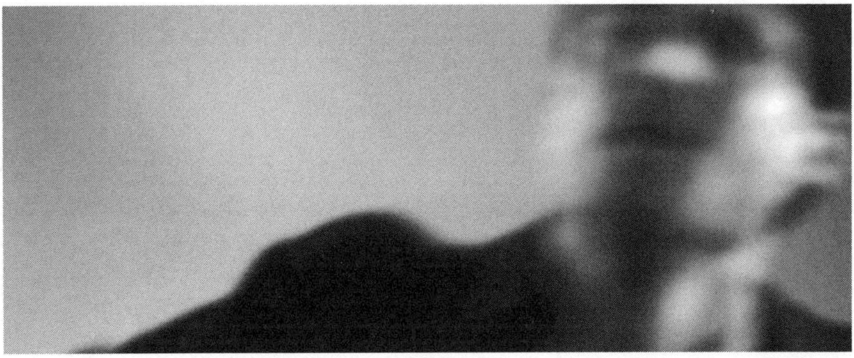

FIGURE 2.19
Tom's jerking movements in the underground as he attempts to pick up a coin. Film still from Omer Fast's *Remainder*. © Omer Fast.

COMPULSIVE MACHINIC EXTERIORITY

For Hegel, the peristaltic rhythm of "pulsation" (*Pulsieren*) remains blood's chief characteristic; it is the "vital point where none of the mechanical explanations of the understanding are of any use."[55] Pulsation is a vital sign that the "absolute interior vibration" of digested otherness remains interiorized and that it is idealized as circulation and a "being-at-home-with-oneself."[56] However, in *Remainder*, this pulsing is always already exterior, mechanical, and pulsatile. During the film's opening credits, we hear Tom's heavy breathing interwoven with Schneider TM's static, glitchy score. A bit further into the film, his breathing is fully mechanical as the machinery he is hooked up to beeps and rasps him like an "electronic metronome" at an interval of three or four seconds (Rem, 4, 54). If the lifeblood that circulates within the body is, as Hegel describes, "connected with the external world through breathing and respiration," from the beginning of *Remainder* that breath of life is already pulsed, pumped, and aerated by an intractable mechanical exteriority.[57]

These scenes offer a literal enactment of the anxiety that Lacan has identified as the trauma of birth as we emerge into the world choking and suffocating, as we inhale a fundamentally Other environment.[58] The narrator's inability to embody and embed in the environment never abates and thus he never achieves the mediation between body and world that habit is supposed to accomplish. Even after the narrator is once again upright, the glitchy electronic metronome of the score's crackling and static soundtrack continues to pulse his movements. When Tom tries to pick up a coin in the underground, his body jerks back and forth at a furious pace, keyed to an arrhythmia that prompts ill-timed contractions and frenetically repeated gestures that never settle into a stable tendency or a disposition to act (figures 2.19 and 2.20). During the film's Madlyn Mansions reenactment scenes, a blood-red "rec(ord)"

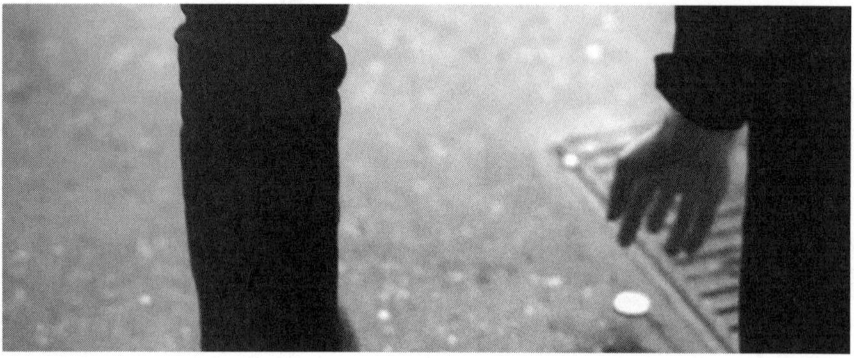

FIGURE 2.20
Tom attempting to pick up a coin in the Underground. Film still from Omer Fast's *Remainder*. © Omer Fast.

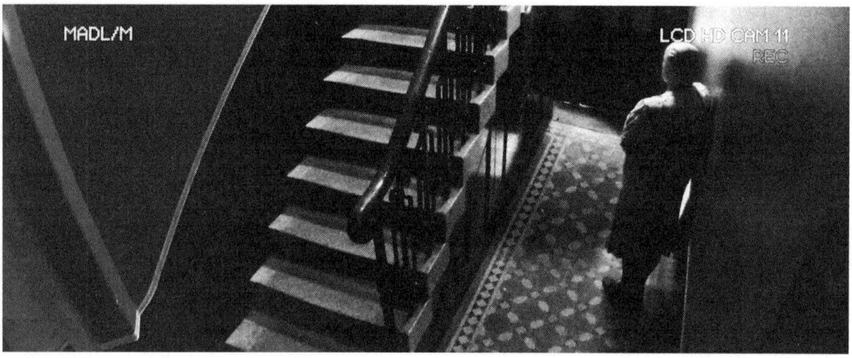

FIGURE 2.21
Pulsating REC(ORD) signal on the CCTV monitor at Madlyn Mansions. Film still from Omer Fast's *Remainder*. © Omer Fast.

indicator pulsates in the upper right-hand corner of the video monitors while Tom's search for immediacy, immersion, and fluidity is breached by a tempo and rhythm that cuts in and out, as he is perpetually suspended between crosscutting shots from multiple CCTV cameras that record different elements of the reenactment (figures 2.21 and 2.22).[59] This stain of the real appears not only as blood red, but also as a queasy, bluish-green light emanating from the CCTV video monitors that suffuses many of the scenes in the film and stains Naz and Tom's bodies in its glow (figures 2.22 and 2.26).

BEING-THAT-IS-DEPOSITED

Habit is often not the cure for the "not-being-at-home with oneself" that characterizes bodily derangement in mental disturbance and illness. Rather,

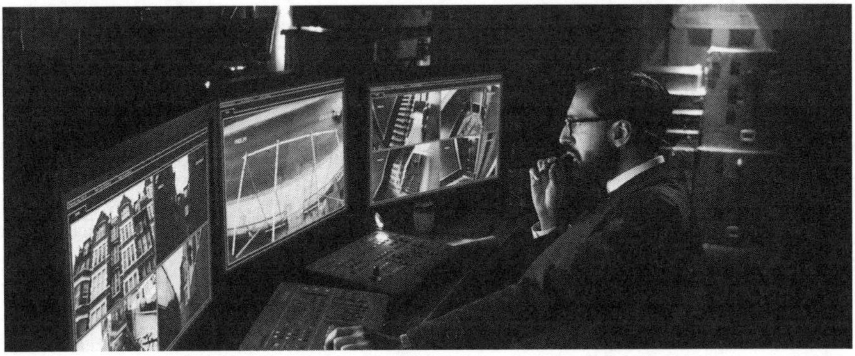

FIGURE 2.22
Naz bathed in the queasy, bluish-green light emanating from multiple CCTV video monitors during the Madlyn Mansions reenactment. Film still from Omer Fast's *Remainder*. © Omer Fast.

it is a further elaboration and intensification of that disturbance. In Hegel, bodily and mental disease (*Krankheit* and *Verrücktheit*) indicate unconscious drives, fixations, and altered states that are bound up closely with nature, inorganic matter, and the body, and habit is not merely prone to regressing to these states but actually generates them.[60] In *Remainder*, habit is not the development of a stable conatus achieved through interiorizing and idealized repetitions that produce a mode of self-preservation that adjusts the bodily organism into balance with its internal and external environment. Instead, the narrator's movements and way of being are precarious and often self-sabotaging. In fact, they are more akin to a death drive that Hegel implicitly accounts for in his persistent linking of death and habit throughout his writings, and that is at the very core of repetition in *Remainder*.

Contrary to Hegel's explicit claims, habit does not stabilize the subject so that it is "no longer dominated by drives" but, rather, it constantly generates such drives, and they, in turn, gear the body into overdrive.[61] If habit is a "universal mode of my own doing" that arises through the repetition of many single units, instances, or actions such that the "individual is appropriated to a universality," in *Remainder*, repetition is the narrator's very undoing.[62] Contrary to the assertion that, in habit, "the moment of corporeity" that is "posited in me" loses its externality and materiality, in *Remainder* that corporeity always remains an "immediately concrete thing" at the heart of any attempt to render it "completely pervious."[63] Thus habit persistently remains "a fragmentary and uncertain actuality" (*eine vereinzelte und unsichere Wirklichkeit*), or what I characterized earlier as an evacuating actuality.[64] Habit is called a second nature, owing to its resemblance to nature with respect to its necessity and immediacy, but those conditions are not natural determinations, rather they are "self-posited." As such, habit establishes a "basic and originary self-reference of subjectivity" that serves as the basis for the further "development" of the capacity to think, and thinking's ability to set itself free as a subjectivity of thinking, which depends much more on the insistence and persistence of automaticity than commentators on habit are willing to admit.[65]

As noted in the previous chapter, the terms positing or self-positing are repeated to such an extent that can only be characterized as a repetition compulsion that registers an intense anxiety around this second nature, which marks the birth of the subject in and as the first form of stabilized subjectivity. The precariousness of this crucial juncture is clearly attested to by the magic incantation of "positing" and "self-positing" that would consolidate these acts of ingraining and sedimentation performed by habit. Thus, in habit, we are not talking only about self-positing, but also about a "being-that-is-[de]posited," to supplement the English translation of *Gesetztsein* from the *Encyclopedia Logic*.[66] These sections in the anthropology of habit show it to be mired in "grains of the real" that perturb and unsettle the corporeal body rather than ingrain and establish its stability.[67]

Thus, habit's "drifting towards waste activity," is originary and generates an ontological "trash can deep within" overflowing with the particular content that it seems to be incapable of sloughing off, recycling, or emptying.[68] The myriad simplifications that habit generates through its economizing function of abstracting do not simply reduce and unify. They also generate off-cuts, dregs, parts, and units that are the correlates to the precipitous acts of abrupt cutting, contraction, and punctuation. These precipitous acts also result in a kenotic spilling out from rims, drillings that do not consolidate through repetition but drain through excessive punctuation, and impeded movements characterized by jerkiness, stumbling, seizure, and collapse. These conditions dominate *Remainder*, driven as they are by the narrator's repetition compulsion. They generate the very unsublatable repetitions that habit is supposed to temper and those material resistances it is meant to infect with its universality. And they are antagonistic to habit's achieving any "simple self-relating unity."[69]

If Hegel has described habit's self-positing as a "*seizure* of the corporeity," this possession is more like an intransitive wrenching and recoil that racks the body.[70] It is also much less controlled and willing than might be suggested by an overly voluntaristic interpretation of the Fichtean dimensions of self-positing in these sections on habit. In the same vein, interpretations of self-positing habit as a kind of weak willing—or, following the same logic, the basis for further elaborations into other more robust forms of intentionality—are inadequate. The drivenness of habit—that forces us to think—is predicated on a drive to break down and breakdown that is beyond the willing principle.

In habit, the corporeal body remains "corpo-Real": it continues to struggle with its own extimity that it can never seem to outwit, no matter what kinds of magic it employs to possess its mechanical, unmediated, and inertial condition.[71] As an appropriation or seizure of corporeity away from its exteriority, habit does not produce a "persevering in oneself," but, rather, a per-severing body marked by self-sundering and getting stuck in circuits of repetitions.[72] The ideal of the habitual body as a pliant and skillful instrument, never countermands its status as an incessantly breaking tool that is unsettling rather than unifying or stabilizing. Habit's failure to mediate its substance is not a momentary pedagogical or epistemological obstacle in the otherwise fluid mastery of a practice. It is not simply a Hegelian "moment," to be sublated and incorporated in spirit's "upward" movement that will result in increasingly complex and accomplished syntheses.

As a way of concluding this section, I want to return to Roupnel's description of acquired habit quoted in Bachelard's *Intuition of the Instant*, and read it against the grain in a way that is fully immanent to it. Roupnel characterizes habit as follows: "Through the effect of acquired habit, an act that begins again does so with more speed and precision. The gestures that carry it out shed their excessive dimensions and useless complication; they simplify and abridge themselves. Parisitic movements disappear. The act reduces outlay and waste to a strict, necessary minimum—both in terms of energy and time."[73] But, by my reading, when the universalizing function of habit fails to subsume the particular or manifest itself in it, gestures do not shed their "excessive dimensions" and "useless complication," rather, they are buffeted by and entangled in particularity; "Parisitic movements" do not disappear in favour of "speed and precision" but manifest as sluggishness and misprision instead; The act does not reduce outlay and waste to a necessary minimum but rather increases them. As Roupnel's quote duly notes, gestures do simplify and abridge themselves, but this does not necessarily result in what Hegel characterizes as "adroitness" and "simplification." Instead, it manifests as an excessive and repetitive cutting out and cutting off, more likely to produce glitchiness, or even a violent short-circuiting, than an accomplished act.

As a result, we are confronted with habit as a corporeal desease that disrupts fluidity (*Flüssigkeit*)—a term that is sometimes translated as "ease" rather than fluidity in Hegel's account of habit—and that is characterized by its modes of fixating, separating, and getting caught up in its parts and drives.[74] This desease extends into the "higher" realms of reason and consciousness, which are always already unsettled owing to their preposterous emergence from and immanence to habit's mode of de-positing, foundering, and sundering. In the *Philosophy of Mind*, Hegel claims not only that habit is the "basis of consciousness," but also that the "form of habit encompasses all sorts and stages of the activity of spirit."[75] One of the primal scenes that habit reenacts is the relationship between understanding and reason in the movement of spirit—down to the very language of fixity and fluidity—that echoes and repeats their crucial role in the Preface to the *Phenomenology* in ways that resist their dialectical reconciliation.

UNDERSTANDING AND THE AESTHETIC IDEOLOGY OF HABIT CHANGE

Strikingly, the crucial role of "understanding" is powerfully invoked in *Remainder*, which casts a very different light on our understanding of understanding's relationship to habit that remains central to all accounts of its corporeal way of knowing. Reading *Remainder* with Hegel forces us to rethink the "revision" in Merleau-Ponty's claim that "the phenomenon of habit is just what prompts us to revise our notion of 'understand' and our notion of the body."[76] Rather than habit proper fluidly permeated by bodily understanding, understanding is cut off in and through habit and its repetitions. It is precisely this cutting off that forces us to think—and to rethink the relationship between, habit, understanding, and the body.

After the accident in *Remainder*, the narrator has lost the proprioception, kinesthetic fluidity, and habitual skills indispensable to the performance of even basic tasks. As a result, he has "learnt to do things slowly since the accident, *understanding* [my emphasis] every move, each part of what I am doing. I did not choose to do things like this: it's the only way I can do them" (Rem, 6). When his "facilitator," Nazrul Ram Vyas (Naz), asks the narrator if one iteration of his Madlyn Mansions reenactment was a success, he replies that it was, up to a point, but the "detour" that separated him from his dream of seamless movement could not simply be "cut off" (Rem, 152). "Had I expected the detour through *understanding* [my emphasis] that I'd had to take in order to do anything for the last year—for my whole life—to be bypassed straight away: just cut off, a redundant nerve, an isolated oxbow lake that would evaporate? No" (Rem, 152). Why not?

At first reading, we might take this emphatic "no" to indicate that the narrator is simply being reasonable, pragmatic, or adapting to his altered circumstances. After the accident, he needs more time and practice to do things fluidly and habitually, we might reasonably surmise, because learning or relearning a skill, gesture, or movement requires conscious attention, but, as that skill becomes more automatic and fluid with practice, that need fades away. The narrator has not yet reached the point where the habitual body's movement and action are no longer, in Merleau-Ponty's gendered terminology, "a handmaid of consciousness."[77] Nor is the narrator's lack of confidence that he will ever be able to bypass his "eternal detour" simply due to an accident that has caused permanent neurological damage, and that prevents him from ever getting completely up to speed (Rem, 23). In the novel, that not-getting up to speed is not merely a deficit. Rather, it is an indication of a constitutive gap, delay, and intractability at the heart of the ontology of habit itself. As the narrator clearly articulates, the accident only highlights that it made him become even more what he'd always been anyway; he was always already "completely second-hand" (Rem, 25, 54).

The dilemma addressed by the narrator recurs in almost all accounts of habit. The discourse on habit acknowledges that the formation of habit requires skill, will, and consciousness. That is why it is called a "second nature": it resembles a natural quality, but it is posited and mediated by us. However, there is always a fear of the inertia and deadening effects of habit, and the loss of freedom and autonomy this entails, when we are, as Hegel aptly puts it, "appropriated to universality" through the abstractions involved in habit formation and thus when thinking goes on automatic pilot. Although through habit we gain a degree of "free thinking" afforded to us by its automaticity—such that we may cast our attention elsewhere while engaged in a habitual act—the freedom gained does not entirely make up for the risks to it engendered by the exteriority and abstraction involved in automaticity. It is common—often the norm—to consider rigid, automatic, and clichéd behaviors—characterized as mechanized, mindless, and repetitive routines posing an imminent threat of becoming calcinated and thing-like—entirely negatively. These are seen as failed, deficient, or bad habits, or mere routines, and thus often unworthy of being characterized as habit at all.[78] This dual nature is captured by Hegel's definition of habit as the mechanism of self-feeling. Because the *gap* in self-feeling (me) is engendered through the automaticity of habit that converts it into a bodily possession (mine), if it is not somehow counterbalanced, it is always on the verge of collapsing into unfreedom, exteriority, and death.

However, *Remainder* seems to present the opposite situation as the predominant concern or impediment. The protagonist appears to be suffering from a hypertrophy of consciousness and understanding, and a complete lack of habit. This state recalls Nietzschean fears about the "hell of a life without habits," which would force one to constantly think and improvise, such that one would be unable to get through the door or brush one's teeth, let alone gracefully and dexterously perform more sophisticated tasks like playing piano. This "hell of a life without habits" can also be seen in another light, as a modernist ethos: what Blanchot would call a form of "habitless inhabiting."[79] But, in the breach, what one is usually talking about is a more moderate, yet bracing, rhythm of habit change, in which Nietzsche's "brief habits" take precedence over "enduring ones": a constant clearing of a path before or as soon as it grows over, or the forging of new and divergent paths that crosscut those pre-established ones. This contradiction at the heart of habit is captured in William

James's and Giorgio Agamben's respective definitions of "genius": the former stating that genius is little more than perceiving in an unhabitual way, and the latter claiming that genius is habit, as it "is our life insofar as it does not belong to us."[80] Cleary, these two positions are not merely opposites, as they both account for the "extimate" nature of habit that is an intimate part of us with an external and alien quality.[81] How have they been reconciled?

Aesthetic modernism imagined that it could close the gap between the habitual and unhabitual through a rhythm of habit change. This rhythm would require a constant shifting between the stabilizing, repetitive, and automatic aspects of habit on the one hand, and the destabilizing, innovative, and attentive, if not conscious or intentional aspects, on the other. This modernist "accelerationist" intervention into the axiomatics of habit change—that change generates habit, but that habit, in turn, is actualized as a habit of changing—would develop a dynamic habit of the interruption of habit.[82] The logic of that dynamic is effectively captured by Charles Sanders Peirce's notion of the "deliberately formed, self-analyzing habit—self-analyzing because formed by the aid of analysis of the exercises that nourished it."[83] The notion of a self-analyzing habit often assumes a relatively balanced rhythm between sedimentation and de-sedimentation, automatization and de-automatization.

This rhythm is ubiquitous and articulated in myriad ways and valences by philosophers from across many philosophical traditions: Dewey's "continuous reconstruction;" Merleau-Ponty's "sedimentation and spontaneity;" Michael Polanyi's "analysis and integration;" Nietzsche's "brief habits" versus "enduring ones"; Bourdieu's habitus involving an "incorporation" and "objectification" of schemas; the pairing of "Addiction and Grace" in Catherine Malabou's title for her introduction to a translation of Félix Ravaisson's *On Habit*; Deleuze's "habitual" and "attentive" recognition; Walter Benjamin's "attention" and "distraction"; Bruno Latour's rhythm between "automatic pilot" and "manual restart"; Taussig's "immersion and intellect"; and Sloterdijk's anthropotechnics of repeated repetition versus repeating repetition. There are also Hegelian versions of this rhythm in accounts of habit as an anti-bildungsroman that continuously undoes itself to avoid the "processless habit" of maturity that is a form of stasis and death.[84] The furthest deviations from it are the versions of habit's "stabilized instability" that were outlined in the introduction.

At times, this rhythm can make it seem like conscious attention is *magically*—read: immediately—available for a "manual restart," in Bruno Latour's vocabulary of habit. That is, it is willing, able, and ready to intervene on habit when it threatens to become too automatic and rigid, as if to reverse engineer how a habit might have started with attention and analysis before sinking into habit. Or, better yet, to foster a condition in which we might inculcate the habit of Peirce's "self-analyzing habit." In cunning, homeopathic, and pharmakon-like ways, habit cures habit by using its mechanical laws in ways that end up enacting the subject's goals.[85] But this account assumes that the automaticity involved in habit is a "petrified intelligence," and that the abstracting and universalizing dimensions of habit never degenerate into pure, mindless, passive automatism. This assumption is common to many accounts of habit. It receives one of its starkest formulations in Bergson's *The Creative Mind: An Introduction to Metaphysics*, where Bergson writes that "Habit ... gives us the living demonstration ... that mechanism is not sufficient to itself; it is, so to speak, only the fossilized residue of a spiritual activity."[86] Thus, only a little quotidian magic is needed to coax these schemas of petrified intelligence back into circulation (which they never really left), and deftly manipulate them so that intelligence, understanding, and intentionality may be brought to permeate the body so it develops the ability to immediately express the inner movement of thought without conscious reflection. Often this language inevitably veers toward a Merleau-Pontyian notion of habit as a corporeal schema of intentional dispositions, or what he sometimes calls "motor intentionality," in which understanding never really withdraws after the learning phase but remains suspended in bodily schemas of intentionality.[87]

The language of magic appears like a rabbit out of a hat precisely when, in a "feigned immediacy," and produced through habit's simplifications and dexterity, attention and understanding have sedimented in and as fluid bodily aboutness.[88] As Hegel notes, in habit there "arises a *magical* relation, an immediate operation of mind on body."[89] Habit's drift toward automaticity and thingness is never allowed to progress to the point where the mechanical rudder of its cybernetic loop cannot be recalibrated by a prodigious manual restart and, in a further feat of magic, reflection, intelligence, intentionality, and rule following are now incorporated such that any "on," "over," "aboutness," or "led by" are transfigured into "in" and "through" bodily means. Of course, even in this immersion and immediacy, there is also an absence and desertion that always has "the shape of something *mechanical*," as Hegel notes—but only after that mechanism has first been ensouled and quickened with spirit through habit, thus ensuring that it will never again fully pass into what Ravaisson calls "the grip of a blind mechanism."[90]

We seem to be in a soup of contradiction. At times, we seem to be speaking about a sequential operation of analysis *then* integration. At other times, we are speaking about a mode of constant vigilance that hovers *over* habit at a minimal distance, ever ready and primed to swoop in when needed, or, more subtly, fluctuating in and out of habit that might suggests bodily versions of what Schlegel calls a "permanent parabasis" in his definition of irony, or thoroughly permeating it as bodily intentionality. But we can find no convincing account of how this rhythm happens, except through the sanctioned modernist paradigms to which the dilemma owes its figuration and force. According to those paradigms, we break out of our habitual way of experiencing things by rhythms of alienation/exteriorization and incorporation/interiorization that represents a more or less "conscious" aesthetic strategy that accelerates the logico-aesthetic rhythm of "present-at-hand" and "ready-to-hand" in Heidegger's proverbial account of the broken tool.[91] In many ways, this modernist aesthetic of habit change remains dominant in our accounts of the culturological—if not ontological—operations of habit.

Tom McCarthy has captured this modernist dilemma well: he calls attention to a very "classical construct," whereby "the dancer and dance should become one"—he is clearly referring to the ending of Yeats's poem "Among School Children" and perhaps Paul de Man's reading of that passage in his essay "Semiology and Rhetoric"—"they should converge so that the experience of them doing it and the act should merge. There shouldn't be any cognitive gap—but then he wants the awareness of the disappearance of the gap. It's an irreducible paradox. He'll never be happy."[92] In his *Encyclopedia Logic*, Hegel calls the cognitive gap referred to here as "thinking over" (*Nachdenken*), a version of the unhappy consciousness in the *Phenomenology of Spirit*, in which a phenomenon is "made double, broken apart into the inner and the outer, force and expression, cause and effect."[93] But, as Hegel notes, in adopting a more speculative perspective on understanding, "the examination of knowing cannot take place other than *by way of knowing*."[94] For Hegel, such thinking over is insufficient because it is a form of finite cognition that is not yet a speculative understanding of the self-generating and immanent movement of thinking as an *impersonal* process.

But the implied balance—or punctuated equilibrium—in the rhythm of habit change often ignores or smooths over the unbearable glitchiness of habit. Habit does not just rock gently back and forth between analysis and integration, obduracy and pliancy. Rather, it is rocked, mired in, and perturbed by the many detours and deviations that understanding generates at the heart of habit via its hyperbolic cutting out and breaching. That process, in turn, produces excess parts and matter that cannot settle down sufficiently to secure the emergence of any stable consciousness that could reflect on its own autogenerated habits rather than recoil from them. There is no smooth way to balance the oscillation between understanding and habit. Nor is understanding opposed to habitual fluidity in the way that the narrator in *Remainder* might lead us to surmise. *Remainder* is not, to my mind, a novel about the loss of "non-conscious cognition" and thus an exaggerated vision of the "*imperialism* of higher consciousness," as N. Katherine Hayles writes, that has to overcompensate for the loss of habit-like fluidity and adroitness that makes life bearable.[95] Rather, *Remainder* enacts understanding's power of separation that is internal to the logic of habit itself. This is the immanent event of habit: a disruption internal to its workings and not simply something external that disrupts habitual fluidity.

VERSTAND AND *VERNUNFT* IN HABIT

Here, we might gain some clarity by means of a detour though Hegel's philosophical system, in which understanding (*Verstand*)—a particular form of consciousness—is contrasted with reason (*Vernunft*).[96] The most succinct account of *Verstand* is found in the Preface to the *Phenomenology of Spirit*: "the act of parting is the force and labor of the *understanding*, the most astonishing and the greatest of all the powers, rather, which is the absolute power."[97] *Verstand* is a hyperanalytic mode of thinking characterized by dividing, isolating, distancing, abstracting, parting, atomizing, anatomizing, dissecting, and severing. In its more frenzied and brutal Dionysian or Gorgonian manifestations, it is a tearing-apart, dismembering, and mortifying gaze. But, beyond separating and dividing, the *Verstand* also "fixes" and reifies—and, one might say, fetishizes—those severed elements. In contrast to these analytic divisions and abrupt separations, speculative reason (*Vernunft*) is the ability to grasp the fluid, organic interconnectedness and plastic exposition of these dead parts as dialectical moments in the "self-moving movement" of the life of spirit.[98]

But speculative reason's drive for dialectical unity cannot simply take a detour *around* understanding to avoid the detours *of* understanding. Nor can it simply extrude the extrusions left as remainders by understanding's incisions, thus taking leave of what is left over. *Vernunft* must tarry with those detours and remainders—double down on them, so to speak—precisely because it is only through these fixations can one see the "one-sidedness" and "abstract" limitations of *Verstand*. Only thereby can *Vernunft* reassemble these parts and determinations into their proper speculative unity, fluid interconnection, and circularity as organs and moments of the whole.[99] Nathan Ross succinctly articulates the dialectical stakes of *Verstand* and *Vernunft* in its starkest terms: "without the stubbornness of the understanding there would be no fluidity."[100] In Hegel's own words, "the common practice of separating understanding and reason is to be rejected on all counts."[101] Or, in a deceptively lyrical passage from the *Encyclopedia Logic*, the "fact that there is rhyme and reason (*Verstand*, *Vernunft*) to the world conveys what is contained in the expression 'objective thought.' To be sure, the latter expression is awkward because *thought* is habitually (*gewöhnlich*) used for something belonging to the mind, i.e., to consciousness and what is objective is for the most part attributed to what is not mental."[102] Of the many difficult issues to address in this stunning passage, let us stick to the simple fact that there is no speculative movement—no objective thought—unless we account for tarrying with the sundering power of the negative in a speculative way.

But this is not a tale of simple progress or of overcoming, in the sense that understanding cuts the parts loose, and gets stuck on them before reason, as the speculative perspective of understanding, unfixes them and ushers them into a "self-moving movement." Fixity is not simply a "moment" within fluidity or an external blockage thereof. If the understanding is the "most astonishing and greatest of all the powers," then speculative reason must incorporate this force: "Spirit is this power only by looking the negative in the face, and tarrying with it."[103] The German term for the activity of *Verstand*'s parting (*Scheiden*) does not just mean separation—it also indicates departing, death, and mortification.[104] In one of the most well-known passages from the Preface, Hegel writes that spirit "wins its truth only when, in utter dismemberment, it finds itself."[105] How should we interpret this "it finds itself"? Spirit, or speculative reason, does not win its truth by simply overcoming dismemberment by making whole again—"re-membering" (*Erinnerung*) that absolute dismemberment into an inwardness.[106] Rather, it does so by finding itself mired in and tarrying with dismemberment, such that fixity is never fully supplanted by fluidity.

Yet, the language of fixity and fluidity in habit suggest that it is one of the privileged places where the nascent spirt of soul begins to overcome fixity. Through habit, the vitality, life, and freedom of the organism begins to assert itself as an inaugural self-positing that begins to round itself off through self-mediation and inner reflection. All these qualities of life and vitality, Hegel insists, are beyond the grasp of *Verstand*, as it remains mired in finite mediation.[107] The *Verstand* in habit is a form of *desperate* vitality that recalcitrantly remains "beyond its grasp," but also beyond the grasp of *Vernunft*.[108] The divisions and gaps generated by habit are not settled and ensouled through the lived body of habit in which—to use Merleau-Ponty's vocabulary from *Phenomenology of Perception*—"grasping a meaning is performed by the body."[109] Rather, habit is often a further punctuation of the gaps in which understanding is cut off.

Phenomenologically inflected and orthopedic accounts of habit tend to "mind the gaps," such that understanding transimmanently remains within the realm of continuity and fluidity. If speculative reason articulates its truth in positing that "the true is the whole" in the Preface to the *Phenomenology of Spirit*, then that truth and its method is relentlessly disarticulated, sundered, and even tortured throughout the body of that text, such that "every moment of its existence, every bone in its body, has been broken on the wheel [of dialectics]."[110] But it is not always easy to recognize that this "whole"—this body of truth—is broken, full of holes, perforated and leaking. Going for broke, all circular or spiraling motion in *Remainder* is ground down into a halting, jerky "cog-wheel rigidity," beyond the cunning of any mechanic to fix. In McCarthy's novel, the first auditioner for the part of the motorbike enthusiast is told

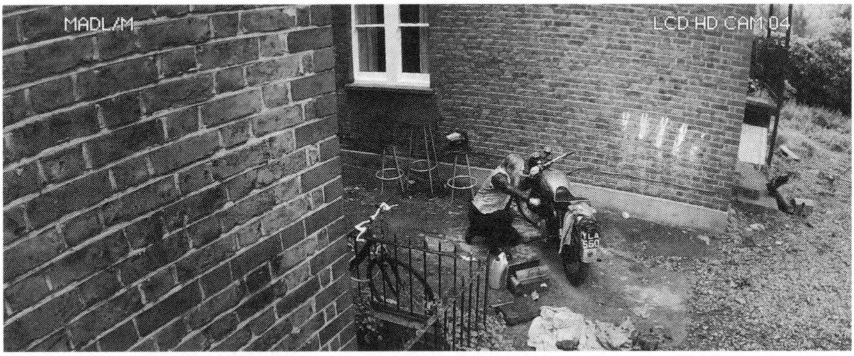

FIGURE 2.23
Reenactor taking apart a motorbike in order to "fix it back." Film still from Omer Fast's *Remainder*. © Omer Fast.

he will be "fixing it," and once it is fixed, he will "take it apart again. Then fix it back" (Rem, 117–118) (figure 2.23). He doesn't get the part perhaps because he thinks that fixing it back means to make the motorbike whole again so that it runs smoothly, instead of getting caught up in the reenactment of an obsessive loop of assembling and disassembling.[111]

Immediately before the novel's sections on neural rerouting, the protagonist enters Green Park tube station. There, he observes a disassembled escalator lying in pieces awaiting overhaul. "You think of an escalator as one object," the narrator muses, "a looped, moving bracelet, but in fact it's made of loads of individual, separate steps woven together into one smooth system. Articulated. These ones had been dis-articulated, and were lying messily around" (Rem, 16). Notably, this escalator is never fixed and put back together seamlessly for the narrator. It remains "lying messily around" in pieces. It also remains with him as a greasy stain on his coat sleave and fingers, left by his tube ticket that was "wedged between two cogs" at a turnstile in the underground (Rem, 16). This image of the disjointed greasy escalator parts returns at pivotal points throughout the novel, disrupting and staining the narrator's dreams of connectivity and fluidity: "this messy, irksome matter that had no respect for millions, didn't know its place. My undoing: matter" (Rem, 16–17, 38, 153–154). Later, when his health is deteriorating owing to his reenactment "addiction," a doctor diagnoses Tom's "cog-wheel rigidity" as an autonomic symptom of his traumatic state, thus recalling the greasy remainder spewed out by the cogs (Rem, 220).

Simply put, we should avoid the trap of seeing McCarthy's "detour through understanding" as something opposed to habit, to be overcome in order to achieve habitual fluidity. Nor should we see the detour as an indication of the loss or absence of habit, or merely an external deviation and blockage that prevents habit proper from forming. *Verstand* is not simply an epistemological model of rational, analytic thinking that is hyperactivated by the accident and therefore overcompensating for the loss of habitual action, thus compelling the narrator to think about or analyze each action before he does it. Rather, understanding is a disarticulation of the mortifying aspects of habit, which are immanent to its *ontology* of abstraction, and not just an external epistemological, pedagogical, or psychological stage in—or external impediment to—the inculcation and functioning of habit proper.

If understanding in Hegel is characterized by sundering, one-sidedness, abstraction, rigidity, lingering, and getting mired in the particular, the narrator never overcomes this "detour" precisely because habit produces detours, parts, cuts, gaps, and excesses, and repetitively gets stuck on and in them. Instead of securing the first stable form of self to emerge—thereby providing the grounds for the emergence of more developed shapes of consciousness, self-consciousness, and speculative reason—the *Verstand* in habit repetitively reenacts the divisions, gaps, cuts, and disturbances that it creates. *Verstand* in *Remainder* is misunderstood when it is pitched solely at the level of epistemology rather than as a mortifying condition that is internal to an ontology of repetition and habit. Habit allows us to see that which are usually considered epistemological limitations as constitutive, internal divisions and gaps within ontology.

Tom's declaration in the film—"I have big gaps"—makes very clear the real ontological stakes of *Verstand*, in which the interruption of habit *by* understanding is actually a disruption and desease internal *to* habit itself (Rem film, 17:24:23). The cuts and fissures in the habitual body are generated by features of habit that exacerbate and immerse us in—indeed impale us on—the "distressing drive body."[112] As such, habit does not necessarily stabilize or distance us from those drives as Hegel seems to claim in his anthropology of habit: "habit is the subject and being is the predicate ... and both have their stability [*Halt*] in habit so that the subject is no longer dominated by drives."[113] The Lacanian claim that the "drive circulates around a hole, a *gap* in the order of being" can occlude the fact that the drive does not circulate around a preexisting gap, but rather it is the drive that *generates* the gaps, cuts, holes and excesses in the order of being.[114]

It is precisely the incisive, mortifying, and death-driven aspects of the understanding in habit that generates a sundered and surded body rather than a "lived" body. That habitual body is not at peace with the unifying and mediating functions of bodily habit as "the harmony between what we aim at and what is given, between the intention and the performance," such that "the body is our anchorage in a world."[115] Recall that, when the narrator in *Remainder* insists that the "detour through understanding" is constitutive of his "whole life," his friend Greg notes that his condition is exemplary, not exceptional.

All the detours and glitches that repeatedly cut in and out in *Remainder* are telling of habit's status as an ontological desease that is a per-severing and hyperbolically driven presence throughout the novel and film, not indications of its absence. As the narrator repeatedly affirms, he is and always was an "eternal detour" and "completely second-hand." This condition demands a strange logic and logistical operation to process these endless detours, mediations, short circuits, and drifts of matter generated by the mortifying and analytic dimensions of understanding and the compulsion to repeat.

DEATH-DEALING MATTER AND FORENSIC ANALYSIS

If the *Verstand* is indicative of a mortifying and grinding analysis, then the logic of habit is always tarrying with the generation of an excessive and death-dealing matter. Here, I shall consider the science, logic, and logistics that are meant to account for the hyperanalytic aspects of *Verstand*, played out in the narrator's fascination with the formal procedures of forensic crime manuals.

Preparing to reenact a murder that occurred near Madlyn Mansions, the narrator spends hours in the British Library reading forensic textbooks, general introductions meant for the public, and complex academic papers addressed to experts in the field. In particular, he focuses on a handbook that every professional forensic investigator "has to learn by rote, and learnt it by rote too" (Rem, 186). Like a medieval scholastic treatise—for instance, Thomas Aquinas's *Summa Theologica*, that was so important for Erwin Panofsky's concept of the *habitus* in his *Gothic Architecture and Scholasticism*, and for Bourdieu's extension of that concept into his own master sociological concept—the textbook's *modus operandi* is manifested in its *mise-en-page* (figure 2.24).[116] It is incessantly subdivided into ever smaller parts, "paragraphs headed by numbers, then by capital letters, then by roman numerals, then by lower-case letters as they indented further and further from the left-hand margin" (Rem, 186).

The text's progress through endless subdivisions invokes the narrator's own breaking down of each movement into its constituent parts before executing it—like the chains, steps, units, and sequences that are involved in the learning phase of habit formation. Each indentation of the manual corresponds to "a step or half-step in the chain of actions you must follow when you conduct a forensic search" (Rem, 186). Like the narrator's hyperanalytic dissection of the specific movements, gestures, or "angles" in his reenactments, the forensic *modus operandi* is extremely formal: "you don't just go ahead and do it—you do it slowly, breaking down your movement into phases that have sections, and subsections, each one governed by rigorous rules" (Rem, 186–187).

But this obsession with analytic procedure and logistics is not pursued to solve any crime; its operations are ill-suited to identify any antecedent causes as it relentlessly fissures and surds the causality of action. Just as the narrator

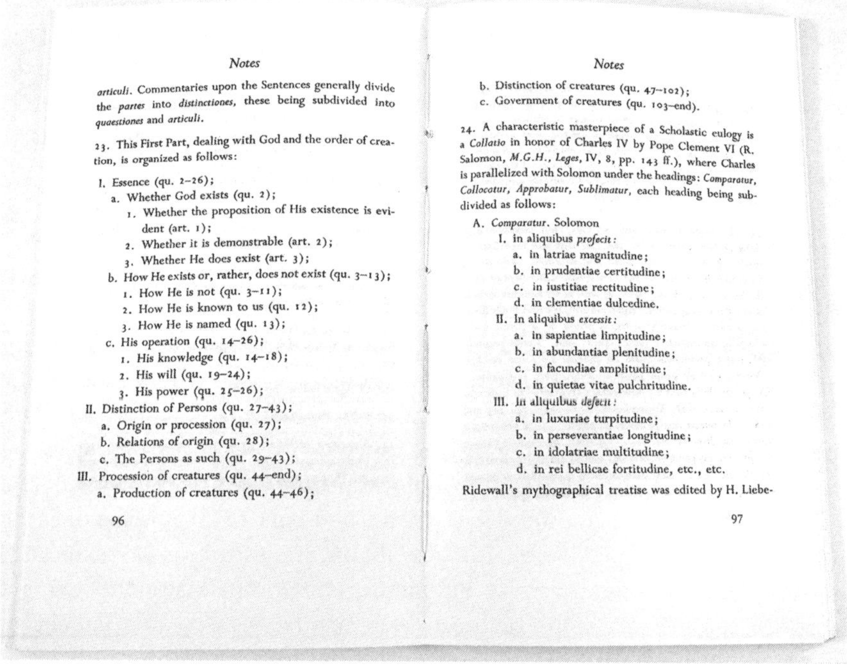

Notes

articuli. Commentaries upon the Sentences generally divide the *partes* into *distinctiones*, these being subdivided into *quaestiones* and *articuli*.

23. This First Part, dealing with God and the order of creation, is organized as follows:

- I. Essence (qu. 2–26);
  - a. Whether God exists (qu. 2);
    - 1. Whether the proposition of His existence is evident (art. 1);
    - 2. Whether it is demonstrable (art. 2);
    - 3. Whether He does exist (art. 3);
  - b. How He exists or, rather, does not exist (qu. 3–13);
    - 1. How He is not (qu. 3–11);
    - 2. How He is known to us (qu. 12);
    - 3. How He is named (qu. 13);
  - c. His operation (qu. 14–26);
    - 1. His knowledge (qu. 14–18);
    - 2. His will (qu. 19–24);
    - 3. His power (qu. 25–26);
- II. Distinction of Persons (qu. 27–43);
  - a. Origin or procession (qu. 27);
  - b. Relations of origin (qu. 28);
  - c. The Persons as such (qu. 29–43);
- III. Procession of creatures (qu. 44–end);
  - a. Production of creatures (qu. 44–46);

96

Notes

  - b. Distinction of creatures (qu. 47–102);
  - c. Government of creatures (qu. 103–end).

24. A characteristic masterpiece of a Scholastic eulogy is a *Collatio* in honor of Charles IV by Pope Clement VI (R. Salomon, *M.G.H.*, *Leges*, IV, 8, pp. 143 ff.), where Charles is parallelized with Solomon under the headings: *Comparatur, Collocatur, Approbatur, Sublimatur*, each heading being subdivided as follows:

- A. *Comparatur*. Solomon
  - I. in aliquibus *profecit*:
    - a. in latriae magnitudine;
    - b. in prudentiae certitudine;
    - c. in iustitiae rectitudine;
    - d. in clementiae dulcedine.
  - II. In aliquibus *excessit*:
    - a. in sapientiae limpitudine;
    - b. in abundantiae plenitudine;
    - c. in facundiae amplitudine;
    - d. in quietae vitae pulchritudine.
  - III. In aliquibus *defecit*:
    - a. in luxuriae turpitudine;
    - b. in perseverantiae longitudine;
    - c. in idolatriae multitudine;
    - d. in rei bellicae fortitudine, etc., etc.

Ridewall's mythographical treatise was edited by H. Liebe-

97

FIGURE 2.24

Analytic subdivisions of Thomas Aquinas's *Summa Theologica* as illustrated in Erwin Panofsky's *Gothic Architecture and Scholasticism* (New York: Meridian, 1951). © Gerda Panofsky.

repeatedly breaks each sequence of a reenactment down to its constituent parts, not in order to fix (correct) the problem, but rather to proliferate, linger on, and "relish" all the way stations that comprise habit as a way of being, the forensic process allows him to tarry with habit's own death-driven ontological crime scene, in which habit is both the cause and the effect of his undoing by matter (Rem, 168). The narrator's obsession with forensic procedure mires him in a surfeit of matter that the process generates and that is in excess of the analytic procedures that are supposed to contain it. His wires are short-circuited such that repeating (automaticity) and working through (understanding) relentlessly collapse into a scene strewn with infinite stuff.

The collapsing relationship between repetition and working through is raised in the narrator's compelling exchange with Edward Samuels, a former armed robber who the narrator hires to "choreograph" the final bank heist reenactment. When asked about the criminal psychology textbooks he has studied, including one entitled the *The Psychopathology of Crime*, Samuels responds: "Reading these was like suddenly being given the key to my own past. Understanding it. If you don't want to repeat things, you have to understand them" (Rem, 246). The narrator, somewhat perplexed, ponders his response: "I thought hard about what Samuels had just said, then told him: 'But I do want to repeat things. ... And I don't want to understand them. That's the ...' My voice trailed off" (Rem, 247). In this exchange, we witness again the collapse of the compulsion to repeat (the drivenness of habit) and working through (understanding) into each other and where understanding is cut off.

When the narrator investigates the scene of a crime he wishes to reenact, he is overwhelmed by information. Myriad substances and markings are either impressed within or strewn across the fissured, cracked, seamed, and cambered surface: water and dirt mixed to form "muddy, pockmarked ridges ... chewing gum, cigarette butts, bottle tops ..." (Rem, 201). He observes that, in just a small, ten-by-ten-centimeter cube of matter from the scene, one could find, "so much to analyse, so many layers, just so much *matter*—that your study of it would branch out and become endless until, finally, you threw your hands up in despair and announced ... *There's too much here, too much to process, just too much*" (Rem, 202). The narrator's preferred "pattern" for moving through the scene, if he were a lead forensic investigator, is a "figure of eight" (Rem, 187). He chooses this pattern precisely because it would entail each person on his team crawling "round the same area in an endlessly repeating circuit, unearthing the same evidence, the same prints, marks and tracings again and again and again, recording them as though afresh each time" (Rem, 187).

This interwoven, endlessly repeating circuit, rerecording as though anew each time, is indicative of speculative movement as such which, in Hegel's discussion of the "circle of circles," winds the end back to the beginning, and in which "each single member ... in returning to the beginning it is at the same time the beginning of a new member."[117] Of course, this entire pattern is an impossible and speculative forensic archaeology; as if by magic, its hyperbolic analytics does not destroy the ground it overturns, and whatever it cuts grows back, in a movement that is a perpetual arriving at a new beginning. It is a repetitious circuit that repeats the repeating by rote of "the chains of actions you must follow" that are supposed to be formal and deliberate (Rem, 186). This figure-eight movement is like a conversion machine, in which the deliberate and formal aspects of "thinking over" abruptly switchover into a drivenness by "the chains of actions you must follow." The *Verstand*-like mortifications that break down matter, action, and meaning are immanent to and generated by the circuits of the topological figure-eight movement in which understanding is cut off.

At any crime scene or archaeological site, recording data constitutes an integral part of the methodological procedures that are meant to compensate for the potential destruction or misrepresentation of data generated in any forensic analytics. In a hyperbolic exaggeration of this need to record, the protagonist in *Remainder* engages in what might be referred to as acts of "absolute

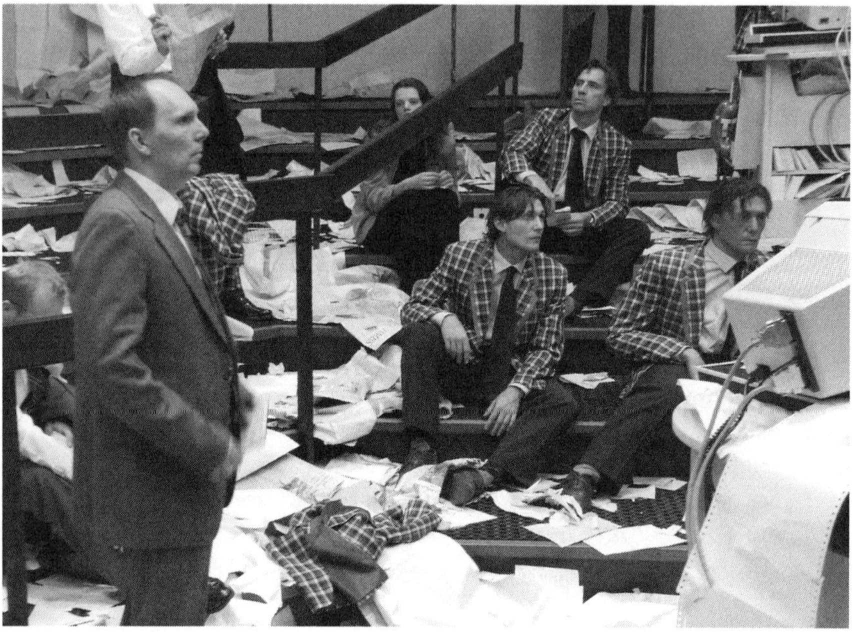

FIGURE 2.25
Still from Aernout Mik, *Middlemen*, 2001. Camera: Bonito Strangio. Directing assistance: Marjoleine Boonstra. Courtesy of the artist and carlier | gebauer, Berlin/Madrid.

rend(er)ing," to slightly twist the preferred French translation—by Kojève, Bataille, and Derrida—of Hegel's *absoluten Zerrissenheit* from the Preface to the *Phenomenology* as *déchirement absolu*: "absolute rending," which does not adhere to Miller's anatomically inflected English translation of the German as "utter dismemberment."[118] In many ways, this rend(er)ing is better able to account for the relentless proliferation and recursion of drawings, sketches, diagrams, charts, indexes, frottage-like impressions, models, and lists generated during the reenactments that do not simply record and synthesize all the patterns, surplus matter, and stains but are of a piece with their analytic proliferation. They accumulate in the novel and film like the "chits of paper" in Aernout Mik's video *Middleman*, which stages a stock trading room right after a market crash, that are spit out by multiple inscriptional devices as they are strewn across the floor in unruly heaps (figure 2.25).[119]

Here and elsewhere in *Remainder*, we see that, contrary to Bergson's claim that in habit repetitive action drives out representation, it can actually generate representations in a very material sense. The narrator in *Remainder* is constantly tripped up by a bricolage of disjointed parts, surplus matter, scraps of conversations, and partial memories that constantly interrupt his attempts to cut out the detour of understanding. What appears external, disruptive, and at odds with any notion of habit as a mode of a fluid bodily understanding that adapts the organism to its environment is in fact internal to it in disturbing and unsettling ways. Let's call this the cunningness of habit at work in *Remainder* that appears to posit understanding as inimical and external to habit proper but is actually driving it—behind its back—in endless deviating circuits, which it is never in control of.

THE MAGIC AND CUNNING OF HABIT

In Hegel, the Cunning of Reason (*List der Vernunft*) usually refers to its manifestation in *Lectures on the Philosophy of History* and *Elements of the Philosophy of Right*.[120] There, the supposed universal reason of history is described as being achieved behind the backs of states, nations, and historical figures. They may think that they are guiding it through their own determinate actions and principles but they are, in fact, the "unconscious instruments and organs of that inner activity" whose shapes they assume pass away, while the work of spirit "in and for itself" continues its speculative movement.[121] Reason's cunning refers to its use of deviation, indirection, distance, and externality to achieve its immanent "purpose": what appears alien and contradictory to reason turns out to be at home with itself in its other. Like a judoka, it allows forces to work against themselves to reveal their contradictions and conflicts.

But the most primal sense of cunning, ruse, or *metis* is the "lever principle," which is intimately related to the mechanisms that outwit and trick the forces of nature, such as gravity and inertia, by their own means.[122] In the *Jena System Lectures*, Hegel articulates this as the "blind doing" of nature's own activity made purposeful in opposition to itself.[123] For these reasons, cunning and magic are central to thinking about habit, a fact clearly reflected in Hegel's characterization of habit as a "second nature," "mechanism of self-feeling," and "spiritual mechanism"; a corporeity made into a supple *instrument* that establishes a "magical" relation between body and mind that is self-acting and allows us to mediate the world behind our backs, so to speak.[124]

Hegel makes clear that it is only when *Verstand* is "pushed to the extreme" does it turn over into its opposite.[125] Only at the extreme point of sundering and finite mediation is the fixity of understanding sublated into the fluidity of speculative reason. In *Remainder*, it would appear *Verstand* is pushed to such an extreme *without* turning over into fluidity. The analytic properties of *Verstand*—posited as external to the achievement of the fluidly of habit in *Remainder*—turn out to be internal to its operation. Understanding's analytic properties are not moments pliable to being sublated within habit's idealizing and synthesizing function, enabling a shift from fixity to fluidity. Rather, by habit, they are ratcheted up to an excruciating intensity. Conditions of deviation, indirection, distance, externality, and sundering are now too close for comfort or stability. In *Remainder*, the cunning of habit is immanently outwitted by its own outwitting—it cannot cut out its own cutting out or bypass its own eternal detour. The magic power of habit, enacted behind our backs, does not adjust bodily means to our goals. It results in endless deviations, detours, isolation techniques, and sleights of hand that founder rather than ground a stable way of being.

The cunning play between immediacy and mediacy in *Remainder* is also manifested in the close relationship between the narrator and Naz that is a further embodiment of the ruse of habit. The narrator hires Naz, a main partner of Time Control, to "facilitate" all his reenactments, employing a word that arises frequently in neoliberal management lingo, and in discussions of habit that refers to the ease and fluidity generated by its repetitions (Rem, 72, 82). Naz is like an "extra set of limbs—eight extra sets of limbs, tentacles spreading out in all directions, coordinating projects, issuing instructions, executing commands. My executor" (Rem, 77).[126] From the outset, the narrator feels a strong affinity with Naz and, through him, the narrator's second-handedness is exponentially extended. Their interaction may be characterized as a strange form of "animal magnetism" that Hegel describes as a "magical relationship," exerting an immediate influence of one mind over another, thus capturing the essence of magic which is, as defined by Hegel, a power and action that that produces effects without any mediation.[127]

This form of magic is considered inferior to the "*Absolute* magic" of spirit as such, which, at this stage in the anthropology of subjective soul, is best exemplified by habit: "With the frequent repetition of bodily activities in the service of mind … there thus arises a *magical* relation, an immediate operation of mind on body."[128] But their "intimate conjunction" is not so easy to parse. N. Kathryn Hayles sees both the narrator and Naz as embodiments of the "cognitive paradigm" of consciousness, albeit manifesting it in differing ways.[129] Whereas the former shows the consequences of consciousness operating without unconscious cognition, the latter manipulates formal symbols as if entirely independent of the inputs supplied by embodied actions. Hayles's interpretation is based partly on the fact that Naz seems to operate like a computational machine, blindly processing information from the narrator, as the following passage suggests: "I explained more things to Naz and he processed them. When his eyes told me to wait I waited; then the whirring behind them stopped and I'd go on again. He never once asked me why I wanted to do all this: he just listened, processing, working out how to execute it all. My executor" (Rem, 89). Although Naz sounds like the "executor of his will," this is simply the ruse of habit whirring away (Rem, 89).

Naz is not simply an "external" processor or executor. Rather, he is of a piece with the narrator himself. It is clear that the narrator's machinic repetitions—his "cog-like status" that perpetually catches, his hyperanalytic, abstract, and formal behaviors producing surplus matter, and his increasing vacant outlook and hypnotic trancelike states—are, in fact, shared with Naz. It is as if one had been split into two. We should also note that, as Mikkel Borch-Jacobsen makes clear, magic is particularly at stake when manipulating symbols, schemas, and mathemes devoid of meaning, a magic that is invoked by Hegel precisely when the abstractions and simplifications of habit have appropriated the body to a universality achieved by its automatisms.[130] Eventually, the narrator realizes that Naz is "completely onside. More than onside: he was as involved as I was—but for entirely different reasons" (Rem, 234). His facilitator, however, is not merely committed in a rational way, befitting his preternatural skill for information management and processing or his talent for logistics. Naz is "driven onwards," "drunk," and "infected" by a bureaucratic "zealotry," a "manic whirring" with the "gears, gone into overdrive, becom[ing] almost unbearably intense" (Rem, 234–235, 255).

During the bank heist reenactment, the walls of Naz's office are "caked with charts: planning charts, flow charts, and Venn diagrams, lists and indexes and keys to charts and indexes to lists," to which he continuously adds further drawings or annotations (Rem, 254–255). This information accumulates to the point of becoming indigestible surplus matter that is generated by the very material inscriptions and visualizing techniques that are supposed to render the analytic procedure perspicuous. Although at one point Naz thanks the narrator for the opportunity to manage so much information, it is clearly *too much* information to process or control, echoing the narrator's claim about the excess matter produced by forensic analytics: "*There's too much here, too much to process, just too much.*" And the sheer numbers that Naz must deal with are staggering. The five tire shop reenactments alone, we are told, required no less than one hundred and twenty actors, five hundred and eleven props, and the involvement—in some capacity or other—of close to one thousand people (Rem, 236–237).

Although it is often noted that habit is a mode of abstracting us from the wealth of information that went into its making—thus allowing us the speed, efficiency, and "economy" to accomplish acts without paying attention to them—I hope it is clear by now that the abstractions of habit also mire us in the surplus matter that is generated through its repetitions. Naz and the narrator do not simply "represent a vision of human cognition that increasingly takes on nightmare proportions," as Hayles argues. Rather, they represent the cunning and magic of habit that tries to outplay its detours, delays, and material excesses in a process that generates even more of them.[131] Rather than simply facilitating communication and connection, like the city workers the narrator stops to watch as they engage in the sacred task of installing wires—"gods laying down wiring of the world, and then covering it up—its routes, its joins"—the driven machinic operations of both Naz and the narrator incessantly cut up this smoothing-over function as they tarry with all the infrastructure's joins, deviant routes, short circuits, and surplus matter (Rem, 103). Even as they attempt to cover their tracks by getting rid of all traces of matter—information and bodies in their final, all-too-real bank robbery reenactment that merges with the real event—the wiring of the world spills out and trips them up (Rem, 265).

A SHORT-CIRCUITING ANAESTHETICS OF THE INFINITE JUDGMENT

The emphasis on magic and cunning when it comes to habit is meant to account for the strange (second) nature of habit that is a mediated immediacy. These magic acts are meant to show how habit overcomes the sundering effects of understanding and judgment in the anthropology of subjective spirit. This is made perfectly clear in Ravaisson's claim that habit "even in the abysses that seem forbidden to it ... illuminates, in the deepest heart of nature, the mystery of the identification of the ideal and the real, of the thing and thought, and of all the contraries that the understanding separates."[132] It is interesting to note that if magic is always about an immediacy that is not determined by the mediation of finite and objective relationships, the implications are that it results, at least in most accounts of habit, as an equilibrium, balance, and harmony that overcomes the dualisms and divisions of the understanding instead of unbearably exacerbating them. Contrary to Hegel's claim about habit as a syllogism, habit often does not dialectically sublate the anthropological moment of judgment, thus restoring the unity of subject and predicate.[133]

Like the speculative sentence—in which habit plays such a crucial role—judgment and understanding continue to disturb the dialectical unity of the syllogism, miring it in particularity, division, and abstract one-sidedness.[134] The firm holding oneself together (*Zusammenhalt*) in habit that is meant to overcome the dividedness (*Entzweiung*) in the anthropological moment of judgment through a coinciding (*zusammenfallend*)—taken more literally, a "falling together"—achieved in and through habit as a simple unity, often fails and "collapses," which is another meaning of this speculative word.[135] This collapsing resonates with Hegel's account of the infinite judgment that "collapses into itself"—or, as it is expressed elsewhere, a "falling apart"—thus expressing the complete incommensurability between subject and predicate.[136]

The *unbearable* contradiction of the infinite judgment speaks to habit's logic of breakdown due to the *Verstand* aspects of habit that I have been exploring in this chapter.[137] The language Hegel uses to describe the infinite judgment's collapsing of two extremes without any continuity, rational explanation, or balanced movement between them—"nonsensical," "absurdity, "senseless," "complete inadequacy," "unyielding extreme," "collapse"—is particularly relevant for my account of habit as resistant to mediation and that is further intensified in recent accounts of the infinite judgment that expands Hegel's vocabulary with terms such as "short circuit," "non-relation," "grotesque discord," "absolute maladjustment," and a "thorough incongruity" to describe the non-relation between subject and predicate, particular and universal, high and low.[138] Although the infinite judgment might appear to be an exceptional species of judgment in Hegel's logic—so odd that at one point Hegel considers them "not judgments at all"—others have seen its strange logic written all over Hegelian speculative dialectics, which seems to be driven to breakdown after breakdown.[139]

The most well-known instance where the sundering effects of judgment are brought to its logical extreme in the form of the infinite judgment is expressed in the paragraphs on phrenology in the "Observing Reason" section of the *Phenomenology of Spirit* as "the *being of spirit is a bone*."[140] It is here that the inert fixity of understanding—and its isolating, rigidifying, and one-sided tendencies—is brought to its extreme point thus instantiating Hegel's claim that only when *Verstand* is "pushed to the extreme" does it "[turn] over into its opposite," i.e., the fluidity of reason.[141] Žižek returns again and again to this infinite judgment to emphasize that the Hegelian system does not sublate or exorcise inertia but rather brings inertia to an extreme in identifying spirit with a bone and getting stuck on this bone of inertia.[142]

I have already drawn attention to the very literal instantiation of this "spirit is a bone" in *Remainder* in regard to the tiny redundant and surplus remainder of bone that remains "jammed between the ball and its socket" of the narrator's kneecap after the accident, such that he twists and catches rather than fluidly turning during his repeated attempts to glide by the kitchen countertop at *Madlyn Mansions*, or the monetary "set-l-ment" that is meant to compensate for the accident, which literally "gags" the narrator and, in regard to the economy of habit, never sediments and ingrains as a dispositional stability that would help him adjust and integrate (Rem, 4, 8). Thus "spirit is a bone" speaks to the fact that subject and substance, universal and particular in habit do not "coincide" in an inner unity but exist as a non-relationship that its repetitions are incapable of bridging due to the unbridgeable gaps and voiding that its renascent scissions generate. If anything, habit is more like a faulty syllogism than a corporeal "*by means of* [*vermittels*]."[143]

There is another dimension of the infinite judgment we need to pay attention to in the *Phenomenology* that does not get as much attention as "spirit is a bone," although it is directly related to it and features in many accounts of habit that I have drawn upon. In the final section of the *Phenomenology* on "Absolute knowing," Hegel notes that like the extreme point reached in the "the *being of spirit is a bone*," which can be expressed in a different way as "the *being of the I is a thing*," can be supplemented with another infinite judgment: "*the thing is I*."[144] These two infinite judgments—that are inversely repeated—resonate with the language of "thingness" that is invoked in habit, for example in Ravaisson's faith that habit can heal the wounds inflicted by understanding thus reconciling "thing and thought."[145] In contrast to Ravaisson's confidence in habit's capacity to illuminate the contraries that the understanding separates, Ricoeur's account of habit always registers a more anxiety-ridden notion of habit's "passion to become a thing."[146] It is worth further running through some of Ricoeur's sentences in *Freedom and Nature* to get a feel for the anxiety raised by habit's "thingifying" tendencies: "the path of automatization lies open ... to what is perhaps the most perfidious of passions, the passion to become a thing"; "when automatization predominates over spontaneity in habit ... man is buried under habits." And to bring this death-dealing automaticity and inertia of habit back around to "the being of spirit is a bone" in Hegel: "ossification is a threat inscribed in habit, but not its normal destiny."[147]

Like most phenomenological and hermeneutically driven accounts of habit, Ricoeur takes flexible habit as the proper and defining starting point of habit and any automaticity or ossification as a threatening deviation from that norm. But, as I have been arguing in this chapter, habit is our "ana-tomical" destiny, so to speak, that is of a piece with its unsublatable exteriority.[148] Habit registers a thing-like otherness in ourselves, in terms of our own bodies, interhuman relationships, and the ability to inhabit "our" environment. Tom's statement "I have big gaps" is repeated in the novel in the collective as "We got cut off" after the narrator calls his lawyer back following one of the many interruptions and cleavages in their conversation that is not merely situational but rather constitutive (Rem, 11) (figures 3.9, 3.10, and 4.2). If habit is marked by a profound failure to mediate, which is the premise and logic of this book, I am not claiming that when it comes to habit that it is unity or bust, as it is clear that any "full" achievement of the plastic ideal of habit would result in a "processless habit" that would be a form of death by the inertia of habit itself that is clearly inimical to Hegel. Yet the requirement for a perpetual reconciliation between particular and universal, inner and outer, that is registered in accounts of habit as a rhythm of doing and undoing, making and breaking, that are so crucial to habit change, often remain within a logic of plasticity that is too well-tempered.

The short-circuiting aesthetic dimensions of habit in *Remainder* operate like a Hegelian infinite judgment manifesting in the starkest ways possible—without any continuity, rational explanation, or balanced movement—the extremes that it is supposed to mediate. These scenes and passages are suspended right at the moment before the extremes collapse and cut into each other, recoil, break down, entangle, and pile up in bits, parts, and heaps, and whose aesthetics are exemplified by the unsettling, static-generating logic of

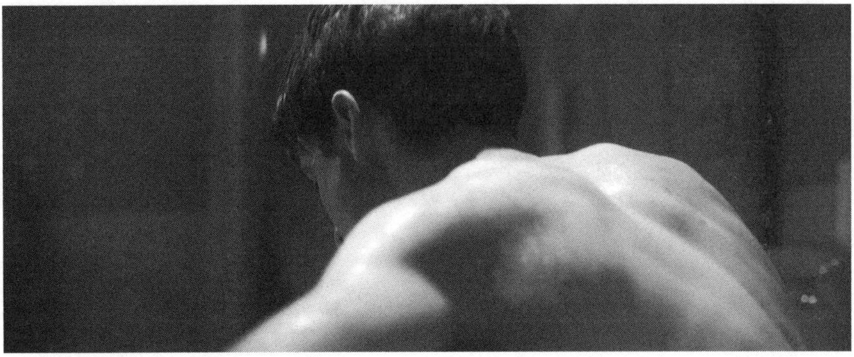

FIGURE 2.26
Tom's Michelangelesque back. Film still from Omer Fast's *Remainder*. © Omer Fast.

habit and its ontology of waste in the speculative sentence. It is at this point that the bridge of the mediating middle has collapsed due to the *explosion* initiated by the "unyielding extreme" of the infinite judgment.[149] Here we might recall that throughout the novel the narrator smells a sharp, acrid, and oddly elusive whiff of "cordite" that is particularly insistent during the liver lady's reenactments that not only infects the vapors of liver fat that "waft" through the Madlyn Mansions reenactment but also permeates *Remainder* through and through (Rem, 70, 87, 208, 225).

At times, *Remainder* seems to be entirely constituted by an unsublatable repetition of infinite judgments as the narrator/Tom is perpetually torn between extreme states of catatonic inactivity and the fury of destruction; seizure as mastery and being seized; being sunk in particularity and possessed by universality via automaticity; suffocating proximity and radical exteriority; acts of levitation and brutal falls; precipitous speeding up and preposterous delays and slowing down; abrupt voiding and excessive spilling out; disappearing and reappearing. In both the novel and film there are numerous instances of nonsensical cuts between states of the body that are logically incompatible, like the hand that short-circuits between its pre- and post-accident states, that is well beyond the logic and rhythm of reparative plasticity and recovery (see next chapter, figures 3.11 and 3.12), or the shot of Tom's back—that can only be described as Michelangelesque—which is immediately juxtaposed with a tracking shot from behind that highlights his emaciated, scarred, and vulnerable body (figures 2.26 and 2.27).

At one point when Tom goes to visit his lawyer, his body cuts into itself (coinciding as collapse) to the point that he disappears as he is cut off by his mirror reflection—like one of Robert Smithson's enantiomorphic mirror chambers—as if to instantiate the extreme contradiction between an "inner reflection" supposedly achieved in the unity of habit as a "self-relating

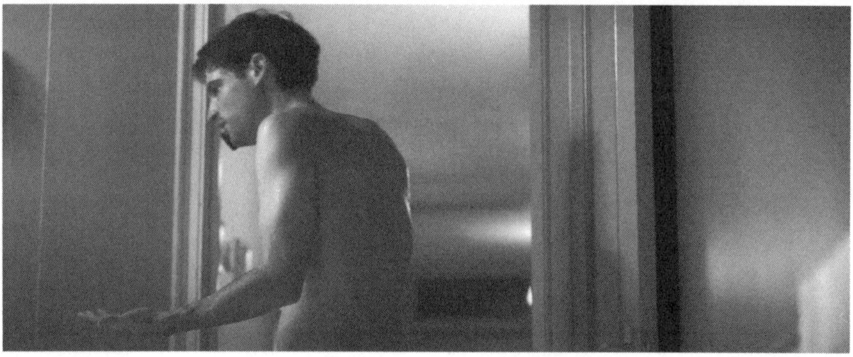

FIGURE 2.27
Tom's emaciated back. Film still from Omer Fast's *Remainder*. © Omer Fast.

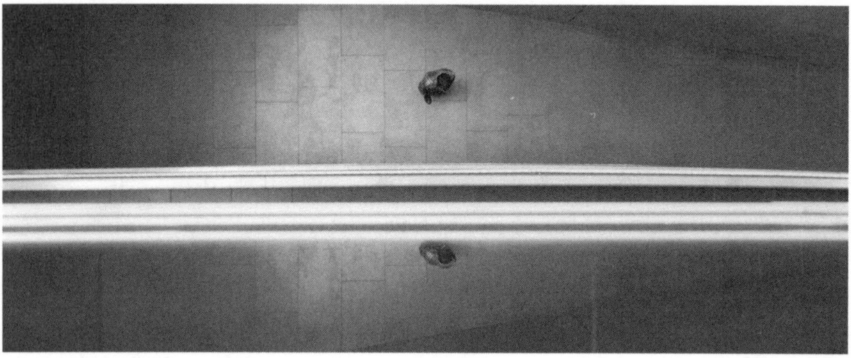

FIGURE 2.28
Tom reflected and doubled by a mirror. Film still from Omer Fast's *Remainder*. © Omer Fast.

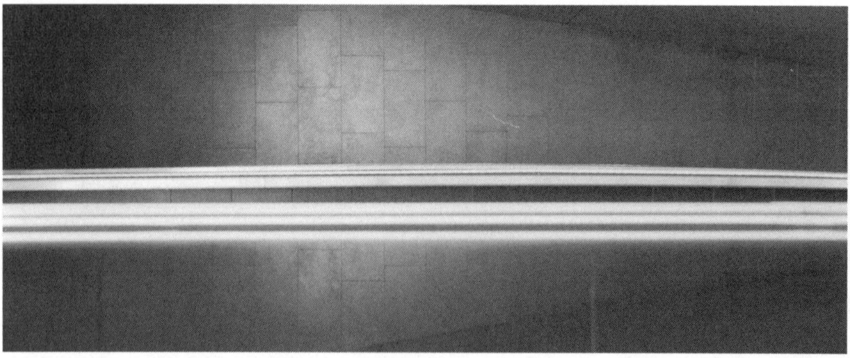

FIGURE 2.29
Tom as a vanished subject of reflection. Film still from Omer Fast's *Remainder*. © Omer Fast.

ideality" and a vanished subject of reflection that has been cut through and off by exteriority (figures 2.28 and 2.29). Conversations, connections, and sentences are perpetually cut in media res, creating short-circuiting leaps between two radically unrelated speech acts, perhaps best exemplified when Tom first meets with Naz in the Blueprint Café to talk about the Madlyn Mansions reenactment (figure 3.18). When the latter asks him: "Is this a childhood home?" Tom responds: "How much do you charge" (Rem film, 40:15:22). In the novel even the incessant use of ellipses in conversations not only suspends, delays, and exhausts speech, it often "vanishes" it as if to emphasize the more abrupt and cutting valences of that Hegelian term. The anaesthetics of the infinite judgment in *Remainder* alerts us to a notion of habit as an unbearable contradiction that remains in excess of and resistant to any mediation.

3

BUFFETING AND BEING SECOND-HAND

MICHELANGELO'S ARTICHOKE

As the narrator begins the process of searching for (or better, finding) the apartment building—later identified as Madlyn Mansions—with the help of his "facilitator" Naz and the Time Control team, he recalls a sculpture class from his youth. They were given large blocks of stone, which they had to turn into something recognizable, like a human figure or building. He recollects the art teacher, Mr. Aldin, explaining the point of the exercise by loosely adverting to Michelangelo's Neoplatonic notion that the finished work is already contained within the block: "'your task isn't to create the sculpture,' he said; 'it's to strip all the other stuff away, get rid of it. The surplus matter'" (Rem, 91–92). The narrator notes that he pondered this lesson about stripping away surplus matter when learning "to eat carrots and to walk," as if the movement was already in place and all he had to do was remove "all the extraneous stuff—the surplus limbs and nerves and muscles that I didn't want to move, the bits of space I didn't want my hand or foot to move through" (Rem, 92).

The issue at stake here, however, is not a matter of overemphasizing acts of previsualization, understanding before doing, or conscious attention involved in the process of reparative plasticity. Rather, it is meant to dramatize the impossibility of removing all the extraneous stuff that would enable a fluid action or gesture due to the incessant generation of surplus matter that is far in excess of the ability to incorporate it. The violent dimensions of "stripping" and "removing" resonate with the narrator's account of how Naz and his crew move through the city in repetitive patterns in order to find Madlyn Mansions in Brixton, burrowing into the city's block and "chiseling away at surplus matter," not to mention the brutal act of gentrification involved in acquiring it and the eviction of its tenants (Rem, 96). To shift the metaphor, they go about their work like beaters scaring pheasants out of bushes for a Lord to shoot (Rem, 96).

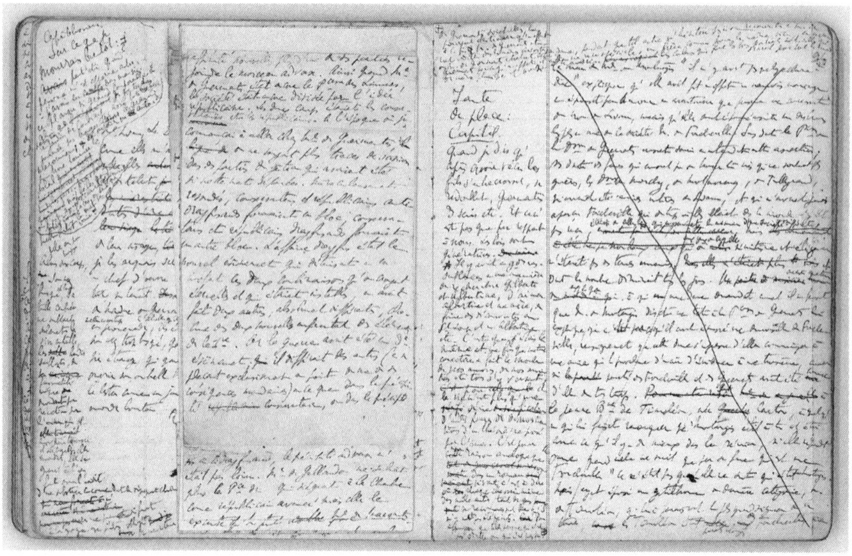

FIGURE 3.1
Proust's *paperolles*. Fonds Marcel Proust. II—À LA RECHERCHE DU TEMPS PERDU, ID/Côté: btv1b6000138g.f69, N.C.(c) BnF.

Throughout the process of "gutting" Madlyn Mansions in preparation for the reenactments precipitated by his Proustian moment with the crack at the party on Plato Street, the site continuously generates massive amounts of surplus matter that neither recedes neatly into the background nor vanishes but incessantly accumulates, staining, spilling, and tracking everywhere. While the narrator and Naz are busy working on the Madlyn Mansions reconstruction, they make their way from a Mayfair piano sales room to a used furniture warehouse, then back to their car and to Madlyn Mansions. Flakes of plaster, the chimes and tinkles of pianos, and a constant "cacophony of modems and drilling and arpeggios and perpetually ringing phones" mingle together in relentless, overlapping waves of noise and matter that they cannot escape (Rem, 113).

Each reenactment, and each subordinate part in the reenactment, is repeatedly reenacted, and the chains of remediation proliferate as the narrator continuously sketches out details, diagrams, plans, stains, and body angles on blank pieces of paper that his déjà vu has released from the crack running down the bathroom wall, including inscriptions and repetitions of that very crack itself. He sketches and marks all kinds of surfaces—ranging from blank paper to "the reverse side of letters, bills and legal documents—whatever came to hand"; a process reminiscent of Proust's *paperolles* that record the relentless revisions as additions that accumulate in the form of diverse and sundry scraps of paper that are affixed to the working manuscripts for *À la recherche du*

FIGURE 3.2

Proust's *paperolles*. Fonds Marcel Proust. II—À LA RECHERCHE DU TEMPS PERDU, ID/Côté: btv1b6000138g.f81, N.C.(c) BnF.

temps perdu (Rem, 73) (figures 3.1 and 3.2). This cascade of renderings requires ever-increasing feats of Kafkaesque logistics to process them. Yet it is all to no avail, as matter is tracked everywhere, so that legibility, meaning, and signification are overridden by the sheer repetitive weight of its quantity and intransitive force.

There is an "inconvenient bittiness" at the heart of all the reenactments, which is facilitated by Naz's "piecemeal" approach to the reconstruction of Madlyn Mansions in preparation for the reenactments (Rem, 231, 111–112). Rather than taking a specific point of departure, working piece by piece in a logical and temporal order, he works on everything at once. The resulting technique fails to draw together and bridge the disparate material and instead creates "huge gaps in between" that perpetually entail new problems of alignment and compatibility, requiring constant corrections that generate increasingly more parts and bits (Rem, 111–112). This piecemeal approach is then carried over into the reenactments, as the narrator and Naz explore endless variations, combinations, repetitions and subdivisions of each scene, part, and action, thus generating further surplus material, gaps, and voids that perpetually spill out beyond their immediate confines, defying all notions of containment, sovereign control, and planning. If the narrator concentrates "on different bits at different times. Different locations, different moments" during the Madlyn Mansions reenactments, that is not because the narrator has lost the synthesizing function of habit but because habit's anatomizing function is always interrupting the capacity to draw disparate elements together into a body of knowledge that would generate a stable disposition correlated to a specific position (Rem, 89). The narrator remains perpetually unable to plug these traumatic gaps with "his memories" since his compulsive repetitions continuously generate them.

In both the novel and the film, these gaps and voids appear within the scene of representation as neutral, blank, and "unfilled" stretches of the apartment building and its contents. They are papered or cemented over—concealed in generic brown wrapping paper in the film—just as some of the anonymous, vague reenactors (at one point the narrator calls them "extras") wear Lycra-like body suits that cover them from head to toe, or, in the novel, ice hockey goalie masks (Rem, 74, 88, 105, 120, 164) (figures 3.3 and 3.4). Like the subject matter of habit, the staging of the Madlyn Mansions reenactments is replete with all the gaps, unfinished patches, stretches of neutral space, wrapped objects, veiled neutral figures, and surplus matter that insistently remain as materialized absences and non-actualities. If the relation of being and having in habit is about appropriating our determinations, then these blank or neutral spaces register how we are dispossessed by our indeterminancies. They register the surplus ontological glitches and gaps—the stain of contingent, indeterminate, and generic matter—that are always within the

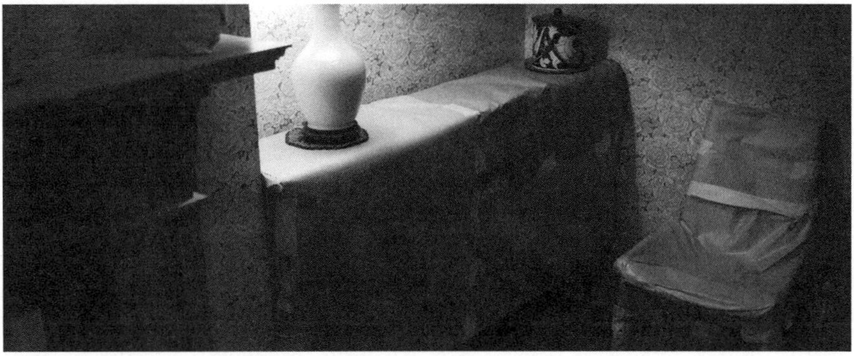

FIGURE 3.3
Parts of Madlyn Mansions wrapped in generic brown paper. Film still from Omer Fast's *Reminder*. © Omer Fast.

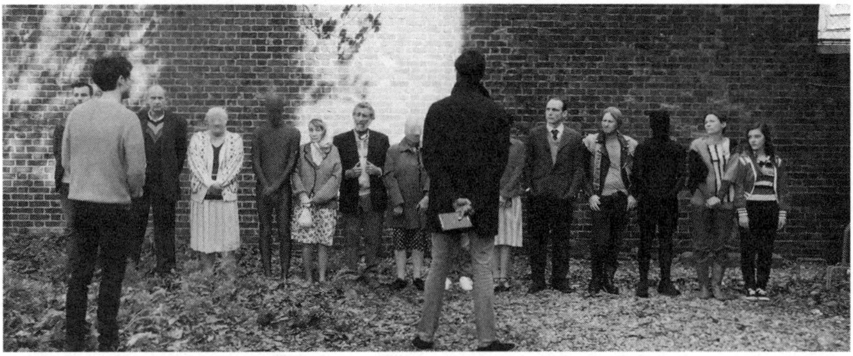

FIGURE 3.4
Reenactors, some wearing body suits and stockings over their heads. Film still from Omer Fast's *Remainder*. © Omer Fast.

scene of representation yet remain recalcitrant to the narrator's capacity to unify, possess, and control.

Surveying the construction at Madlyn Mansions, the narrator observes that the process of undoing and removal invariably seems to result in the carting away of more building material than is used for its reconstruction—a condition that is axiomatic for all the reenactments in *Remainder*. Turning aside to Naz, he quips that this "surplus matter" is like an artichoke: there is always more on your plate at the end of your meal than before you started (Rem, 127–128). The logic of the artichoke is a counterimage to the veiling, abbreviating, simplifying, and unifying functions of acquired habit that are achieved by stripping away and sublating any surplus matter, parts, and units. The logic of the artichoke in *Remainder* shows how habits often do not shed their excessive dimensions and useless complication or slough off parasitic movements. If inanimate matter, thingness, and inertia are seen as threats to the smooth running of habit, then these incessant remainders are the very stuff of habit in *Remainder* and do not simply vanish. The narrator's desire to feel himself into the very "interior" of things—to inhabit without gaps or detours—is countermanded by his compulsion to repeat that mires him ever deeper in externality, like the pulpy, bruised artichoke petals that proliferate the more we consume. This process equally constitutes spirit's movement as recounted in Hegel's Preface to the *Phenomenology of Spirit*; we linger, tarry, and get caught up within all the accumulation of parts, determinations, way stations, shapes, and picture-thinking, such that they are never unfixed and rendered fluid in and through spirit's "unhalting" (*unaufhaltsam*) movement.[1]

Perhaps Bruno Latour's analogy that bad habits are to good ones what spam is to electronic messages—"shreds of existence" and "rootless utterances" floating around without an author, a responsible party, or a receiver and polluting the world—should be seen as a more ordinary ontological condition and effect of habit that is generated by its repetitions rather than simply its pathological condition.[2] Latour's particular wording—"shreds of existence"—resonates with a passage that Malabou includes in her account of destructive plasticity: "When a psyche is shredded it corresponds to the birth of a new, *unrecognizable* person."[3] But are not Latour's "shreds of existence" and Malabou's "shredded" psyche also a more quotidian effect of habit—something that habit generates—that is beholden to neither the veiling function of habit nor the complete breaking of habits that produce a total metamorphoses of identity? As Agamben aptly notes, the "ontological squandering that we bear within ourselves far exceeds the piety of our memory and consciences. Its persistence determines the status of all knowledge and understanding."[4] Although Malabou is attentive to how traumatic events always derive from an indivisible intimacy between the outside and inside, perhaps she is less attentive, as Adrian Johnston has suggested, to the "disavowed familiarity" of senseless materiality rather than the "different-in-kind foreignness" of external senseless traumas.[5] To adopt Malabou's own terminology of the external accident, bodily habit itself is often "constitutively inassimilable" and a "brutal event, without signification" that is of a piece with its generation, and not just the matter of a traumatic event that intervenes and severs previously acquired habits and skills.[6] In *Remainder*, habit is a breakdown that lodges an external meaninglessness, a thing-like contingency and opacity within oneself, that generates an anxiety-ridden condition of tarrying with this internal impediment.

If the past is "sedimented" in the body through habits, as most analyses of habit suggest, the implication is that this past is implicitly there in the body, ready to be called up in the present through a gesture or action and held "virtually" in reserve and "suspended" for inventive and unpredictable actualizations to come. However, I propose to focus on a condition and aesthetics of sedimentation and suspension in which precipitates are not soluble and "ingrained" as a fluid and supple virtual potential.[7] In the aesthetics of habit that I pursue, these precipitates are not settled—they do not accumulate "grain on grain," to employ William James's disavowed "partial" wording, which is meant to suggest how the slow sedimentation of particulars over time consolidate in and as the solubility and fluidity of an ingrained habit—but rather are continuously agitated by the repetitions of habit. In fact, as we have seen, the very word "Settlement" is incessantly repeated and imparted in *Remainder*, and left over as an indigestible remainder that continues to agitate the text (Rem, 4). More often than we would like to admit, we are stirred and perturbed by multiple contractions of emergent, overdetermined, half-baked, or failed habits that do not slough off these insistent remainders and grounds.

THE STATIC LOGIC OF HABIT

Hegel's speculative philosophy and its manifest emphasis on fluidity and the unhalting movement and mediation of the concept comprised of dynamic and dialectical moments would suggest that his notion of habit is the very opposite of a "static logic." But it is precisely the static-generating logic of repetition that I focus on in my reading of habit in Hegel and *Remainder*, in ways that emphasize its noise, grounds, and impeded (*aufgehalten*) movement generated by the novel's incessant feedback loops.[8] In fact, the word "static" is compulsively repeated in *Remainder* as a thoroughly speculative word. First, it alludes to the fact the narrator was "hit" at the start of the novel and film because he was standing still (or still standing, if we want to engage with *Remainder*'s spiralling circularity in all its topological and temporal complexity)—that is, static and exposed where he was and "not somewhere else" (Rem, 63). And he continues to be hit because he continually drags his "thing" around with him, like the real that is stuck in place wherever it goes.

Even when the narrator thinks he has found a more advantageous "position" to occupy or demands that his reenactors remain "static" for hours on end—or even when he has fallen into a catatonic state owing to his reenactment addiction—this frozen condition is always unsettling; it drags, catches, sizzles, spits, whirs, and recoils. In *Remainder*, the inconsistency, static, and noise of matter is fostered and transmitted through the emphasis on low-resolution analog technology where the ratios of noise to signal, inertia to spontaneity, fixity to fluidity, and background to figure are drastically altered, ranging from the graininess of Polaroid cameras and the incessant "crackle" generated by two-way radios, to the narrator's "jerking back and forth" that is likened to a paused video image on a low-quality machine that is constantly freezing and pixelating, to the "static crackle" of the liver that sizzles and pops on the hob (Rem, 14, 44, 127, 140, 142). Owing to these repetitions, reenactments, and deviations, we receive a vast accumulation of data well in excess of any possible gathering and containment or fluid retrieval. Even the newer panes of glass that are initially ordered for the Madlyn Mansions "rehab" are replaced by older ones, as "new glass is totally consistent, doesn't gloop and run and crimp the things you see through it like old glass does" (Rem, 130). We might recall that "glazing" is an older word to describe habit's smoothing-over function, but here that function is declined in favor of inconsistency, imperfection, material occlusion, and viscosity. Moreover, as the many references to "bits" and "circuits" in the novel suggest, the issue of surplus matter is not simply nostalgia for older, slower analog technologies—like the novel itself in the age of information overload—but about the very logic of ontological delay, drag, and dregs.

The excessive slowing down that the narrator imposes on himself and others during his reenactments is intended precisely to enable him to experience the unsettling agitation and unruliness of matter that habit, as a medium of otherness, can generate. The slowing down and stretching of time brings out the crater or sponge-like topological relief of matter as replete with holes, rough edges, cracks, and grains. The pianist reenactor's repetitions and temporal stretching of musical passages lands him in a barren field of isolated notes with barely any redress except through precipitous upticks in tempo that create more opportunities for collision, collapse, and muddle rather than affording the recovery of a well-tempered rhythm. When the liver lady turns to communicate with the young boy in the corridor during a key sequence in the Madlyn Mansions reenactment, her indecipherable words emerge as a garbled, "meaningless sound" (*sinnloser Laut*), or a murmuring (*Rauschen*) glossolalia.[9] It is as if she is "swallowing a mouthful of water" rather than articulating and projecting a voice that universalizes and preserves itself by "vanishing" (*verschwinden*) as it mixes with the air—such that its "disappearing itself is thus immediately its lasting" (figure 3.5).[10]

The status of communication in *Remainder* is always curdled by the viscosities of matter, like the tea that becomes the "main currency" between the narrator and Catherine—"a kind of milky, sickly substitute for actual connection"—or the pile of "residual voice-scraps" ("Heyy!"; "Heyy dude!"; "Stop!") that litter the text and barely function as phatic statements or interpolations making particular or meaningful commands (Rem, 28, 52, 62–63, 74, 98, 115–116).[11] All we receive is the grain and strain of the voice, or the dross, delay, and blurriness of a "grubby coin"—usually a fifty-pence coin—that is handed back and forth between Tom and the young boy in the film (figure 3.6). This is not simply a "stamped coin" that has discarded "the slag from pure metal" but an eroded one—a condition enhanced by the blurred, out-of-focus shots that capture these exchanges as an anamorphic stain "that

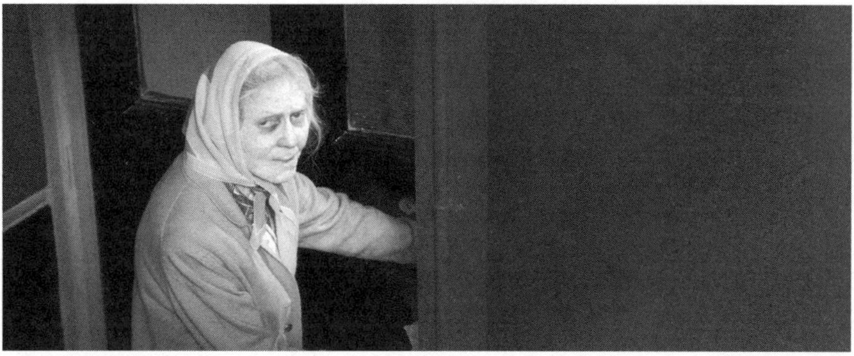

FIGURE 3.5
The liver lady turning to speak with Tom in the stairwell of Madlyn Mansions. Film still from Omer Fast's *Remainder*. © Omer Fast.

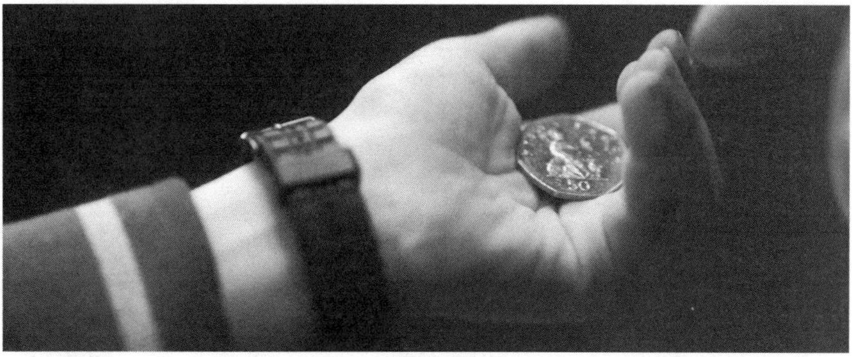

FIGURE 3.6
Fifty-pence coin that is handed back and forth between Tom and the young boy. Film still from Omer Fast's *Remainder*. © Omer Fast.

people pass from hand to hand," and that retains its value only as a worn-out "*tessera*."[12] This coin is always "the fifth quarter"—to use Leopold Bloom's term in *Ulysses*—that is "surplus to a thing's integrity," as McCarthy notes in his essay "Why *Ulysses* Matters."[13]

The constant slowing down (or becoming static) in *Remainder* is not simply a sign of the narrator's need to hyperconsciously control his environment to compensate for the supposed loss of speed, fluidity, and the abbreviating aspects of habit due to the neurotrauma he has suffered.[14] In fact, this slowed-down tempo and motion often results in subtle investigations of the recalcitrance of matter, conditions of velleity, and all the recoils in any given action that blow back far in excess of their aims and goals. For instance, in the slowed-down tempo of firing a gun in a murder reenactment carried out in the street, the narrator's repetition compulsion returns him to a static, passive, prone, and deponent state that loops back again to the speculative sentence about "being hit" on the first page of the novel: "We weren't doing them: they were being done. The guns were being fired, I was being hit, being returned to the ground" (Rem, 216). He never actively leaves the scene and has "vague memories of being lifted ... handled tenderly, and delicately" in a kind of prosthetic resurrection that is always followed by other brutal drops, collapses, ratcheting movements, and more extreme forms of levitating, vaporizing, or vanishing that inevitably blow back in overflowing waves of surplus matter that knock him down again and again (Rem, 217). In the filmic version of the murder reenactment, Tom is continuously and willingly tasered until he can no longer stand up and is plunged into a trancelike state at the edge of inertia and passivity, but he is driven to keep repeating his "compulsion to re-enact" his reenactments (Rem, 186, 219–221).

BUFFETING AND BEING SET ADRIFT

The narrator's last clear memory "before" the accident is "being buffeted by wind twenty or so minutes before I was hit" (Rem, 7, 87). This "buffeting" scene is repeated throughout the novel and film whenever the narrator has a feeling of being at one with his movement and gestures, without detour or separation. "Just being," as the narrator calls it, as if to suggest that the "having" of being is not obtrusively external but is fully incorporated as a way of being (Rem, 24, 67). At these moments of "just being," when his having of being seems to have settled into a second nature that is at home with itself, his body feels both "intense" and "serene," "unbearably light and unbearably dense at the same time"; a state often characterized by the narrator as a "fluent, gliding, feeling" mixed with a sensation of "tingling" that courses up his body as he is locked, trance-like, in place (Rem, 9, 44, 83, 96, 106, 108, 151, 161, 177, 264, 293). While "just being," the narrator often closes his eyes and extends his palms outwards, recalling the figure of Saint Francis in a Renaissance painting receiving the stigmata, an Early Christian Orans posture, or a beggar figure asking for alms (figure 3.7).[15] At these moments in the film, the young boy usually appears, out of focus and blurry, sometimes handing a fifty-pence coin to Tom or another character in a manner that recalls the messy, redundant, and surplus remainder of the monetary, bodily, and linguistic "*set-l-ment*" to which the narrator is bound (Rem, 4, 8) (figure 3.6). At first glance, these bodily states seem to be where habit is "ensouling [*beseelen*] the body," resulting in the graceful, light, and "smooth elaboration and fluent force of all the members," as if the dead weight of externality, picture-thinking, and detour had been permeated by a fluid inner connectedness that is at home with itself.[16] Yet the very language in which these blissful states are

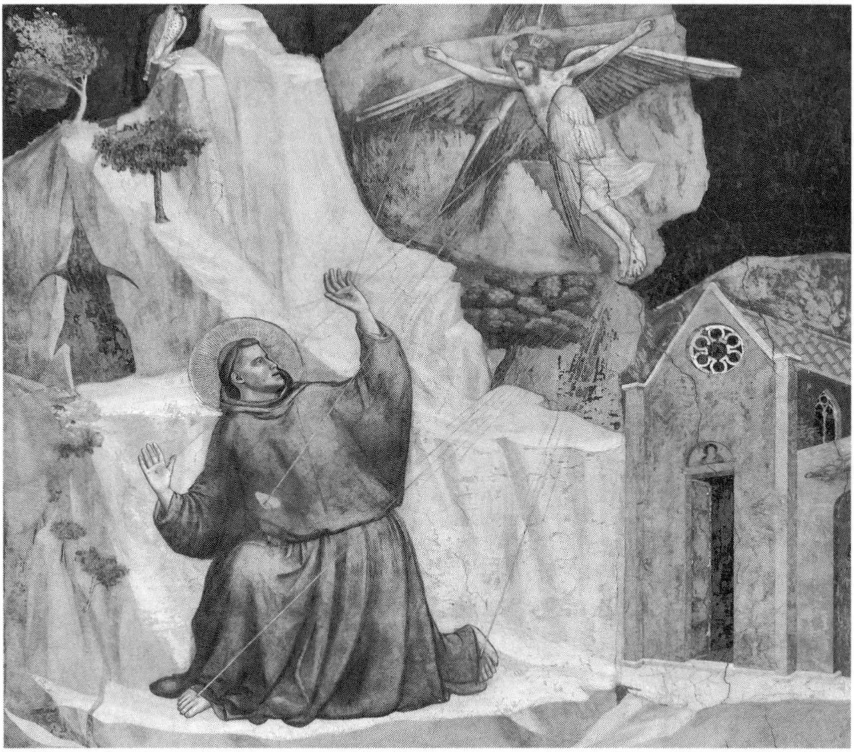

FIGURE 3.7
Giotto di Bondone, *St. Francis Receiving the Stigmata*, 1320–1325. Transept, external part of the Bardi Chapel, Capelli Bardi, S. Croce, Florence, Italy.
© Ghigo G. Roli/Art Resource, NY.

described—"buffeted," "static," "intense," and "tingling"—articulate unbearable speculative tensions.

First, the phrase "buffeted by wind" suggests exposure to an excessive and contradictory agitation, akin to a vessel caught between countervailing gusts and "marooned in constant motion."[17] Buffeting in *Remainder* is akin to neither stagnation nor standstill; it is not a state of being in the doldrums, in which the wind has gone out of a boat's sails, thus immoblizing it on a calm sea. Nor does it suggest a gentle, aimless drifting, enabled by a soft wind stirring the waters in a rhythmic motion, thus preventing stagnation and generating the kind of subtle peristaltic waves and ripples that are the very conditions and movement of aesthetic autonomy.[18]

The narrator's body is not just the object of these buffeting forces but also autogenerates an infra-buffeting that never settles into a form of embodiment that possesses "within itself the determinateness of its bodily nature in a perfectly fluid form."[19] Rather, his body remains driven and possessed, such that he is rendered in a condition of paralyzed unrest as he is set adrift. Thus, buffeting is always on the verge of turning these drifting waves (*Wellen*) into a swelling (*anschwellen*) of wave upon wave rather than resulting in a harmonic (*Oberwellen*) wave of aesthetic pleasure. An evocative sentence from *Remainder* invokes the disturbing waves of interference that perpetually inundate the narrator during the Madlyn Mansions reenactments: "The static crackle of the liver broke across the orphaned signals cast adrift from radios and television sets" (Rem, 142). This feedback and reflux of matter is relentless and never abates. The sizzling and spatting liver repeatedly infects and clogs up the atmosphere at Madlyn Mansions, and Schneider TM's score punctuates the film as a "fizzle like static electricity," such that the narrator is perpetually entangled in a "wave-tossed breakdown" of air, noise, silt, and detritus from which he incessantly sub-emerges.[20]

The constant reference to "buffeting" in the novel is another bodily sign of the repeated anxiety and "conflict with air" that marks *Remainder*'s thoroughgoing anxiety of beginning.[21] In the *Phenomenology of Spirit*, Hegel calls attention to the abrupt and precipitous arrival of spirit's "break of day" and compares it to a child's first breath that "shatters the gradualness of only quantitative growth."[22] Elaborating on Freud's work in *Inhibitions, Symptoms and Anxiety*, Lacan also emphasizes this shattering at the birth of a new world, in which the trauma of the first breath is the "inhalation, into oneself, of a fundamentally Other environment."[23] This externality persists in *Remainder*'s "buffeting" that is akin to what Lacan calls a "gust effect" (*soufflage*): a drivenness that topologically disrupts inside and outside, before and after, front and back, goal and aim.[24] This gust effect blows holes, gaps, and craters via the overpunctuation of grammatical marks at the level of the sentence in *Remainder*, the ventilating pumps that play the narrator like an unruly metronome, or the riveting soundtrack by Schneider TM that manifests the narrator's *inability* to mediate, aerate, and enliven his own rigid body.

Although the narrator's body seems to be relatively at peace in these moments of buffeting—in contrast to the dizziness, vertigo, and nausea he experiences when he does not feel connected—it is, in fact, of a piece with his disorientation. In these moments his body is suspended in a state where fixity and fluidity excessively *overlap*, generating *currents* of jouissance that are profoundly unsettling beyond any state of equilibrium or homeostasis that might be inferred from the enjoyment he derives from them. In fact, the narrator's memory of being buffeted "before" the accident is akin to his being hit by the aftershocks of the accident itself, in an ongoing reverberation and feedback loop of "the gap—the crater—that the accident had *blown* [my emphasis]" in him (Rem, 3). At one point in the novel the protagonist hurries to his bedroom to close the window as he hears a "rustle" from an evening breeze that is "tugging" and seeking to "unpick" the myriad diagrams and sketches tacked to his wall (Rem, 76). Unlike James's account of the uncanny feeling of first occupying a new room—"we do not know what draughts may blow in upon our back, what doors may open"—this unsettling condition is never stabilized by habit's coming to "feel at home."[25] Although the narrator manages to shut the window before the sketches are torn off, more often than not he autogenerates the unpicking of his tenuous adhesive stuff by his own hand, as he is constantly breaking down his reenactments into endless parts and deviations or endlessly correcting them in ways that generate ever more acts of gluing and ungluing, doing and undoing, that are compulsive and unhinged.

Thus, being set in motion in *Remainder* does not generate a habitual body that might ground our "throwenness" into the temporal ecstasies of past, present, and future, as the term *Bewegtheit* indicates in Heidegger. Nor does it enable the reconciliation of fixity and fluidity in the "movement" (*Bewegung*) of the concept that is characterized by Hegel as "quiescent unity" (*ruhige Einheit*).[26] Nor does it converge in the coordinated economy and balance of a bodily aboutness that is "lived" through as a "motor intentionality" that constitutes our "anchorage" in objects and tasks—and ultimately a world—as Merleau-Ponty argues. Habit in *Remainder* is always on the verge of a more violent wrenching and recoiling of the body as it becomes mired in the wake of its own buffetings and static. Thus, buffeting in *Remainder* is not equivalent to, nor adequately explained by, what Hegel calls "trembling" (*Zittern*).[27] What I wish to emphasize is that buffeting does not occur without real agitation/restlessness (*Unruhe*) that is never dissolved into the "absolutely fluid," which is meant to describe the movement of self-mediation as a state of "endless, unbroken unrest."[28] These buffetings are the sign of a "self-repulsion/self-repelling" (*Sich-Abstoßen* or *[sich] von sich selbst abstoßende*) that does not result in an "*absolute* internal *counter-repelling*" (*absoluter Gegenstoß in sich selbst*), but rather in unsublatable division.[29] I propose to home in on the ways in which habit generates this unsettling anxiety owing to the excessive proximity of a body that has not mastered its drives through the unifying and binding work of habitual repetition.[30]

If habit brings stuckness, inertia, excess, and surplus matter to a maximum intensity and extreme, it is not simply to reach a "crisis point" as a necessary "moment" that enables the fluidity of speculative movement to occur. Rather, as the logic of *Remainder* makes clear, what happens at this point of short-circuiting is a gushing, overflowing, or drunken reeling; a shredding, catching, halting, grinding, and grounding that keeps the precipitate and sediment perturbed rather than dissolved, fluidified, or settled. The extremes of fixity generate something other than fluidity, and it is imperative that we remain and tarry with that fixity itself in order to register the anaesthetic particularities that it generates. Fixity is unrelenting and remains insoluble and resistant to any "universal fluidity" in and as a "*fluidity* of the differences."[31] If there is any "settlement" occurring in *Remainder*, it is not in the sense of sedimentation as a an "absorption" or "ingraining," such that habit tempers the extremes it mediates—or incorporates our bodily aptitudes as mediator of a world, like a musician who "settles into the organ as one settles into a house," as Merleau-Ponty evocatively suggests—but rather as a getting stuck in the real turmoil of the disturbing impingements and upheavals of habit that refuse to settle and ingrain.[32] The narrator's repetitions bind him to a buffeting by habit that renders him static and intransitive no matter how much he moves or reaches out to grasp objects or to communicate with others. These buffetings register the anxiety-ridden nature of the habitual body's constitutive desease as it is repeatedly spun around, set adrift, and knocked off course by the aftershocks of its own unsublatable repetitions that generate drifts of surplus matter in its wake.

TINGLING AND THE TINNITUS OF THE BODY

The narrator's "fluent, gliding, feeling" is always accompanied by a "tingling" that courses up his spine as he is locked in place (Rem, 9, 44, 83, 96, 106, 108, 151, 161, 177, 264, 293). McCarthy has specifically written about the word "tingle" in his account of Lewis Carroll's so-called "nonsense poem," *The Hunting of the Snark*, in a report from the International Necronautical Society, titled "Navigation Was Always a Difficult Art"—thus adding another dimension to the pelagic connotations of buffeting and being set adrift.[33] In *The Hunting of the Snark*, the boat's captain—the Bellman—steers his nine crew members on their venture, refusing all standard navigational props and relying solely on his one notion for crossing the ocean: "to tingle his bell." This word, according to McCarthy, captures the whole mood of dread, horror, and mortal danger that accompanies their venture to hunt the Snark.[34]

What these crew members dread is an excessive materiality, which is overwhelming, weighty, and too close, as they move in a haptic space without direction or perspective so that the boat collapses and "snarks" in on itself as the "bowsprit" gets mixed up with the "rudder"; the boat, like the Baker describing his heart, is "like nothing so much as a bowl/Brimming over with quivering curds!"[35] The Bellman, as McCarthy notes, is a literal *kubernetes*, a helmsman and navigator, unable to steer the feedback loops, as he himself is a virtual effect of the innundating waves of matter, cast adrift and rudderless by the "tinnitus of existence."[36] McCarthy characterizes this as a condition of "un-masterable drifting"; an infinite and immanent "dy-*ing*" drive that snarks everyone in its wake.[37] Or, worse, the Bellman is a defective autopilot, recalling the automatic, mechanical aspects of habit that distance us from ourselves.

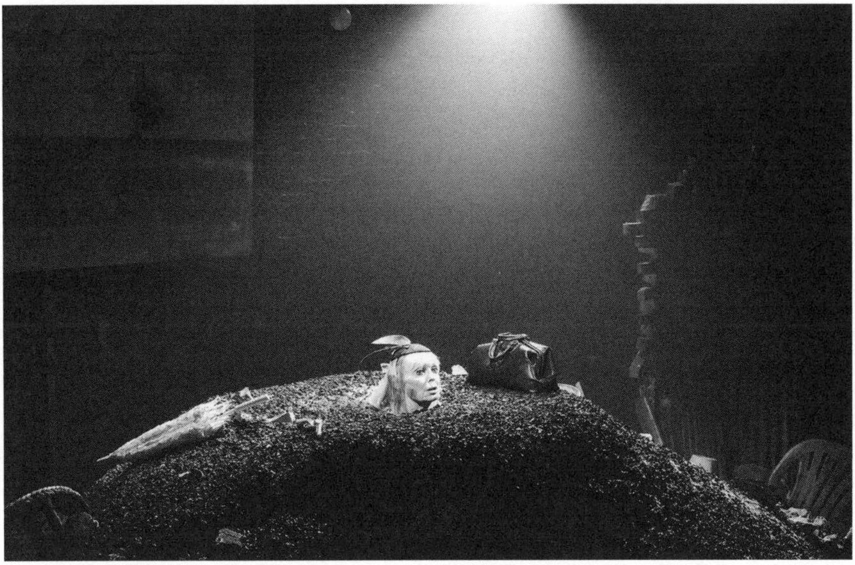

FIGURE 3.8
Belinda Giblin in Samuel Beckett's *Happy Days*, Sydney Australia, 2021. Directed by Craig Baldwin, set design by Charles Davis, lighting designer Veronique Bennett. Produced by Red Line Productions at the Old Fitz Theatre. Photo by Robert Catto.

The narrator's "tingling" body in *Remainder* is not the "absolute quivering" or "quiescent" state that Hegel invokes to describe digested otherness in the body's "aliveness," nor is it the tingling of aesthetic pleasure, although the word "beautiful" often comes into play when the narrator feels he is inside things and has "cut out the detour." This tingling is more indicative of anxiety or jouissance, variously described by Lacan as an eruption and overflow of enjoyment as a result of repetition, a pain-in-pleasure, a "disturbed relationship to one's own body," or a "backhanded enjoyment"—states that are not antithetical to conditions of entrenchment, suffocation, paralysis, and short-circuiting.[38] In fact, the narrator often describes this tingling as slowly creeping up his legs and into his neck, recalling Winnie from Beckett's *Happy Days* as she is ensnared and buried up to her neck in habitual repetitions and reenactments of those repetitions by the second act of the play (Rem, 9, 96) (figure 3.8).[39]

The repetitive, noisy clanging, pinging, and striking of matter as it reverberates and echoes is what McCarthy calls the "tinnitus of existence," and it is always too much to navigate or handle. The forceful breeze that blows on the body, tugs at the narrator's tenuously affixed drawings, or the more violent gust following a catastrophic impact, indicates that habit is a driven force that winds us and knocks us off course. Rather than a quickening of the body by spirit, the habitual body is shaken to the core.

FULGURATING LIGHTNING RODS

One of the most overworked metaphors of habit is the "lightning-conductor" that absorbs and converts difference and otherness into the stabilizing and deadening aspects of habit. Beckett's formulation is the best-known version of this trope: "habit is a compromise effected between the individual and his environment, or between the individual and his own organic eccentricities, the guarantee of a dull inviolability, the lightning-conductor of his existence. Habit is the ballast that chains the dog to his vomit."[40] The assumption here is that habit dampens, dulls, and distributes the external shocks of existence. It is the grounding mechanism that incorporates the flashes of spontaneity and creates the continuities, adjustments, and compromises with life that are always inseparable from habit's nascent deadening effect.

Yet habit, rather than working as the lightning rod that prevents short-circuiting, instead perpetually generates it. At one point the narrator recalls an "intense and overwhelming tingling that had fulgurated" in him as he lays passive lying on the tarmac after one of his reenactments (Rem, 241). Habit does not just dampen shocks; it is also the crack of the real that fulgurates and far exceeds any ability to secure the inviolability of its dullness or veiling-over function. If habit is precisely what creates a break in the immediacy of "self-feeling" in and as a "mechanism of self-feeling," that gap is rendered inviolable as its repetitions do not simply produce the "protective shell" that would secure its distance from the discordant jolts of matter that might engulf it. In *Remainder*, the narrator is never able to "plug" the gap or crack that the accident has blown in him since he is of a piece with that crack. When the narrator's friend Catherine comes over to his apartment, she comments on the phone unit that he had pulled out of the wall a while earlier when trying to call his lawyer, now lying in a heap of plaster and wire in the novel: "'Wow! Did it get hit by lightning?' she said—then, with a gasp, added: 'Oh! I'm sorry. I mean, I didn't ... I know it wasn't lightning, but ...'" (Rem, 29) (figures 3.9 and 3.10). The narrator's response to Catherine's observation is equally over-punctuated in ways that short-circuit their conversation, generating further jolts that generate virtual incompletion and cuts in continuity, communication, and meaning.

Here we also glean more about habit as an anxiety that "chokes off" the functions of speaking and communicating, so that the very sentences themselves have inwardly fallen into dissolution and collapsed under their own suffocating weight.[41] Instead of vanishing (*verschwinden*) into air—which is how Hegel describes spoken language's form of universalization as it takes leave of the individual—the conversation drops, stains, excessively punctuates, cuts off, and entangles, much like all the myriad "stuff" that falls in *Remainder* as a perpetual echo and recoil of the initial accident.[42] Habit as a fulgurating lightning rod manifests the temporality of delay and precipitousness that marks

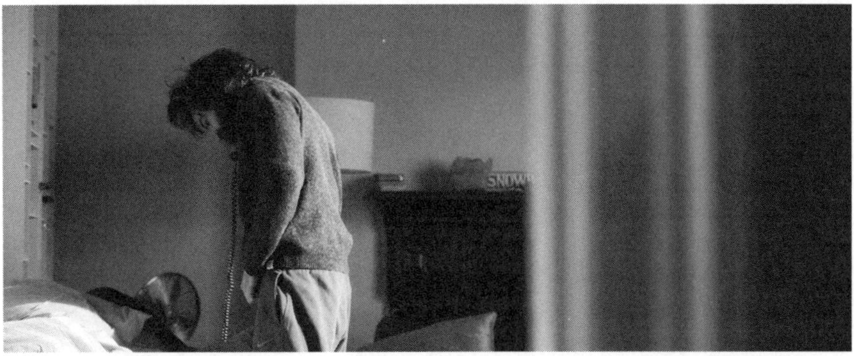

FIGURE 3.9
Tom talking to his lawyer. Film still from Omer Fast's *Remainder*. © Omer Fast.

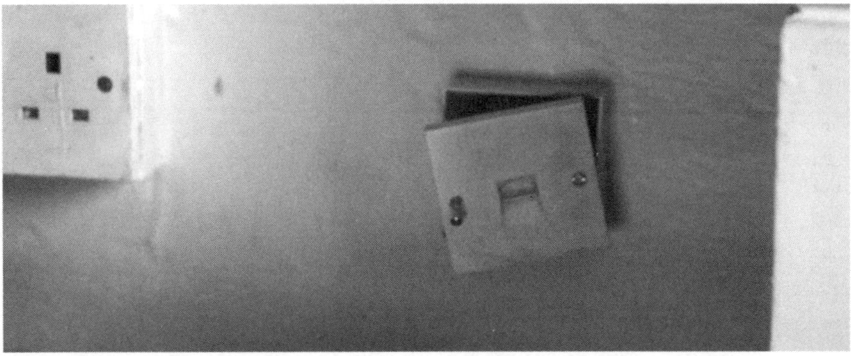

FIGURE 3.10
Phone cable yanked out of the wall. Film still from Omer Fast's *Remainder*. © Omer Fast.

speculative movement that is characterized by jerks and jolts, rather than by a grounding that simply absorbs fulgurations like a lightning conductor. Like habit, and punctuation itself in its speculative and psychoanalytic dimensions, lightning always strikes (at least) twice.

One begins to suspect that the notion of habit as a lightning conductor that dampens disruptive energies is a defense mechanism against habit as a disturbing "tinnitus of existence," just as the characterization of Hegel's *Phenomenology* as a "circuit breaker" that absorbs all the jolts of difference and singularity in identity thinking is a disavowal of the fact that its circular movement—or more accurately, its "circle of circles"—is always tripping, breaking, isolating, and cutting off, like an annulating machine spiraling out of control at the heart of its enclosing and rounding-off function.[43] Unlike a lightning flash that seizes and consolidates the "simple unity" of the conscious

"I," habit can sunder and tear the subject apart. The narrator is a fulgurating lightning rod always immanently generating perturbances that are never adequately dampened or unified. Habit perpetually cracks the subject, a crack that the narrator is committed to keeping open by incessant acts of repetition and ren(de)ring that are attentive to its spectral yet material specificity, which cannot be definitively placed, contained, or remembered: "I stood there staring at the crack. It all came down to that: the way it ran down the wall, the texture of the plaster all around it, the patches of colour to its right. That's what had sparked the whole thing off. I had to get it down somehow—exactly, how it forked and jagged" (Rem, 67). It is a crack that continues to spark, flash, and lacerate the narrator throughout the novel and film like a wound that never heals; in fact, it is perpetually ripped open, rendered, and filled with a multitude of other cracks, like a crater within a crater.

If, in the high modernist tradition of Walter Pater, Viktor Shklovsky, and Samuel Beckett, habit is often regarded as the lightning rod that dampens the jolt of particularity, smothering our sensitivity and deadening us to the world that deadening is also a site that gives way to a procedure of undeadening, in which the particularities of matter and time become unmoored and untethered. Perhaps habit demonstrates what Alain Badiou has called a "generic vacillation" that puts differences to the test without any supporting base.[44] In any case, it is precisely the veiling, smoothing-over, or, more pejoratively, deadening function of habit that is overridden by a mode of habit that generates excesses, gaps, divisions, and ruptures. It is this per-severing unbearability that is explored in *Remainder* and that is generated by the repetitions that are internal to the regular workings of habit itself.

If the narrator is continuously knocked down and collapsing, as explored in earlier chapters, such a falling must be taken as a rigorous exposition of the very tenuousness of standing upright, which Hegel describes as the "absolute gesture" (*absolute Gebärde*), or ground zero, of habit in that it does not require an effort of conscious willing but still needs to be "pervaded by our will if we are not momentarily to collapse."[45] *Remainder* is constantly tarrying with an immanent collapse of the body that is evoked in Hegel's claim that "Spirit only wins its truth by finding its feet in its absolute disruption."[46] If this sentence from the Preface is one of the ways in which Hegel characterizes knowing's movement as "the path of despair," the narrator in *Remainder* articulates his own path of despair as a lamentation on the (second) hand and its inability to grasp the surplus matter at hand: "just so much *matter*—that your study of it would branch out and become endless until, finally, you threw your hands up in despair and announced … *There's too much here, too much to process, just too much*" (Rem, 202).[47] In what follows, I want to consider the bungled action (*Vergreifen*) at the heart of grasping (*begreifen*) in the per-severing second-handedness in *Remainder* alongside Hegel's notion of the concept (*Begriff*), conceptually comprehending thinking (*das begreifende Denken*), and his philosophy of the hand. What happens when the hand resists its own graspability or when the concept of habit—which, as we have seen, is often articulated through the metonymy of the hand and acts of handling in phenomenological terms such as it is "the body which 'catches [*kapiert*]' and 'comprehends meaning,'" "taking in hand," "knowledge in the hands," or the "grasping of meaning is performed by the body"—is caught up in its own perturbations, such that it is no longer able to get a grasp on itself and its ability to handle its own otherness?[48]

THE RECOIL OF *VERGREIFEN* IN *BEGREIFEN*

Almost every account of Hegel's philosophy notes the close etymological connection between the concept (*Begriff*), which can also mean "the grasp or grip," and the verb *begreifen*, which means conceptually comprehending, and because it is derived from the verb *greifen*, it also connotes "to grasp" or "to seize." A speculative taking in hand is meant to sublate a certain "fixed" notion of grasping, as the Hegelian concept is not a "fixed entity distant from comprehension" but a (self-moving) movement of comprehending that takes its own subject matter in hand.[49] The grasp (*Be-griff*) of the concept (*Begriff*) is meant to take hold of itself through an action (*Handlung*) of reaching through (*durchgreifen*) and embracing (*umgreifen*) the actuality of the movement of comprehending in its universality and individuality.[50] In many ways, the hand is itself the "concrete universality" of the concept and its grasping. In turn, this grasping and taking hold of its own self-moving movement is a metonymy for habit in Hegel's sense that "after the organ of speech, it is by and large the hand by which a person brings himself to appearance and actualizes himself ... we may say of the hand that it is what a man *does*."[51]

The connection between the logical and physical aspects of grasping in Hegel is further pursued in different stretches of his writing where he develops a philosophy of the hand in relation to habit, decay, disease, and the relationships between actuality and non-actuality, part and whole, universal and particular. Closely following Aristotle's accounts of the human hand in *De Anima* and *De Partibus Animalium*, Hegel describes the hand as an "absolute tool" (*das absolute Werkzeug*), or the "tool of tools" (*Werkzeug der Werkzeuge*), that is indicative of the sedimented and incorporated refinements of habit, which begins with the most apparently automatic and external actions that involve a minimal willing—such as the "absolute gesture" of our human, upright posture—and culminates with the hand that is a "flexible instrument" adapted for a multitude of conscious and willed activities.[52] But there are other, more anxious aspects of the hand that never seems to take hold of its objects; that does not take the matter in hand; that is disconnected from the body; and that is characterized by a compulsion to repeat that per-severs and disarms the willing activities of the grasping hand.

Remainder is preoccupied with the hand that from before the very beginning has difficulty coming to grips with its own material consistency never mind completing an action. In *Remainder*, the grasping hand is always dropping and recoiling from its actions and objects, as if it had internalized its accidents but in ways that are never stabilized. Simply put, the hand in *Remainder* never gets a grip on its ability to mediate and actualize itself, thus enbabling it to make itself at home within its surrounding environment. The hand is just as likely to seize up, drop its object, and fail in its attempt to grasp or even enact any capacity to have, hold, or more generally to "[keep] a grip on it" (Rem, 41). This is not a trivial issue in *Remainder*, as the narrator believes that he is "completely second-hand," and always outside himself in a perpetual condition of detour, delay, and repetition both before and after the accident (Rem, 54).[53]

The grasping hand in *Remainder* is more likely to result in what Freud calls a "bungled action" (*Vergreifen*) in *The Psychopathology of Everyday Life* than in a grasping (*begreifen*) of the concept (*Begriff*).[54] *Vergreifen* refers to all those cases in which a wrong result, i.e., a deviation from what was *intended*, seems to be the essential element, or when the whole action seems to be inappropriate, primarily manifested in actions that result in all manner of stumbling, falling, breaking, and self-injury. However, I am not strictly following Freud in developing this line of thought, as I am not claiming that bungled actions are deviations from, or repressions of, an "unconscious intention." Rather, I argue that they are recoils from the untamed drives generated by the effects of habit that supposedly ground intentionality in a lived body.[55]

It is precisely the *ver*-, a per-severing prefix that is ubiquitous in the Freudian and Hegelian lexicon, that best captures the detours, delays, repetitions, gaps, and surplus matter that the narrator in *Remainder* is perpetually caught up in and disarmed by. As Katrin Pahl notes, the German prefix *ver*- expresses both the thorough accomplishment *and* the negation of an action expressed in the verb it modifies, in the sense of carrying something through and the very failure to do so. Mladen Dolar has further suggested that these *ver*- words are indicative of getting caught up in and derailed by a failed negation in Hegel and Freud.[56] This "failed negation" articulates the limits of self-positing—anxiously and repeatedly invoked in Hegel's account of habit as second nature—that Hegel succinctly defines in *Science of Logic* as a "*turning back* of the negative into itself."[57] Thus, these *ver*- words speak to the limits of habit as a "posited universality" able to subsume and coordinate its particularities into a speculative unity. Instead of habit as a form of corporeal absolute negativity that "simply" has otherness in its own self, this is a concept of habit that is shattered and stained by material excess, resistance, untamed drives, and excessive forms of depositing generated by its kenotic modes of self-divestiture.

We have already encountered many of the oddities of these *ver*-derived terms in the account of *Verstand* and *Vernunft* in the previous chapter, which manifest as the deviations, recoils, and repetitions generated by the "under-stumbling" of habit in *Remainder*.[58] But there are many more *ver*- words in Hegel, such as *verschwinden* (disappear/vanish), *verfaulen* (putrefy), *Verhältnis* (relationship/comportment), *Verleiblichung* (corporeity or embodiment), *Vermittlung* (mediation), and *Verwirklichung* (actualization)—to name but six additional words intimately connected to habit. In addition, there are the five *ver*- words that, as Dolar notes, are central to the Freudian vocabulary of (failed) negativity, and the many *ver*- words that comprise the "slips," "misses," and "forgettings" that comprise the parapraxes (*Fehlleistungen*) in Freud's *Psychopathology of Everyday Life*, including *Vergreifen*, which means not only "a bungled action" but also "committing a violence or assault."[59] The latter meaning of this term is the one emphasized by Hegel's apparently singular use of *sich vergreifen* in the *Phenomenology of Spirit*; both dimensions of the word are at stake in *Remainder*.[60]

THE EGO-FUNCTION OF AN ORGAN IS IMPAIRED

Remainder begins with Tom *about* to be hit by falling debris. Yet it is apparent in the odd way in which Tom holds his mobile phone, gripped between his third and fourth fingers, that he has always already been accidentalized *before* getting hit by the "external" accident (figure 1.4). This disruption persists throughout the film, as we are precipitously launched between shots where Tom's compromised grip is evident in his awkward manipulations of a pen, a utility knife, or his ever-present mobile phone and then, suddenly, those where his hand engages in a fully functioning grip, for instance when Tom firmly takes the "kink" in a carpet in hand during the bank robbery enactment (figures 3.11 and 3.12). But the cuts between these states are too exaggerated, precipitous, and jarring to be subsumed into a bildungsroman of the ups and downs or the progressions and setbacks involved in the recovery from a neurological trauma requiring relearning and rewiring, with a two steps forward, one step back, or two steps back, one step forward rhythm. The neurologically compromised grip precipitously and inexplicably reverts to a firm one and back again in a way that short-circuits any attempt to read these cuts in terms of a montage-as-narrative of the inevitable "daily marathon"—the myriad travails, setbacks, and incremental advances—involved in healing after a neurological trauma.

The odd status of Tom's per-severing hand is the focus of attention from the very beginning of the film. An initial probing shot of Tom's wounded and bloody head is followed by an out-of-focus panning shot that comes to a stop on the other side of the heap, where we see a close-up of Tom's twisted upturned left hand that looks as if it were another piece of fallen detritus,

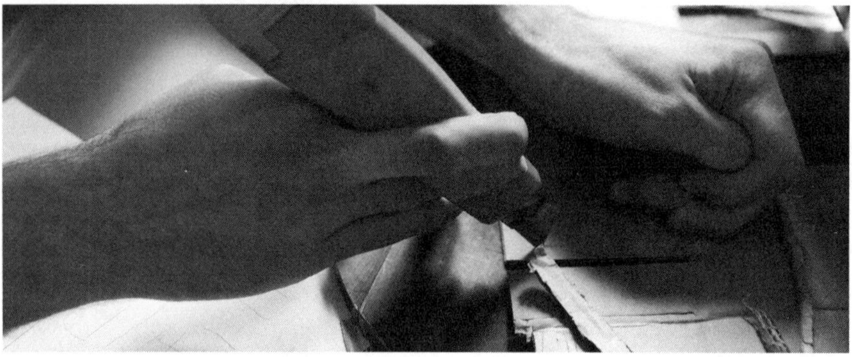

FIGURE 3.11
Tom's odd grip as he makes a cardboard model of Madlyn Mansions. Film still from Omer Fast's *Remainder*. © Omer Fast.

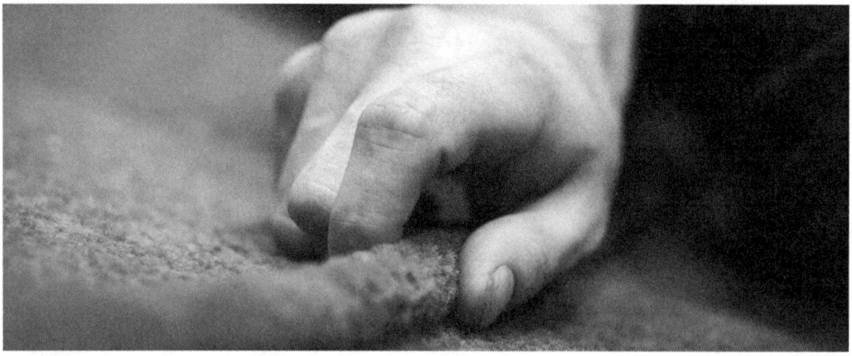

FIGURE 3.12
Tom firmly gripping a kink in the carpet during the bank robbery reenactment. Film still from Omer Fast's *Remainder*. © Omer Fast.

almost completely severed and separated from the rest of his body buried under the heap of debris (figure 2.6).

One of the persistent references to the hand in Hegel's writing—articulated in slightly different ways in *Philosophy of Nature*, *Encyclopedia Logic*, and *Elements of the Philosophy of Right*—occurs when a hand is separated from the body or a finger is cut off from the hand; it is no longer a "living" finger or a hand in "actuality" (*Wirklichkeit*) but only in name, as "the individual members of the body are what they are only by means of their unity and in relation to it." Although "[a] hand which has been cut off still looks like a hand and exists ... it has no actuality"—with the phrase "no actuality" indicating that the concept (*Begriff*) and its grasping (*begreifen*) has lost the power of necessity and thus its "true actuality."[61] In the Preface to the *Phenomenology*, the "non-actual" is defined as "what is separated," and ultimately, to "what is dead." But this death is clearly not just physiological death.[62] As explored in the previous chapter, there are ways in which an organ "establishes itself in isolation and persists in its particular activity against the activity of the whole, the fluidity and all-pervading process of which is obstructed."[63] But this per-severing and stuckness is not simply a matter of disease, putrefaction, pathological deviation or a dismemberment caused by the sundering acts of understanding as *opposed* to the unifying effects of spirit-suffused habit. On the contrary, it is one that is fully immanent within the assumptions of fluidity itself and these sundering effects of the understanding are of a piece with habit's self-positing non-actuality.

To clarify these ideas, let us return to the ubiquitous example of piano playing as the privileged example of habitual skill and fluidity discussed in the previous chapter. The evidence that all the parts, units, or steps of an action have been incorporated into a unified and fluid act often refers to fingers that "glide" across the keys in such a way that mindedness, intelligence, and knowing have drifted toward the organ of the hand. Two examples drawn from Merleau-Ponty's *Phenomenology of Perception* and Walter Benjamin's essay "Rastelli's Story" suffice to make the point. In Merleau-Ponty's account of piano playing, he speaks about "knowledge in the hands," while in Benjamin's account of the accomplished Italian juggler Enrico Rastelli's dexterity, he notes that "the will abdicates its power inside the body in favour of the hands, such that the hand has taken the matter in hand and joined forces with the object" (figure 3.13).[64] These passages suggest that intelligence, know-how, and understanding have bypassed conscious volition and that the hands are operating without conscious guidance, thus invoking a mode of bodily understanding, in which, to use Merleau-Ponty's phraseology, "grasping a meaning" is performed by a bodily member that is precisely *not* a part.

Merleau-Ponty is at pains to emphasize that even when he refers to "knowledge in the hands," such knowledge does not exist without the habitual effort of the body and cannot be "formulated in detachment from that effort."[65] For Merleau-Ponty, the grasping of a meaning is performed by a bodily habit in which the hand is not separate from the body but is more like a bud on a fully thriving plant, with the fingers representing its organic flourishing.[66] The gliding fingers are a sign of an achieved fluidity that does not pay heed to the individual steps, parts, or units of which it is composed. But what happens when the "ego-function" of the hand—or even the fingers—is not working and bodily derangement has not been "disarmed" by the universalizing and generalizing aspects of habit? What if the organist's hands and fingers "have a mind of their own," never fully becoming her hands and never integrating themselves into the fluid movements of the instrumentalist's "consecratory gestures."[67] What if these hands and fingers persist as "part-objects," "little passive selves," "larval contemplations," or "an organ without a body"? What

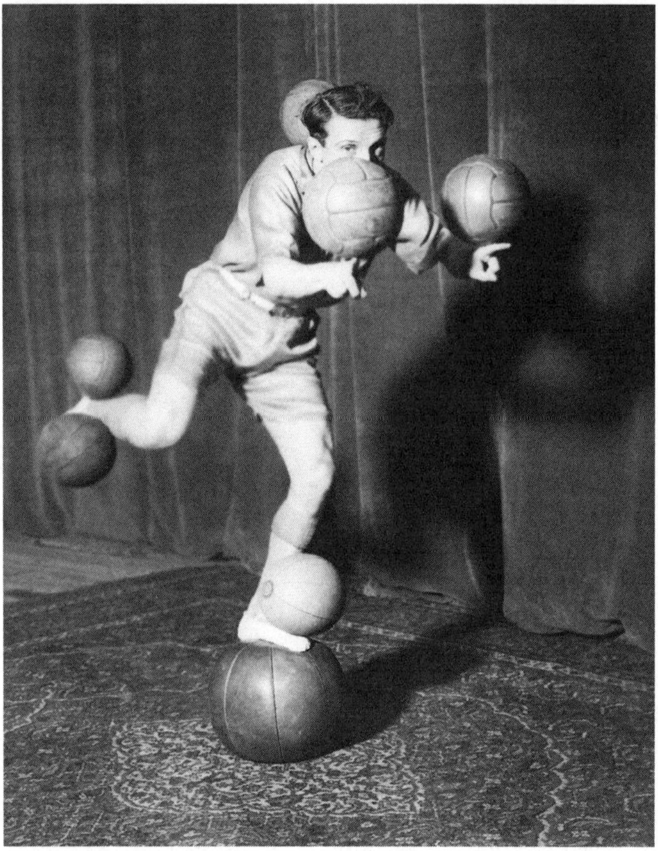

FIGURE 3.13
Publicity photograph of Rastelli reenacting the pose of an Etruscan sculpture of a juggler. © Ullstein Bild.

happens when, in contrast to Benjamin's story about the juggler Rastelli, the hand or the fingers do not take the *matter at hand* in hand, joining forces with the object behind our backs?[68] What if an arm is detachable, can fall off or be left behind?

In what seems like a direct riposte in his *Seminar on Anxiety* to Merleau-Ponty's account of Anosognosia in the *Phenomenology of Perception*, Lacan homes in on this "taking up arms" in a brief discussion of the arm as an "instrument" that is an "intermediary" between will and act.[69] In doing so, he raises the issue of not just the possibility of the arm's removal but, more importantly, its "non-control"; the fact that someone might seize possession of it, or leave that arm behind, for instance, like an umbrella misplaced at a subway station. Of course, that other who does the "seizing" does not have to be literally someone else; moreover, this leaving behind and separating off might have other causal, temporal, and material implications in terms of "deciduous appendages" that bring forth a sundering complication of the "body participating in its totality" though habit's molding an aim that "shows the corporeity rendered completely pervious, made into an instrument."[70] Habitual understanding does not necessarily enable the body to achieve a fluid harmony between what we aim at and what is given, between intention, performance, and accomplished act.[71]

Toward the beginning of *Inhibitions, Symptoms, and Anxiety*, Freud specifically refers to piano playing when he discusses activities that are impeded owing to neurotic inhibitions, or the fact that the physical organs brought into play, such as the fingers, are too strongly eroticized, thus impairing the "ego-function of an organ."[72] Drawing on Freud's language, and perhaps alluding to this specific example, Lacan refers to this impairing as an "impediment" (*empêchement*), echoing the Latin *Impedicare* that he chooses to inflect in terms of "*to be ensnared*" rather than merely as a "halting of movement."[73] Pushing further, he claims that these inhibitions are not simply a matter of interrupting or disrupting an action or function as a literal English translation of the neologism "parapraxes" ("faulty function") might suggest—or even an interpretable psychoanalytic symptom as indicative of an unconscious intentionality—but rather they are "truly and verily the subject."[74] Lacan emphasizes the "objectality" of the partial body, a term he uses in deliberate opposition to the term "objectivity," and that is defined as "the correlate to a pathos of the cut."[75] This "corporeal morsel" or "part-object" is a lost cause that can't be retrieved and remains as "this bodily portion of ourselves [that] is, essentially and functionally, partial."[76]

Thus, the per-severing nature of such arms and hands is not just a matter of neurotic inhibitions, putrefaction, or a diseased, pathological condition, but an excessive state of drivenness intrinsic to habit that the "will" never overrides because the hands are "fixated" (have a drivenness of their own) in ways that are not dictated by a unified, habitual body. Although we often encounter such hands in animation, film, or literature—the withered hand of the narrator's grandmother repeatedly pulling at the bedsheet on her deathbed in Proust's *À la recherche du temps perdu* is one striking example that comes to mind—that condition is not solely a scene of death encountered at the biological end of life but is fully akin to the static logic of habit as a constitutive desease. Perhaps the very status of the human hand as not simply a tool but the "tool of tools," suggests that the hand is always already subject to repetition, second-handedness, and failing to grasp.[77]

Although we might try to comfort ourselves that we can control, possess, grasp, and take this unruly otherness in hand, or, to use the language of habit, get a hold of ourselves in the sense of stabilizing our way of being in a fluid and unified bodily action or socialized habitus, in *Remainder* that jubilatory discourse is always shattered. In an observation relegated to a footnote in the *Psychopathology of Everyday Life* on the German verb *versteigen*, it notes that the prefix *ver-* "here not only suggests mis-climbing" but also in its figurative meaning, a surplus and excess: "to over-reach oneself."[78] In his *Seminar on Anxiety*, Lacan persistently mocks any sleight of hand that takes seriously the mastery—the cunning that believes it has complete control over its cunningness—that would convert our being seized by an anxiety that exceeds our grasp into an ability to grasp the Other in a sovereign act of the grasping hand.

In fact, Lacan seems to rehearse, mock, and lure us in in ways that recall Freud and Hegel's characterization of anxiety as a way of forestalling the loss of the object après-*coup* by generating an anxiety that would master an event ungraspable in the first place. In the *Phenomenology of Spirit*, Hegel calls attention to the inherent instability and violence that consciousness suffers at "its own hands" by perpetually overreaching itself and, as a response, "might well withdraw and strive to hold on to what it is in danger of losing."[79] In failing to acknowledge that in its essential function the object "steals away at the level of our grasp," we might, for example, attempt to "tame the gaze" (*dompte-regard*), perhaps by taking an oculiform amulet in hand, in order to reassure ourselves that the evil eye "*cannot* be out there, because I have it right here in my hand."[80] Or, consider "the odd little twisting object" that Lacan constructs for the participants in his *Seminar on Anxiety*, "putting it in [their] hands" like a consecrated host, thus allowing them to grasp and handle the "short-circuiting" that is demonstrated through the little missing portion that results from the central cut of the figure eight in the form of a "cross-cap."[81]

This non-graspability at the heart of Hegel's *begreifen* is perhaps most directly addressed in the hand's gasping of "the thing" in "the being of spirit is a bone" passage, as if one could take spirit as a thing to be literally grasped, thus attesting to the necessity and limitations of any picture-thinking to do justice to the concept, as the whole truth is precisely what is never fully grasped.[82] It is not that this grasping of "thinking is a thing" is untrue—in fact Hegel explicitly states that "*Thinking* is *thinghood*, or *thinghood* is *thinking*."[83] And Lacan does indeed mean that the gaze is an object—however it is never just an object but always an objectality and thus partial.[84] A hand letting go and letting drop is an articulation of the acceptance of non-actuality as part of the movement of actuality and the limits of any subjectification of the concept that would limit its self-moving movement to a finite theory of subjectivity. In *Remainder*, however, these movements and gestures are excessively cutting, pulsatile, kenotic and stained by an unruly "matter at hand" in ways that suggest more brutal acts of letting go.[85]

"NOT A MEMBER IS SOBER"

There is an important and frequently cited sentence in the Preface to the *Phenomenology of Spirit* that might be brought to bear on the question of the hand as a part-object in relationship to corporeal unity: "The truth is the bacchanalian revel [*der bacchantische Taumel*] where not a member is sober [*kein Glied nicht trunken ist*], because, in isolating himself from the revel, each member is just as immediately dissolved [[*sich*] *auflöst*] into it—the ecstasy is likewise transparently and simply motionless [*durchsichtige und einfache Ruhe*]."[86] In *Philosophy of Nature*, Hegel characterizes nature as a "Bacchic god unrestrained and unmindful of itself"—a point echoed later in the *Phenomenology*: "In bacchanalian enthusiasm, the self is external to itself."[87] Although the "whole" movement of truth does not shy away from lingering and tarrying with the negative, it does so in such a way that the negation of negation is a form of dissolving/disappearing/vanishing within the movement of the whole—"the vanishing of the vanishing"—and does not exist as something cut off from it.[88]

The sign that these "members" are precisely members and not external and aggregate parts is that they are dissolved just as quickly as they isolate themselves in their lurching/tumbling/reeling (*taumeln*). Particularity does not "actually" die off but disappears (*verschwinden*) in and through its universality, and these members remain essential and therefore are not "something fixed, something cut off from the truth, which along the way is to be set aside (who knows where?)."[89] The logic of this passage on the "bacchanalian revel" is elaborated in many passages in the *Phenomenology of Spirit* and *Science of Logic*: "The equilibrium in which coming-to-be and ceasing-to-be are poised [*setzen*] is in the first place becoming itself. ... Becoming is a ceaseless unrest that collapses into a quiescent result."[90] Like the "universal bloodstream" of the absolute concept, the bacchanalian revel is "pulsating within itself without setting itself in motion; it is trembling within itself without itself being agitated."[91] In this pulsating circulatory system, there is apparently no "sluggish blood" or stumbling and staggering members that might interfere with the organic fluidity of a body.

If this passage from the Preface is meant to show that these "drunken members" are not cut off from and set outside the whole but are inextricable and necessary "moments" or "determinations," "dissolved" in the "whole of movement," I take these drunken members quite literally to mean a recalcitrance to speculative fluidity. These intoxicated members—unbalanced, unhinged, and uncontrollable—are not dissolved, vanished, or fluidly unfixed into a quiescent unity but are at best lingering, tarrying, pitching, and reeling at different tempos and rhythms, like the electronic metronome that plays the narrator at different speeds, or at worst clogging up the whole system, like the excess materiality that the liver lady in *Remainder* produces by her repetitive actions, and which accumulates as congealed and vaporized fat in and around the elaborate extraction system constructed over her cooking range that is meant to facilitate the "wafting"—Hegel uses the language of "diffusion" and "pervasion"—of its infectious and even noxious cordite-inflected scent throughout the apartment building (Rem, 70, 87, 155).[92] In *Remainder*, the unruliness of the "parts" of the hand and the action of grasping never dissolve as quickly as they isolate—rather, they stagger and are out of sync, such that there is no equilibrium of coming-to-be and ceasing-to-be but a more abrupt punctuation that cuts out, off, and on. The disturbed "pulsatility" of these members is the primary indication that their ego-function is impaired: a body-in-pieces that is unable to adequately unify and coordinate its movements.[93] This disarmed hand and these unhanded fingers are directly at stake in an important section of the novel when the narrator is relearning to grasp a carrot as part of his "rerouting" training after the accident.

GRASPING AT THE PRINCIPLE OF CARROT AND STICK

The narrator begins by visualizing simple things like lifting a carrot to his mouth in the hope that this rerouting will ideally establish new routes through the brain to compensate for the damage caused to the left hemisphere—which controls the motor function of the right side of his body—in order "to cut and lay the new circuits" for commands to be successfully transmitted (Rem, 19–20). When he has visualized grasping a carrot—that is, has gone through all the "steps" and "sequences" in the process of neural rerouting, and lifted more than a thousand imaginary carrots to his mouth—he finally attempts to hold this "gnarled, dirty and irregular" thing in his hands (Rem, 20). At this point, his physiotherapist back aways, as if he was "a house of cards" that might collapse at any moment, thus articulating the precipitous temporal logic of a "not yet" that circles around an accident that has yet to come and has always already happened.

When the carrot is finally in his hand and he has closed his fingers around it, the narrator is shattered by its materiality and thingness that cannot be grasped or controlled. He calls it the "surge of active carrot," which starts "short-circuiting the operation" (Rem, 21). As he moves into "phase two, the hoist," he feels the "surge of active carrot input scrambling the communication between brain and arm, firing off false contractions, locking muscles at the very moment it was vital they relax and expand, twisting fulcral joints the wrong directions" (Rem, 21). The carrot rolls, slips, and plummets away, and the narrator remarks: "'At least it didn't fall on anyone'" (Rem, 21). Although the last passage makes it sound as if the carrot is just an external object he is attempting to grasp, it is precisely a part-object, of a piece with the indeterminate accident that is the object-cause of his repetitions. Even when the narrator gets it right, factoring in the "surplus signals," or eventually comes almost up to speed in terms of his adroitness, he is still unable to stomach carrots or cut out the deviations, delays, and detours. Instead of newly wired circuits that would fulfill the "promise of connection," the narrator remains perpetually cut off (Rem, 15).

The accident that blows a crater in the narrator—and in the very act of narration—is also a crater blown within matter itself. As Hegel makes clear in the Preface to the *Phenomenology*, "however much this negative now initially appears as the inequality between the I and the object, still it is just as much the inequality of the substance with itself. What seems to take place outside of the substance, to be an activity directed against it, is its own doing, and substance shows that it is essentially subject."[94] It is not simply that the narrator subjectively feels the vitality of the active carrot with its complex texture and mass, but that "it felt": "I closed my fingers round the carrot. It felt—well *it felt*" (Rem, 21). The narrator senses the carrot's own disruptions, gaps, and excesses. As the narrator is at pains to note, it is not simply a matter of his hands, fingers, or rerouted brain as "active agents" and the carrot as simply a passive "no-thing—a hollow, a carved space for me to grasp and move" (Rem, 21). The "surge of the active carrot"—"the way it bumped and wrinkled, how it crawled with grit"—voids, overflows, and falls outside itself, such that is not simply a matter of the hand (subject) dropping the carrot (object). This ensnarement is "truly and verily the subject."[95]

We might think about the ensnarement in this scene in relation to one of Picasso's preparatory drawings for *Woman Ironing (La repasseuse)* (figure 3.14). The act of ironing is one of the privileged metaphors of habit in its quotidian, repetitive, mechanical aspects, and the exhaustion, fatigue, and boredom resulting from this act is well-captured in impressionist and post-impressionist figurations, which also grasp its veiling function.[96] Less common are depictions of the violence and disruption that these repetitions do not iron out. The laundress's body in Picasso's study shows the immanent loop of habit cracking, opening up, and overflowing with accruals and irruptions of substance.

To borrow Hélène Cixous's pithy and apt account of Picasso's drawing, "this Woman Ironing hurts us," as the excess of black ink furiously rendered in and as swirls and stains in the right shoulder spread and "infect" other areas of the body. The body is "broken and streaked with strokes … blows, of bruises and even of blood." Picasso's laundress is "tumefied," just as the narrator's body in *Remainder* is bruised from his repeated attempts to brush past the kitchen counter in his Madlyn Mansions reenactments.[97] Like Picasso's drawing, the narrator's arm, hand, and fingers are short-circuited, locking muscles and twisting fulcral joints the wrong way, stained by surplus signals as they close around the gnarly, dirty carrot crawling with grit. In Picasso's drawing it is "*death* that is passing through the Woman Ironing"—just as "the

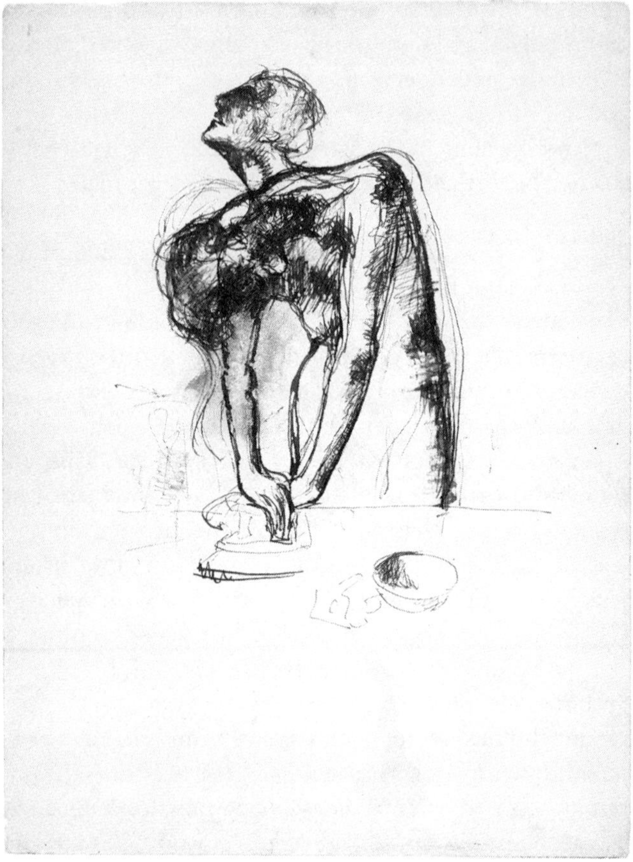

FIGURE 3.14
Pablo Picasso, study for *Woman Ironing* (*La repasseuse*), 1904. Pen with black and brown ink, stomping, 37.2 × 26.9 cm. MP480. © ARS, NY.
Photo: Mathieu Rabeau. © RMN-Grand Palais/Art Resource, NY.

ink-itself" of the forensic diagrams with which the narrator is obsessed in *Remainder*, "vibrates with an almost intolerable violence" (Rem, 185). In the film, Tom's pen furiously overwrites the proper noun "Madlyn Mansions" in his drawing of the building that renders an automaticity in overdrive, generating an overflow of meaningless material marks that stain and disrupt its legibility (figure 3.15). These viscous and inky stains of grease, tar, oil, and black goopy coffee grains relentlessly spill and spread throughout the novel—due to the incessant repetition of words, sentences, phrases, ideas, and images—as they comprise the act of writing as such, which, in McCarthy's wording, is a messy process of "ink polluting [mulchy] paper." *Remainder* is—in the language of book design—all "gutter."[98]

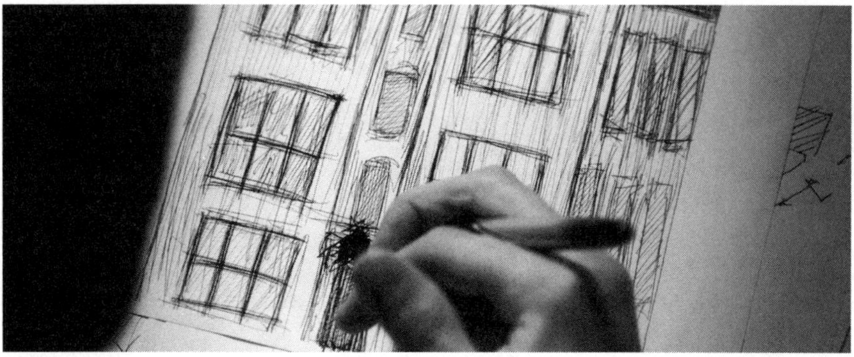

FIGURE 3.15
The violence of ink rendering automaticity in overdrive. Film still from Omer Fast's *Remainder*. © Omer Fast.

If in his rerouting training he imagines grasping the nonbeing of the carrot, that virtual dimension is never bypassed when it comes to grasping the "actual" carrot. It is not simply a discrepancy between the narrator running through the sequences in his head versus the actual movements involved in carrying out the act by means of a real carrot. The coexistence of the virtual and actual imparts to the carrot itself an odd immateriality that is both saturated, buzzing, and crawling, and precipitously voided; it short-circuits the clean, quick, and goal-directed movement of the hand as well as the status of the carrot as an intentional object. The narrator's incessant drive to slow things down creates a void or echo chamber that allows him to generate and hear the "tinnitus of existence": the discordant and buzzing reality of the carrot that manifests as a recoil and errancy that is more likely to curve, pool, and collapse than to result in an accomplished projection, goal-directed activity, or intentional act.

Here, we should remember that *Vergreifen* does not simply mean a bungled action but also a violent act—a point made clear in Freud's *Psychopathology of Everyday Life* and in Hegel's *Phenomenology of Spirit* and that is indicative of the self-destructive and daemonic forces at work in Freud's notion of a repetition compulsion that repeatedly brings us back into the situation of the traumatic accident. In one film sequence, Tom's lower arm pivots at the fulcrum of the elbow, swinging down in a repetitive fury of piston-like blows administered with his right fist, which destroys the cardboard model of Madlyn Mansions—an externalization of his jerrymandered and fragile montage-driven stuff that is assembled and violated by his own hand—and owing to the speed of the movement as it is pulped, registers as an anamorphic blur (figure 3.16). This scene brings to the fore the self-destructive aspects of Tom's repetition compulsion and highlights the recoil of an automaticity in overdrive that is

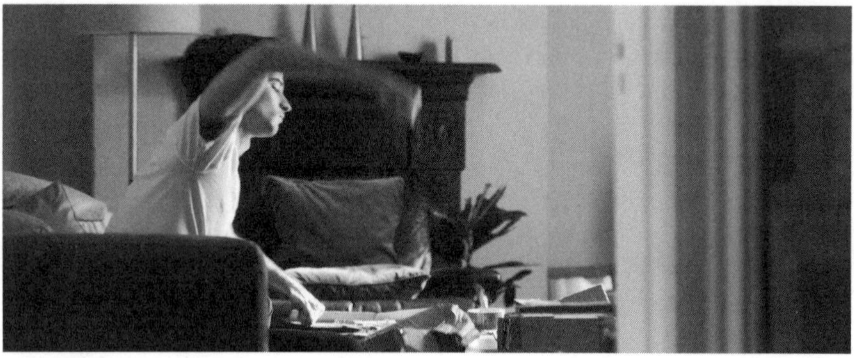

FIGURE 3.16
Tom's fist as an anamorphic blur as it repeatedly strikes the montage-like cardboard model of Madlyn Mansions. Film still from Omer Fast's *Remainder*. © Omer Fast.

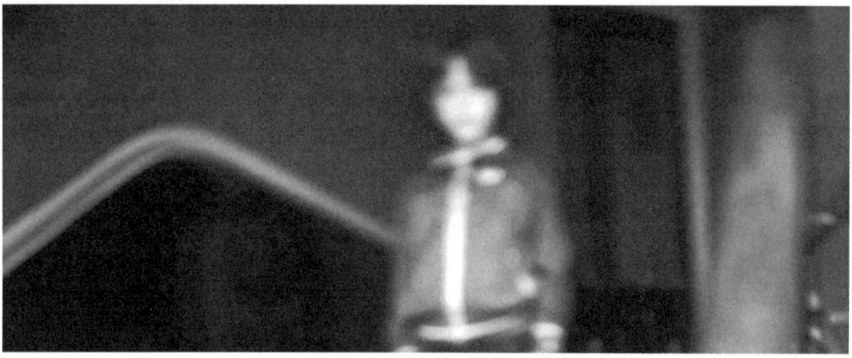

FIGURE 3.17
Blurred image of the young boy. Film still from Omer Fast's *Remainder*. © Omer Fast.

now more indicative of a "*passage à l'acte*" that identifies with the stain itself rather than an acting out.[99] And as is the nature of the gaze in its refracting, flooding, pulsatile, dazzling, and spread-out function, this anamorphic stain punctuates many other scenes in the film, including the often blurred image of the young boy (figure 3.17), and a scene where the narrator first meets Naz in the Blueprint Café and that is hyperbolically studded with anamorphically distorting lamp shades registering the "inner rift of visible reality" that does justice to the incessant and indeterminate oscillation between different registers of the Real and (diegetic) reality in the novel and film (figure 3.18).[100]

In these scenes, as well as in the passages discussing the grasping of the carrot, accidents do not happen to a passive or immobile subject in the manner

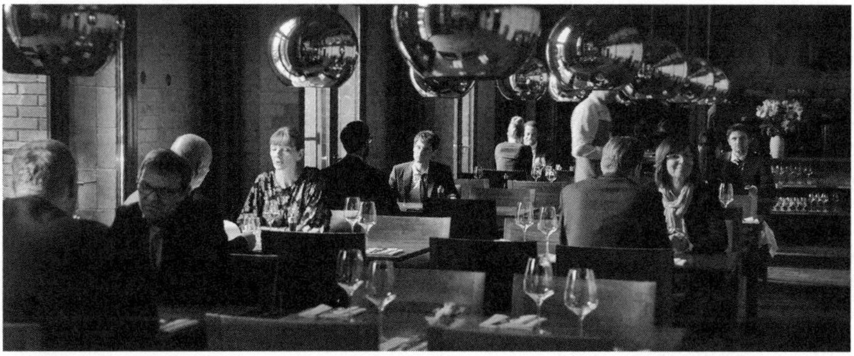

FIGURE 3.18
Anamorphically distorting lamp shades in the Blueprint Café. Film still from Omer Fast's *Remainder*. © Omer Fast.

of a predicate assigned to a subject (and criticized by Hegel in his account of the speculative sentence). Rather, the accident is of a piece with the expiration of the subject and how it arrives by falling outside itself, a point emphasized by the physiotherapist who backs away from the narrator as he is attempting to grasp the carrot as if he was a "house of cards" on the verge of collapse (Rem, 20). This ontological anxiety cannot simply be taken hold of and tempered, as it is autogenerated by the compulsive repetitions that continually return the narrator to and immerse him in accidents that create surplus accidents, which can never be adequately bound and stabilized by the repetitions that habit is supposed to universalize. Thus, the carrot is not simply active in a way that resists our grasp—its substance is neither consistent nor at peace with itself. It is this very weakness that creates the conditions of excess. The narrator's hand does not merely recoil from the carrot and its surcharge of energy; it recoils from the uncanniness of its own part-body that is charged with excessive currents of jouissance driving it beyond its living and organic connections. In other words, it recoils from its own recoil.

Thus, goal-oriented activity, as exemplified by the proverbial carrot, is reenacted in such a way that the narrator is caught up in the surplus materiality engendered by his incessant repetitions, which short-circuits any fluid movement of accomplished grasping. The hand cannot grasp the carrot as it recoils in contact with the disjunctions between its unwieldy contractions and the carrot's resistances and excesses. Here, we literally perceive the grasp as a spasm resulting in short-circuiting, rather than an accomplished habitual gesture. In contrast to this goal-oriented activity, the narrator is forever caught up in and by its materiality, partially engendered by his incessant repetitions, which short-circuits these smooth movements. Instead of a grasping (*begreifen*), we get a bungled action (*Vergreifen*).[101] The "endlessly repeating" reenactments are not a precondition for a smooth and fluid arc of bodily intentionality and "aboutness" that might link aim with object.

The internal divisions that habit generates in the body are evidenced in the film by the narrator jerking back and forth in a glitchy way, as if the body is searching for itself in a coil of precipitation and delay, perpetually catching up and running too far ahead, and thus in a constant state of bodily dispossession and intractability (figures 2.19 and 2.20). The narrator's timing is perpetually off-kilter, as different parts of his body are operating at different tempos and he is pulled like a defective marionette whose wires are crossed, tangled, and caught up by the uncoordinated contractions that mark his spatiotemporal disconnection with people and things.[102] In both the novel and the film, matter, words, and gestures perpetually spill forth, pool, and are drawn back into the abyss of ellipses, unfinished sentences, disconnected circuits, and abruptly interrupted conversations so that the "promise of connection" that the narrator is so desperately searching for is never accomplished. The arrhythmia of his "electronic metronome" results in multiple ill-timed contractions and frantically repeated gestures that never really settle into a stable disposition or fluid action as his body parts are unable to pull together and (virtually) coordinate in and as a "lived body."

A caveat is in order. I am not suggesting that habitual movements literally require all parts or members to be moving fluidly in time with each other. In fact, "internal discordance" is required for movement, as Merleau-Ponty makes clear in the *Phenomenology of Perception* and "Eye and Mind," ensuring that "the body's animation is not the assemblage or juxtaposition of its parts."[103] It is precisely here that the language of cunning, magic, and dexterity aligns with the language of virtuality: "movement is something *conspired* between legs, trunks, arms, and head in some locus of virtuality."[104] Merleau-Ponty's notion of the "body-image," or "corporeal schema," is his preferred language to suggest this virtuality taking form in and as a unified gestalt. Virtuality also attests to the suspension of potentiality within the actuality of habit that is not used up or determined by its present actualization or determinations. Virtuality speaks to both the universality, stability, and hardness of habit that persists and that is not reducible to or exhausted by its specific manifestations, and to a contingency within the becoming necessity of the accident of habit, which also accounts for a freedom that does not merely repeat the past or anticipate and absorb the future but is attentive to a virtuality in the past's actuality as well as in that past's future.[105]

But virtuality is also a crucial dimension to habit in a more disturbing sense; it speaks to the unruly dimensions of temporality, spatiality, and materiality that are neither fluid nor animating. I want to articulate a sense of virtuality that can account for how the part-body of habit is operating at different tempos that pull it apart, so that habit never seems able to gather itself together sufficiently to move in the ways suggested by Merleau-Ponty, and one that does justice to an abstract negativity that stains, partitions, and cuts off, thereby embracing the more unruly dimensions of the non-actual within the actuality of habit. Drawing on Lacan's notion of the real, *objet petit a*, and the part-body, Deleuze notes that the virtual is never subject to the global character that affects real objects. Even when incorporated in real objects, the virtual is always a "partial object"—a fragment, shred, or remainder that resists integration and "remains planted or stuck there." The virtual, in this sense, derails and detaches body parts even within the outwardly appearing unified body. And, like the Lacanian real, virtual objects "have the property of being *and* not being where they are, wherever they go" thus attesting to the "un-matter" and "not without having" at the heart of habit's acts and actuality.[106]

JOAN OF ARC'S GAUCHERIE AND THE STAINED SOUL OF HABIT

Perhaps a detour through another act of picture-thinking might help us grasp the concept of the hand as a per-severing partial object that resists fluid and unified bodily incorporation. Jules Bastien-Lepage's painting *Jeanne d'Arc* (1879) features in Ben Lerner's novel 10:04 and is subject to an astute analysis of its strange form of embodiment (figure 3.19).[107] Like many nineteenth-century French critics, Lerner is particular fascinated by what he calls a "glitch in the pictorial matrix," which is produced by a tension between the metaphysical and physical realms in the painting—that is to say, the "failure to reconcile" the "three translucent angels" hovering at the upper-left side of the painting, rendered in a sketchy and ethereal manner, with the more solid naturalism of the "future saint's body" that is summoned by them to rescue France and who is still resolutely a laborer working at a loom in her parents' garden. Although the intensity of this "extreme contradiction" permeates the pictorial logic of the painting as such, it manifests itself most insistently in Joan of Arc's left hand, which, according to Lerner, seems to be dissolving and vanishing into the non-actual and immaterial realm of angels—her future self—while the rest of the future saint's body remains insistently actual in the carnal solidity of her laboring body. But this way of parsing the actual and non-actual does not do justice to the "dividedness" at stake here in this odd painterly configuration of the unsublatable contradictions of this not yet beautiful soul.

Lerner writes that Joan of Arc appears to stagger toward the viewer, perhaps in the swoon of receiving the angelic summons, while her left arm reaches out, apparently to stabilize herself. But instead of "grasping branches or leaves, her hand ... seems to dissolve," as the "background swallows her fingers." But, if one looks closely, the fingers are not swallowed by the background but, in a kind of reverse Hegelian "letting go" or "releasing," the painted vegetation squishes up between her fingers and "remains planted there," as it begins to spread and stain. Joan of Arc is not a "dissolving subject" but one

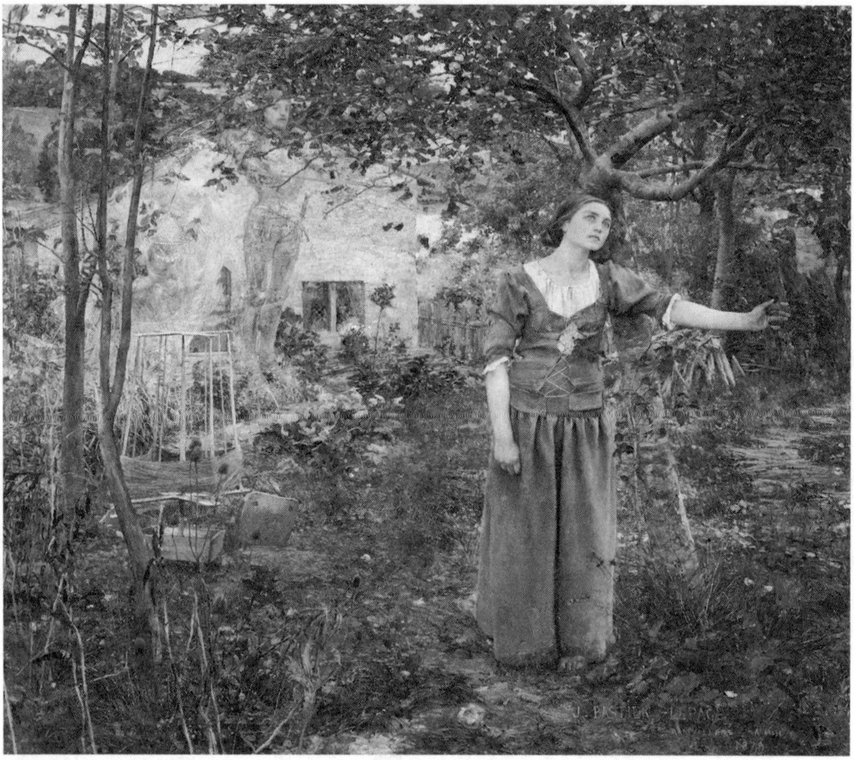

FIGURE 3.19
Jules Bastien-Lepage, *Joan of Arc (Jeanne d'Arc)*, 1879. Oil on canvas, 8 ft. 4 in. × 9 ft. 2 in. (254 × 279.4 cm). Metropolitan Museum of Art, New York. Gift of Erwin Davis, 1889 (89.21.1). © The Metropolitan Museum of Art. Image source: Art Resource, NY.

who insistently remains and stains. Her spiritual calling, like all such awakenings in Hegel—including his specific reference to Joan of Arc's exaltation in the *Philosophy of Mind* as a "kind of magnetic state"—is unruly, precipitous, and strangely unmediated.[108] The Hegelian vocabulary of "contagion/infection" (*Ansteckung/Infektion*) and vanishing, which is, as we have seen, often used to account for the odd temporality, materiality, and spatiality of spirit, frequently veers away from the very language of quiescence, stillness, and balance it also invokes. If the three angels are rendered in a way that captures the "angelic ideality of evanescent air," Joan of Arc's own body also partakes of that immateriality—as do many other aspects of the painting—but in ways that do not "vanish like a shapeless vapor dissolving into thin air," to borrow Hegel's words to describe the beautiful soul's inability to actualize itself, and instead remain as a persistent stain of non-actuality within the actual body of Joan of Arc.[109] Here, the Hegelian "vanishing of vanishing" does not suggest quiescence, but rather the more disquieting words that often accompany the term vanishing in Hegel, such as "fury" and "suddenly," thus attesting to the short-circuiting of appearance and disappearance, actual and non-actual, of the future saint's bodily presence. Although "vanishing" is often meant to suggest how parts become moments and how differences and particularities are dissolved in and as the pulsating "universal blood," here we are exposed to the unruly dimensions of vanishing, which do not reconcile dividedness and inner contradiction but punctuate it.

In *Joan of Arc*, it is the repetitive labor of weaving—one of the primary instantiations of gendered and quotidian habitual actions, along with ironing—that exposes the disturbing relationships between repetition, temporality, and ontology.[110] In the painting, the habitual movements at the loom have been interrupted by an insistent, immaterial presence that possesses and "infects" Joan of Arc in such a precipitous manner that the stool upon which she sat while spinning her cloth is knocked over. What Hegel calls the "mute weaving of spirit"—the bloodless and noiseless infection that has always already occurred before it is consciously thought—is precipitously interrupted by a "noisy ruckus" whose static is woven into the warp and weft of this muteness.[111]

Before Joan of Arc is even aware of what has happened to her, it has already started to happen, just as we are suddenly and inexplicably struck, after a slight delay, by the fact that the vaporous bluish-white clouds that color the evanescent fabric of being in which the Angels manifest themselves, also suffuses the skeins wound around Joan of Arc's spinning wheel, pervade her bodice, and infect the lighter, flesh-toned skin patches around her neck. Expressed in Hegelian terms, the recursive interweaving of cause and effect, beginning and ending, suggests that it is this angelic and immaterial fabric of being that is always already and not yet woven by Joan of Arc's spinning—as rendered by and through the the painter's brushstrokes—which generates the glitchiness of the pictorial matrix. In many ways, Bastien-Lepage's painting draws out the unruly and unmediated dimensions of habit that summon forth the odd material, spatial, and temporal qualities of its subject matter as it obstinately refuses to be mediated into the organic unity of a body or into a unified pictorial composition.

4

PIECES OF (FIGURE) EIGHT AND THE CRUX OF THE MATTER

HABIT AND "UN-MATTER"

William James notes that "the moment one tries to define what habit is, one is led to the fundamental properties of matter."[1] *Remainder*'s trenchant exploration of habit as a profound failure to mediate the world generates an odd materiality that does not behave: it is unruly, volcanic, excessive, overflowing, and messy; it spews forth, empties out, and vaporizes; it is recalcitrant, intransitive, and lingering. The strange and unsettling matter generated by habit's repetitions is fundamentally disruptive rather than stabilizing: "My undoing: matter." (Rem, 17). McCarthy characterizes this unruly matter at different points in his writing as "surplus matter," "un-matter," a "material negative," or the Real of matter (Rem, 91, 171).[2] The phrase "material negative" suggests that immaterial processes are always material and that material processes are always insubstantial, immaterial, virtual, and non-actual. Like the matter generated in psychoanalysis, the matter which habit always returns us to, is shot through with negativity, gaps, virtuality, senseless signifiers, and spectrality.

Hegel's account of habit in the anthropology of subjective soul is often read in hylomorphic terms as a way of articulating that soul is inextricably material and immaterial.[3] But the disruptive aspects of this im-materiality is often underplayed and too well-tempered. The ontology of habit is often an oversaturated phenomenon, rather than a "corporeity saturated by soul," that is overflowing with a strange "universal immaterialism," a term Hegel uses to describe soul in (second) nature early in the *Philosophy of Mind*.[4] To make an analogy, soul in the ontology of habit is like Hegel's hyperbolic account of art as a monstrous "thousand-eyed argus," which oversaturates and overexposes the plastic ideal of corporeity at every point, such that second nature is exponentially and excessively multiplied. Habit is not so much a mediating term between corporeality and spirit as it is a jouissance that is excessive and overflowing.

In *Remainder*, the immanent loop of habit is always cracking, spreading, and overflowing with accruals and eruptions of "un-matter." If habit proper is supposed to permeate matter with spirit, rendering it pliable and less resistant, matter in *Remainder* is always resistant, as it blows back, spills out, stains, or remains prone to fissuring and heaping. The repetitions of habit do not simply overcome material resistance, thereby generating consistency and stability; rather, its compulsive repetitions exacerbate the tensions between particularity and universality and bring them to a toxic level such that the infection of matter with universality remains as a glitchy and unruly abstraction in matter that unsettles it in perturbing ways. The static crackling that permeates the novel and film at the level of both form and content is the "logic of the negative" that punctuates and drills everything it touches with an ineradicable degree of abstraction and automaticity, from sentences, to breathing, to gestures, to the coloring of the body's flesh.[5]

In *Remainder*, matter is not-there like the sponge that McCarthy repeatedly invokes and that is (drilled) full of holes—or like the "ghost kink" ("the kink the other kink left when we took it away") that one of the reenactors trips over during the bank robbery reenactments—as a result of the odd immaterialities generated by habit's repetitions (Rem, 289–290, 296) (figures 1.6, 1.7, and 3.12). The narrator's compulsive repetitions and reenactments void even as they generate excess matter. This unbalanced logic of overflowing and emptying out often materializes the void as a meaningless surplus where understanding is literally cut off and proliferates as a compulsion to cut and get stuck, much like the blank sticky notes that completely cover the pastedown and flyleaf of his subsequent novel, *Satin Island* (figure 4.1).

The materiality of second nature is infected by soul in ways that are intermittent and glitchy; thus, they do not temper and permeate matter with spirit but rather wrench and twist it. The tarrying function at play throughout *Remainder* creates all kinds of delays, fissures, and excesses that derail the causality of action, putting a spanner in the works of habit as a "body schema" or "motor intentionality."[6] As a result, the habitual body is always catching and recoiling in unruly ways that defile its operation as a middle term between self and environment. In habit, the means of forging the relationship between universality and particularity is obtained by a mechanism—an automatic procedure—that persists as a lived abstraction in the narrator's body as it is pulled by the extremes of its entanglement in particularity and its possession by an abstract universality characterized by a "rigidity of being" (*Härte des Seins*).[7] Hegel's definition of habit as the "mechanism of self-feeling" and a "spiritual mechanism" indicates that it is shot through with an intractable exteriority, and thus it is one of the primary instances of the "mechanics always at work in speculation," in which mobilism, fluidity, and incorporation

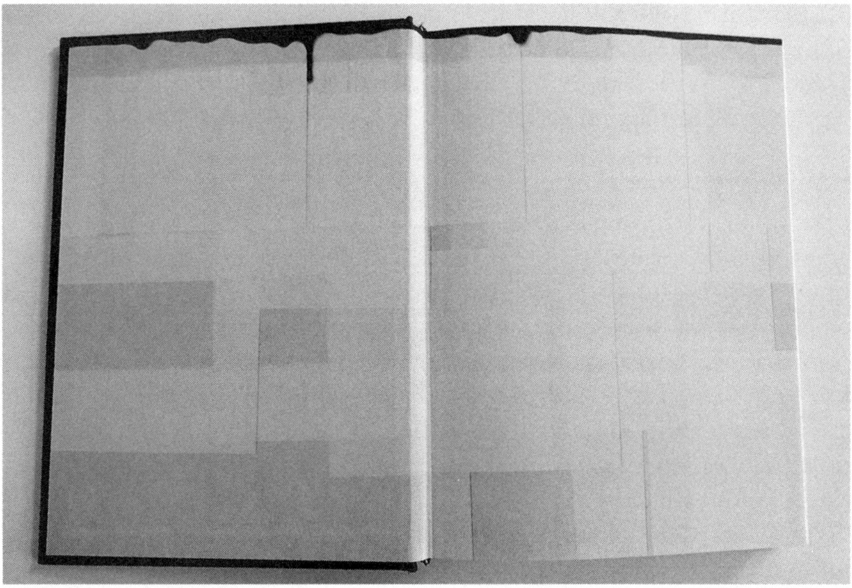

FIGURE 4.1
Proliferation of blank sticky notes, front pastedown and flyleaf, Tom McCarthy, *Satin Island*. © Suzanne Dean.

are subject to an automaticity, machinic repetition, punctuation, and drilling that resists interiorization.[8]

The narrator breaks down each reenactment into ever further constituent parts, and those parts are endlessly repeated and broken down as each part is "relished" (Rem, 162). The parts are then reassembled so that the narrator can relish the whole—that is to say, take it apart again. Here, "relish" means not only an intense enjoyment but also to add something. Moreover, according to its roots in the Old French *relais/reles*, it means "something remaining, that which is left behind."[9] Nothing is left complete or finished in *Remainder*; in fact, an accomplished ending and closure is precisely where the "repetitive function" of habit begins to work against the "restitutive function" of composure and the already composed.[10] In a revealing conversation between Tom and the pianist reenactor, the former tells the latter to "compose" Chopin. The pianist replies: "Chopin is already composed." Tom responds: "Then compose him again" and "when you have done—start over" (Rem film, 44:45:14). All the "ontological waste" generated by habit's fixity and repetitious "fixing back"—all the accidents, contingencies, failures, gaps, indeterminate stuff, inconsistencies, and undigestible matter; all the leftover and fallow patches of our minds; all the circuits that cut off rather than facilitate; all the bungled actions; all the half-digested, indeterminate memories, units, and parts; all the senseless material signifiers lodged in our mind and bodies are far in excess of what anyone can bear. Like McCarthy's description of *Ulysses*, *Remainder* is "packed to overflowing" with excreta: "whatever is excessive, leaking, training, dragging or trascining."[11]

A KENOTIC ANAESTHETICS OF HABIT

In *Remainder*, the process of generating surplus matter and its precipitous emptying out is best described by the Greek word *kenosis*. It is precisely in the culminating section of the *Phenomenology of Spirit*, "Absolute Knowing," where this emptying out of subject and substance is dramatized, resulting in an exteriority that perpetually spills out, remainders, and stains. In the kenotic "letting go" in *Remainder*, liquids are constantly spilling out from their containers as they pool, stain, and mire the body in all kinds of sticky matter. They take on infinite variations and reenactments that recall the last lines from Hegel's *Phenomenology*, which is a syntactically altered fragment from Schiller's poem "Friendship": "Out of the chalice of this realm of spirits/Foams forth to him his infinity."[12] Here, absolute knowing does not mark an end but an "end that keeps going," a closure that keeps opening, a circle that keeps on circling, a crack of subjectivity that is repeatedly fissured.[13]

The *Phenomenology of Spirit*'s last section is headed *Das absolute Wissen* in German, which is sometimes translated into English as "Absolute Knowledge"; however, in A. V. Miller and Terry Pinkard's translation, it is presciently rendered as a gerund, "Absolute Knowing." McCarthy has written about the temporality of the gerund, the verbal form that serves as the present participle that is indicative of an ongoing action that creates a rupture within time and temporality.[14] It is a "time-out-of-time" in the sense of lodging an "eternal" and ongoing immobility within the flow of time that would "suspend" conceptual mastery and achieved action though an "incessant imminence" and an "eternally arriving." This infinitization of the movement of kenosis in *Remainder* keeps repeating precisely because those repetitions are how the subject matter of habit is voided, generating an inconsistency and instability at the heart of subjectivity.[15]

As explored in previous chapters, kenosis has its "techniques" in *Remainder*: modes of riveting, drilling, glitching, and buffeting that wrench not only the body but also matter from itself, causing it to overflow, spill, and stain. This emptying/spilling out is often due to precipitous and more or less violent contractions that are not rhythmically peristaltic but more like seizures, abrupt recoils, or short circuits. At times, these contractions are so abrupt that they can manifest as a disconnection, cutting off, and maladaptation to our body, its actions, other people, and the environment. In what one might call a hyletic reduction, in contrast to a hylomorphic aesthetic, all the forms and substances in *Remainder* that "contain" matter are overturned and emptied out, unsettling the grounds for any stable form of habits to emerge. The generation of these senseless material disruptions is precisely what manifests the odd material aesthetics of habit in *Remainder*.

Once a notion of kenotic insistence is taken seriously, this changes the status of an alienated externality that needs to be internalized, incorporated, sublated, and mediated. In turn, this has huge implications for those aspects of habit at its worst—its automaticity, thingness, rigidity, and inertia—that are often seen merely as falls, deviations, or malign inversions from habit proper and that must quicken with spirit lest they deaden, or even kill. A kenotic anaesthetics of habit puts pressure on its mediating and stabilizing functions over its unsublatable staining and depositing aspects. The *kenotic* anaesthetics of habit in *Remainder* swings wildly between a voiding and an excess engendering of matter that hardly measures up to any sculptural ideal of modulated plasticity. Rather, the incessant spilling out and staining leaves the narrator in a radically exposed condition; moreover, he seems driven to double down on this condition rather than overcoming it through the formation of a disposition that would allow him to establish a stable position and anchor his ontological grounding and connectivity.

VANISHING, VAPORIZING, AND OVERFLOWING

Remainder is a trenchant intensification of the vocabulary of *Vershwinden* in Hegel's speculative philosophy, a term that is translated into English as vanishing, disappearing, or destroying.[16] In the *Phenomenology of Spirit*, vanishing often refers to how a materially resistant "part" is sublated into the flow of speculative movement and thus is transfigured into a "member" or a "moment" that changes its material status within the whole. In this way, it is like a drunken member that drops out of a bacchanalian revelry, such that that it remains but also "disappears" and does not impede the flow of the event. As such, vanishing is also a dimension of letting go indicative of the "self-moving concept" that is the subjectivity of the concept itself. At other moments in the *Phenomenology*, *Verschwinden* is a much more violent force in the sense of a "fury of disappearing" that is more indicative of abstract negativity and "one-sidedness."[17] In other instances, it is more abrupt and fragmentary, like the oft-cited "night of the world" passage from the Jena System Lectures, in which "a wealth of infinitely many representations" shoot up "in phantasmagorical representations" and then "disappear as suddenly" (*verschwinden enbenso*).[18] These phantasmagorical representations are not sublated moments; rather, they are where "the contradictory is held in *external moments* ... parading before consciousness without reciprocal contact."[19] As such, they are more reminiscent of all the exoscopic body parts that Lacan raises in the "Mirror Stage" article, drawing on Bosch's *Garden of Earthly Delights*, that haunt the imaginary and specular logic of the ego. Indeed, the vocabulary of vanishing is explicit in Lacan's account of the pulsatile nature of the unconscious that is gapped through the on-and-off rhythm of appearance and disappearance, fading in and out, marking the "*aphanisis* of the subject" that is resistant to mediation and synthesis.[20] *Remainder* is a hyperbolic exploration of a vanishing of the vanishing of vanishing that pushes a kenotic anaesthetics of habit toward the extremes of the abrupt disappearance of matter and its excessive reappearance and overflowing.[21]

If, as I have been arguing, habit brings stuckness, inertia, excess, and surplus matter to a maximum intensity, this is not done simply to reach a crisis point as a necessary "moment" that enables the fluidity of speculative movement to occur. Rather, as the logic of *Remainder* makes clear, anything that happens at this point of short-circuiting is a gushing, an overflowing, or a drunken reeling; it is a shredding, catching, halting, grinding, and grounding that keeps the precipitate and sediment perturbed rather than settling or resolving it. If the "vanishing of the vanishing" in Hegel articulates how these parts and units do not disappear but rather are sublated and universalized in quiescent unity, in *Remainder* the logic and aesthetics of that vanishing is pulsatile, short-circuiting, and overflowing. Nothing escapes the "static crackle" that punctuates every aspect of the novel and film. Like the ants in M. C. Escher's woodcut *Mobius Strip II–(Red Ants)* that grace the cover of Lacan's *Seminar on Anxiety*, matter precipitously appears, disappears, and then reappears.[22]

Perhaps the oddities of matter in *Remainder* are at their most disturbing when massive amounts of matter cunningly vanish and vaporize upward only to gush forth and overflow with even more insistence. When the narrator notices he has a flat tire, he returns to the tire shop he had briefly paused beside on the day his settlement came through. After seeing that his windshield wiper reservoir is empty, he has it filled, but when he pushes the "spurter button," no liquid appears. One of the boys working at the shop looks in the empty reservoir, then under the car for a "patch" where it might have leaked, but none is to be found. Another liter of liquid is poured in with the same result. It had, as the narrator notes, "vaporized, evaporated" (Rem, 170–171). The narrator is elated by this miracle of transubstantiation that he has witnessed, in which "surplus matter" becomes "un-matter" (Rem, 171). He returns to the car and turns the ignition key in its slot. The engine catches, and as it does, the vanished matter suddenly "burst[s]" out of the dashboard in a "torrent" of blue liquid (Rem, 171). This liquid gushes back to hit the narrator with the force of a breached dam, staining him from head to toe in an act of what McCarthy elsewhere calls a "*reverse* alchemy" or "desublimation."[23] Matter's magical disappearance, countering the "very laws of physics," comes crashing down, turning the "scene of a triumphant launch into the scene of a disaster, a catastrophe" (Rem, 174).

After this scene, the narrator rents a warehouse to create a full-scale reproduction of the tire shop down to the last detail, and he has several teams of reenactors that are rotated "constantly, round the clock" to reenact this miracle of transubstantiation and its failure (Rem, 175). Unsatisfied, however, with the "mini plumbing system" created to siphon off the blue liquid into a sack, which is triggered to rupture when the ignition is turned on a second time, he now wants it so that matter "disappears from the reservoir, then doesn't reappear again. Just disappears" (Rem, 178, 181). His assistants respond that it is impossible but they nevertheless find a cunning way to enact that impossibility, bringing about the magical levitation and disappearance of matter by funneling the liquid into a system of tubes from a holding tank up through the roof. This system vaporizes the liquid into the sky, "sprayed upwards in a fine mist" (Rem, 182). Like Hegel's beautiful soul, it "vanishes like a shapeless vapour dissolving into thin air."[24]

In the "final" bank heist reenactment, the narrator and his facilitator Naz contemplate the need to "eliminate" and "vaporize" all their material traces (Rem, 268–275). This encompasses every reenactor—narrator and facilitator included—as well as all "back-up people" and "sub-back-up people" to cover their crime and prevent information from "leaking out" (Rem, 275). But no matter how many cunning prosthetic devices the narrator constructs to siphon the material way, or how many necronautical vehicles he commandeers to carry all the bodies and make them "disappear" into the sky, there is always a "residual"; as Naz explains, one of the significations of this speculative word is "what remains after a process of evaporation" (Rem, 269). It is this pulsatile ontology and radical kenosis of the vanishing of the vanishing of vanishing ... that is plotted in the "figure of eight" movements in *Remainder*.

PIECES OF (FIGURE) EIGHT

From the outset, the narrator is drawn toward and disturbed by the figure awarded for the settlement of his injury—eight and a half million pounds: "The eight was perfect, neat: a curved figure infinitely turning back into itself" (Rem, 8). Although the amount is already monetarily excessive, it is the half that brings out the logic of its too-muchness: "But then the half. Why had they added the half? It seemed to me so messy, this half: a leftover fragment, a shard of detritus" (Rem, 8). While the narrator ponders this figure, he simultaneously moves in a figure-eight pattern through the city, searching for a phone booth to call his lawyer after their call has been cut off by the narrator tripping in his apartment and pulling the phone wires out of the wall (figures 3.9 and 3.10). Finding a phone booth, he inserts a fifty-pence coin to reestablish contact with the lawyer, only to be cut off again (figure 4.2). After multiple circuits "kinking back" between his apartment and the phone booth, he stops, pauses, and jerks back and forth at the crossing of his figure-eight movements through the city (Rem, 14). The narrator's Proustian moment in the bathroom that "pops up" during a party at a friend's apartment is engendered by

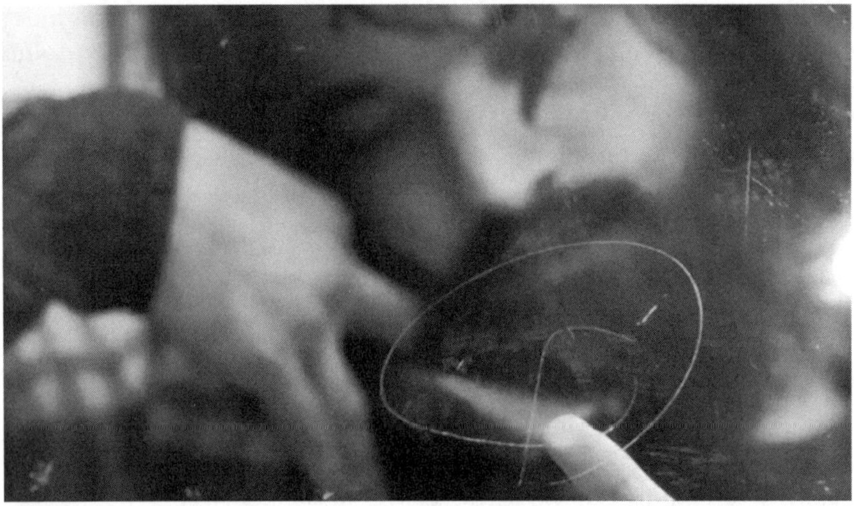

FIGURE 4.2
Tom tracing his finger over an "inner eight"/"circle of circles" in a phone booth. Film still from Omer Fast's *Remainder*. © Omer Fast.

his movement "in the pattern of an eight" (Rem, 64). Subsequently, he finds Madlyn Mansions in Brixton through his pattern of "turning," "overshooting," and "doubling back" through city streets (Rem, 96–102).

In the tire repair shop reenactment that is run through "round the clock" with multiple teams of reenactors, he orders the car to be run in a "figure of eight" pattern that leaves complicated markings on the pavement (Rem, 179–180). The figure-eight pattern is also the pattern he would choose when sweeping through a crime scene if he were the lead investigator (Rem, 187). And the final figure eight in the novel is produced from the vapor trails left by the plane—"turning back, then turning out. Then turning back again"—that the narrator hires to vaporize all remainders after the bank robbery reenactment, which is staged in a real bank during working hours (Rem, 307). Even when the figure eight is not specifically named in the novel, it is invoked by the incessant references to looping, turning back, redoubling, kinking, circuiting, and short-circuiting.

Remainder's obsession with this topological figure and movement is hardly surprising given McCarthy's specific understanding of plotting and narrative that is not about psychological depth or content but about "angles, arcs, and intervals ... geometry is everything."[25] Intriguingly, McCarthy notes that "geometry is not just an aesthetic: it is, to borrow a term from Deleuze, our 'habitus.'"[26] In *Remainder* this geometry is often deadly and more like an accident site than a field of vectors and arcs of action, gesture, or movement that one might fluidly inhabit, thus enabling us to coordinate aim with intention,

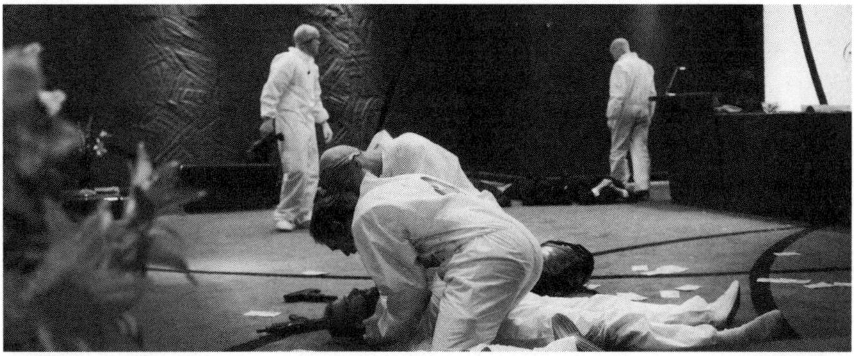

FIGURE 4.3
Reenactors collapsing in a heap on the geometrically patterned carpet during the bank robbery reenactment. Film still from Omer Fast's *Remainder*. © Omer Fast.

act with object, body with environment. Merleau-Ponty's beautiful image of an organist settling into an organ like one settles into a house, with "consecratory gestures" like an "augur delimit[ing] the *templum*," is always defiled in *Remainder*.[27] Fluid arcs of gesture and movement are broken, and the ballet-like choreographic preparations of the bank robber reenactors are upended by the accident of the non-kink in the carpet. It trips them up and triggers the gun that blows a deadly hole into the body of the adjacent reenactor. As a result, the reenactors collide and collapse in a tangled heap on the arc-like designs inscribed on the floors and walls of the bank's architecture in the film (figures 1.6, 1.7, and 4.3).

In *Remainder*, habit is linked to a geometry and topology that trips up and impedes the "perfect circularity" of being and having. The figure eight is not a "single rounded totality," but rather more like a Lacanian "inner eight," which is his symbolization for the topology of the subject that cuts into itself.[28] The figure eight is a "double-circuit topology of the hole" that recalls Hegel's elaboration of speculative movement's circularity as a "circle of circles that returns into itself," like an annulating machine that generates parts, units, and accidents that are not necessarily fluidly reincorporated back into that circular movement.[29] This "inner eight" or "circle of circles" is scratched into the glass phone booth, and Tom slowly traces its circuitry with his finger while the connection to his lawyer is repeatedly cut off (figure 4.2).

There is always a mechanism and automaticity at work in habit that gives it a semblance of unity, in which "the connection remains nothing more than *composition*, *mixture*, *aggregate*, etc."[30] Even the writing of the "figure of eight" in *Remainder* is an unruly and excessive act of epistrophe that marks the impossibility of its abbreviation as an "accomplished return-into-itself."[31] The relentless looping and kinking back in *Remainder* that is driven by the endless repetitions and reenactments throws up excessive drifts of matter in its wake. This occurs as an overturning that is infinitely unsettling; a turmoil that prevents habit from definitively settling down as a solid ground or foundation. It is a movement that both buries the body in the inertia of matter and levitates and voids it in ways that are not the opposite of inertia but rather instantiations of its uneven, inconsistent, and pulsatile logic. Grounding in *Remainder* is an infinite gerund-like act that is simultaneously a sinking, burying, and absorption in recoiling repetitions that generate surplus subject matter and a hollowing out that then spews out disconnected bits and pieces without inner connectivity.

If cunning and magic are at the heart of habit, which accomplishes its grace behind our backs, the topological figure eight precisely avoids adhering to any straightforward logic of front and back, inside and outside in a "*not without cunning*" that outwits its own outwitting.[32] It is a perpetual turning and cutting over to the other side through its imminent "one-sidedness," which resists all forms of tempered mediation between extremes. This movement is often abrupt and kenotic in ways that inflect the speculative language of "throwing back" and "circling back into oneself" into a more violent scene of recoiled bodies, brutal falls, sudden twists, relentless overflowing, and static punctuation.[33] The figure eight is a trickster figure that outwits itself in ways that are not even recuperable in the Hegelian dialectic of extremes—for instance, in the proverb "Too much wit outwits itself," which Hegel invokes in the *Encyclopedia Logic* to demonstrate dialectical reversal at the breaking point of extremity.[34]

The figure eight, as the topological figure of the movement of habitual repetition, is resolutely *not* "the place in which, with a perfect circularity, having, which derives from being, appropriates the latter to itself."[35] It is not the "*point* [my emphasis] at which subjectivity seeks to make itself a master of being."[36] The figure eight's inflection point in *Remainder* does not mediate the double curve's folding back on itself.[37] As Deleuze asks in *Difference and Repetition*, "What, then, would be the ego, where would it be, given its topological distinction from the Id, if not at the crossing of the 8, at the point of connection between these two intersecting asymmetrical circles, the circle of real objects and that of the virtual objects or centres?"[38] It is precisely the "crux of the matter" at the intersection of this double curve that resists the reinscription of the drive into the economy of the ego and its imaginary and specular image of control, coordination, and mastery.

THE DISINHABITING RING OF HABIT

The crossing point of the figure eight in *Remainder* is almost always accompanied by sticky patches of "surplus matter" that pop up in conjunction with its movement. During his circuit of eight pattern as he is "looking for a ... for a thing" at the apartment on Plato Road, the bathroom where the crack in the wall triggers the narrator's déjà vu of Madlyn Mansions "popped up beside it like the half had in my Settlement: offset, an extra" (Rem, 64). Just to the right of the figure eight generated in the tire repair shop reenactment, a "large, sticky patch" made by the "repeated gushing of hundreds of litres of blue liquid" stains the floor (Rem, 180). And at the end of the novel, the figure-eight pattern of the banking plane leaves a vapor trail drifted to the side, "discarded, recidual, a remainder" (Rem, 306). And the narrator's excessive jerking back and forth occurs at the point where he redoubles back through the city in his figure-eight circuit (Rem, 14). In every instance, this topological pattern engenders surplus material remainders through its overturning.

Drawing on Terry Pinkard's preferred translation of the term *die Sache selbst* in the *Phenomenology*, we might call these accumulations of surplus matter at the crossing of the figure eight "the crux of the [subject] matter." The figure eight is a "circle of circles" that loops, and infinitely cuts across itself—marking the constitutive failure of sublation to fully close the loop of habit—and that precipitates the explosion of surplus matter in *Remainder*.[39] The narrator's repetitious movements keep immanently opening the closed loop of habit by doubling, crossing, and twisting it, thus impeding its consistency and unity.

The crossing of the figure eight is the impasse of habit's formalization at the impossible point of its multiple inscriptions, determinations, and repetitions. It is the point where the abbreviation and simplification of habit that is meant to appropriate the body to universality through its automaticity is at its sharpest cutting point; where it breaks off and spills out rather than quickening into a simple unity that has sublated its mediations. In *Remainder*, the crux of the figure eight is a flailing and foundering Hegelian "turning point" where negation is not internalized but rather remains a choking point—"a *circle* that winds around itself"—marking the vanishing of the vanishing point of absolute negativity.[40] This choking point is of a piece with all the breathlessness and buffeting, which is the static crackle of a subjectivity that is perpetually driven back and forth in the kinking movements that are a feature of both the novel and the film. It "murmurs and rustles" with an ineradicable automaticity and exteriority that permeates speculative philosophy—as well as habit.[41] The crux of the figure eight is not an Hegelian turning point that transforms the "*in-itself* into *for-itself*"; it is not an absolute negativity that is rounded off in a quiescent way.[42] Rather, it is an overturning and reeling rotary device without a fly-wheel to stabilize it.

It is precisely at this crux of the matter where habit is caught up in its overturning, deviating, and short-circuiting, which engenders it as an evacuating actuality. If the (death) drive—characterized by is compulsion to repeat—is a fundamentally topological and ontological notion characterized by its rotary movement, its voiding mechanism erupts at its most contracted point in *Remainder* as an inability of habit to master repetition, resulting in a breaking point in which the narrator is recoiled and hit by waves of surplus matter that are never adequately stabilized.[43] As Lacan notes about the compulsion to repeat, "nothing has been more enigmatic than this *Wiederholen* (repetition), which is very close, so the most prudent etymologists tells us, to the verb 'haul' (*haler*)—hauling as on a towpath—very close to a *hauling* of the subject, who always drags his thing into a certain path that he cannot get out of."[44] The narrator in *Remainder* is continually dragging himself into and exposing himself to the disturbing point of what McCarthy elsewhere calls the "violent" or "catastrophic real."[45] In an interesting discussion of a patient who remains "stuck on a problem, going around in circles," Félix Guattari suggests that the only way out of this circuit is "to choose here between a mechanical conception of deathly repetition and a machinic conception of processual opening."[46] Guattari chooses the latter—what he calls the "drive machine"—but the degree of openness is not just a matter of the "capacity of welcoming asignifying singularities" *into* this circuit; rather, it is this vertiginous closure of deathly repetition that generates them precisely through its mechanical drilling.[47]

The crossing of the figure eight is not a circuit breaker but a breaking point in the circuit.[48] It is this disruptive anaesthetics of habit that is at stake in *Remainder* and erupts at the rims, jointures, and rotating points of its repetitions and reenactments. The figure eight is an articulation of the impasse of habit stuck at the point of nonmediation between particularity and universality, abstract and absolute, substance and subject. Rather than rounding off the edges, veiling and burying the cuts, or defensively encircling itself in a sheltering enclosure generated by habit, the topological circuit of the figure eight generates a disinhabiting ring. Rather than a sublatable moment, kenosis is a relentless logic which leaves no enclosures in place for inhabitation to take place.[49]

AUTOPILOT, THE NOT YET, AND *REMAINDER*'S NONENDING

The spilling out of surplus matter and all matter of breakdown and breaking down in *Remainder*—material, bodily, and narrative—does not simply exhaust in the sense of a death-driven repetition compulsion that returns matter to an inanimate and homeostatic state, thus placing its energetics and movement within the logic of the Freudian pleasure principle. Although the narrator's addiction to repetition and reenactment results in all manner of slowing down, inertia, exhaustion, passive states, catatonia, and cog-wheel rigidity, this does not bring about stasis but rather a kenotic insistence (Rem, 178). It is this strange intransitive transitivity that gives the machine-like trajectory in *Remainder* its unruly energy and desperate vitality that always returns to the circuit of the figure eight to be repeatedly reenacted and further broken down in a manner that I have characterized as the static logic of habit.

It is precisely the "half-trip," which the robbery reenactor has practiced relentlessly, and which has "become instinctive, second nature," that trips him up on the "ghost kink" during the bank robbery reenactment in the real bank (Rem, 290). Like a virus that infects repetition in unruly ways, this "half" keeps multiplying in and as a division, delay, and suspension. Earlier in the novel the narrator invokes Fisher Price "wind-up musical toys," in which the "mechanism" might slow down as it unwinds to the end, but with a little nudge, the toys continue with "one last half-chime, and another half-half-chime, and still more, less and less each time, for up to hours—or weeks—after they first ground to a halt" (Rem, 164–165). This logic is repeated in the tire repair shop reenactment, in which the windshield wiper liquid "even when it seemed to have dripped itself dry … still managed to grind out another half-drip a few seconds later, and another half-half-drip a few seconds after that" (Rem, 172).

These "slight mistimings" and misprisions create a defile in time that fissures and surds the arrival at any breakdown that would result in an end that winds down or a winding down to an end (Rem, 265). All manner of vaporization and vanishing in *Remainder* continues to perpetually grind out more vanishing of vanishing of vanishing that continues to burst open and spill out. As Alex Dubilet notes, kenosis is not a matter of purification, nor does it result in a perpetual weakening; rather, it persists in an insistent and immanent kenotic process of self-emptying and externalization that remains at the end and keeps on emptying and spilling beyond the end.[50] The novel "ends" with an airplane that suspends all the reenactors and their support team in a necronautical vehicle that is on autopilot as it banks back and forth in a figure eight waiting for the fuel to run out, like other instances of "trailing off" and "petering out" in *Remainder*. But this winding down is also a winding back. The inertia of repetition drags the figure eight around again as the "end" is thrown back to the beginning and we try to catch up with an accident that both has already happened and has yet to happen, with the implication that the falling debris that "trips him up" at the beginning of the novel is perhaps coming from the future anterior of his own death.

The tenacious repetitions in *Remainder* do not adapt us to any given teleological ends but rather result in a "time that exceeds the end," a hyperbolic temporal and ontological logic of the not yet arriving at the beginning.[51] This collapse of future and past into a suspended present generates a dead time overflowing with voiding, virtuality, and non-actuality.[52] At the "end" of the film, the "being *about* to be—hit" in the novel is infinitized. The camera pans around Tom in a slow, three-hundred-and-sixty-degree movement as he repeats—with a difference—the opening and ending lines of the novel: "About the past, I can say very little. Something fell down from the sky. Technology. Parts. Bits squishing me onto the pavement … eventually the sun will

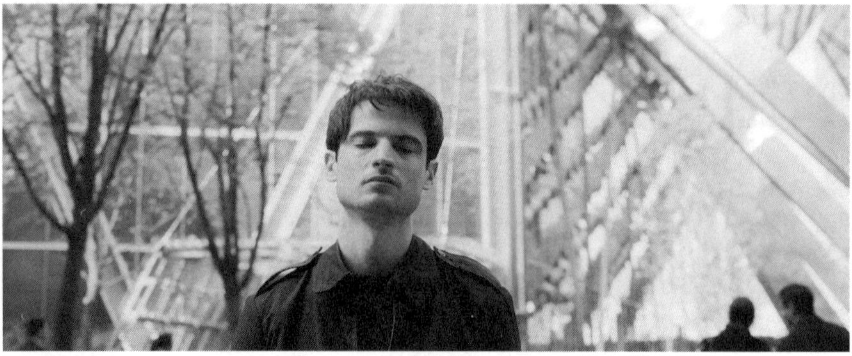

FIGURE 4.4
Tom repeating the opening and ending lines of the novel while the camera pans around him. Film still from Omer Fast's *Remainder*. © Omer Fast.

set and the universe will run down like a toy whose spring is unwound ... no more loops ... for now though the clouds will part and something will fall down, turning, returning, heading back, getting nearer. Here I am. Reborn. And waiting ... again" (Rem film, 1:38:04:03) (figure 4.4).[53]

The repetition of all these "turning backs" in *Remainder* throws us back to the beginning again so that we might free the ending from its routine framework.[54] We do so not by exiting habit—or by avoiding the extreme implications of the autopilot of repetition at the heart of habit—but by collapsing into the logic of habit as breakdown. Once again, for the first time, habit as our "immanent not-yet" can arrive at the beginning of a breakdown that has always already happened and has yet to happen. It is within this defile that we might break down differently into the unbearabilities that catch us up.

ACKNOWLEDGMENTS

This book has taken a long time to write; I have been thinking about habit for even longer. And as is often the case, living its implications longer still. My work on habit has shifted in abrupt and unforeseeable ways over this time, and, as a result, there are some who have been along for the ride from the beginning, and some who have joined me later in the ideas that are more directly related to this book. I could not imagine a life without the close friends, colleagues, and family who have maintained this book with me over its many twists and turns. I am grateful to Amanda, with whom I have shared these ideas over so many years, and whose passionate intelligence is important to me. She knows better than anyone what this book is about. I am thankful to Michael, a great friend, who remains important for me to think with; Suzette, a dear friend who died almost thirteen years ago, but whose memory is still present to me; Derek, Odette, Hanne, and Jan, whose generous friendship and warm intelligence I have depended on; and Gunnar, Marina, and Marco, who helped me work through difficult times. For Wendy, my mother, whose love and intelligence have been essential to me.

A special thank you to Mladen Dolar and the editorial team at the Short Circuits book series, Slavoj Žižek and Alenka Zupančič, and to Tom Weaver, my editor at the MIT Press, for their support of this book from the very beginning. I am grateful to Kathy Caruso, Judy Feldmann, and Liz DeWolf's care and insight with the copyediting and proofreading stages of production.

To Tom McCarthy and Omer Fast for their challenging work and for engaging with me about habit and repetition in the form of a public conversation at The House of Literature (*Litteraturhuset*) in Oslo in 2016, and for their visit with students in my seminar on habit at the University of Oslo. And to the undergraduate and postgraduate students who have taken my courses on habit and related topics on ethology, dwelling, indifference, visuality, aesthetics, temporality, and historicity over the years; I have learned much from them. I am grateful to Jorge Otero-Pailos, with whom I have exchanged ideas on preservation and habit, and who has always supported my work and generously provided me with venues to work through the vectors of this project. Over the past six years, I've been fortunate to be part of the Temporal Experiments research group at the University of Oslo (with Marit Grøtta, Bruce Barnhart, Christian Refsum, Tina Skouen, Per Sigurd Tveitevåg Styve, and the doctoral research fellows affiliated with the group: Emma Helene Heggdal, and more recently, Sofie Njålsdatter Johannessen, Lukas Lehner, and Else Werring). This group offered me the time and space to ruminate in ways that have been important to the way this book has unfolded. Thank you to my colleagues in Art History and Visual Studies for their collegiality and support, and to the Department of Philosophy, Classics, History of Art and Ideas for support with the publication of this book.

I have honed many of the ideas in this book through conversations with friends and colleagues, and via generous invitations to speak, write, and teach about habit. In this regard, I am very grateful to the following: Mattia Biffis, Ting Chang, Swati Chattopadhyay, Whitney Davis, Caitlin DeSilvey, David Gissen, Michael Ann Holly, Michael Kelly, Bente Larsen, Reinhold Martin, Emil Leth Meilvang, Stephen Melville, Andreea Mihalache, John Mitchell, Gaby Neher, Michael Osman, Seunghan Paek, Jasmine Rault, Johanne Sloan, Will Straw, Ileana Parvu, Rose Marie San Juan, Olga Schmedling, Susan Siegfried, Jonathan Tallant, Kerstin Thomas, Kostas Tsiambaos, Pasi Väliaho, Kamini Vellodi, Bronwen Wilson, Richard Wrigley. Thank you to Alex Potts who, in a brief conversation at The Clark, intuitively suggested I read Tom McCarthy's *Remainder*, considering my interest in habit and repetition; and to John McCumber for introducing me to Hegel on the subject of habit so long ago.

LIST OF ABBREVIATIONS

The following abbreviations have been used in the text for frequently cited works.

G. W. F. HEGEL

EPR Hegel, G. W. F. *Elements of the Philosophy of Right*. Edited by Allen W. Wood and translated by H. B. Nisbet. Cambridge: Cambridge University Press, 1991. (*Werke*, vol. 7.) Cited by section (§) in the English translation and German critical edition

ESL Hegel, G. W. F. *Encyclopedia of the Philosophical Sciences in Basic Outlines, Part I: Science of Logic*. Translated and edited by Klauss Brinkman and Daniel O. Dahlstrom. Cambridge: Cambridge University Press, 2010. (*Werke*, vol. 8.) Cited by section (§) number in both the English translation and German critical edition.

LPS Hegel, G. W. F. *Lectures on the Philosophy of Spirit, 1827–8*. Translated and introduction by Robert R. Williams. Oxford: Oxford University Press, 2007. (VPG.) Cited by page number in both the English translation and German critical edition.

PM Hegel, G. W. F. *Hegel's Philosophy of Mind: Part Three of the Encyclopaedia of the Philosophical Sciences (1830)*. Translated by W. Wallace and A.V. Miller. Oxford: Oxford University Press, 1971. (*Werke*, vol. 10.) Cited by section (§) number in both the English translation and German critical edition. Hegel's *Philosophy of Mind*, which contains his main discussion of habit in §409 and §410, is often cited as *Philosophy of Spirit*, as many commentators prefer to substitute "spirit" for "mind" following Michael Petry's three-volume translation and commentary (for good reasons), but for ease of access and reference for the reader I will, for the most part, use Wallace and Miller's title and translation. The broader section that "habit" appears in is "Subjective Mind" ("Subject Spirit" in Petry's translation), the subsection in which the discussion of habit appears is referred to as "Anthropology of the Soul," and the specific sections on "Habit" appear under the heading, "The Feeling Soul." Sections §409 and §410 are often referred to as Hegel's anthropology of habit.

PN Hegel, G. W. F. *Hegel's Philosophy of Nature: Part Two of the Encyclopaedia of the Philosophical Sciences (1830)*. Translated by A. V. Miller. Oxford: Oxford University Press, 1970. (*Werke*, vol. 9.) Cited by section (§) number in both the English translation and German critical edition.

PS Hegel, G. W. F. *The Phenomenology of Spirit*. Translated and edited by Terry Pinkard. Cambridge: Cambridge University Press, 2018. (*Werke*, vol. 3.) Cited by section (§) number in the English translation and page number in the German critical edition.

PS 1977 Hegel, G. W. F. *Phenomenology of Spirit*. Translated by A. V. Miller. Oxford: Oxford University Press, 1977. (*Werke*, vol. 3.) Cited by section (§) number in the English translation and page number in the German critical edition.

SL Hegel, G. W. F. *The Science of Logic*. Translated and edited by George di Giovanni. Cambridge: Cambridge University Press, 2010. (*Werke*, vols. 5–6.) Cited by page number in both the English translation and German critical edition.

VPG Hegel, G. W. F. *Vorlesungen über die Philosophie des Geistes, Berlin 1827/1828*. In *Vorlesungen: Ausgewählte Nachschriften und Manuskripte*. Transcribed by Johann Erdmann and Ferdinand Walter, edited by Franz Hespe and Burkhard Tuschling. Hamburg: Felix Meiner Verlag, 1994, vol. 13 in the series G. W. F. Hegel, *Vorlesungen: Ausgewählte Nachschriften und Manuskripte*. (LPS.) Cited by page number.

WERKE Hegel, G. W. F. *Werke in zwanzig Bänden*. Edited by Eva Moldenhauer and Karl Markus Michel. Frankfurt am Main: Suhrkamp Verlag, 1986. *The German critical edition corresponding to the English translation is cited as *Werke* followed by the volume number and section (§) number or page number.

A AND Z For the Hegel citations above, "A" refers to Hegel's own "remarks" (*Anmerkungen*) and "Z" to "additions" (*Zusätze*) from student lecture notes added as clarificatory material by Hegel's posthumous editors.

TOM McCARTHY

REM McCarthy, Tom. *Remainder*. New York: Vintage, 2007. *Remainder* was initially published in 2005 by Metronome Press in a print run of five hundred copies. Since this first edition is not readily accessible to most readers, I will cite the more accessible Vintage edition in the body of the text followed by the page number, i.e. (Rem, 5).

OMER FAST

REM FILM Fast, Omer. *Remainder* (2016). Written and directed by Omer Fast, based on the novel by Tom McCarthy. Dialogue from the film will appear in the text followed by time stamp, i.e. (Rem film, 48:07).

SIGMUND FREUD

SE Freud, Sigmund. *The Standard Edition of the Complete Psychological Works of Sigmund Freud*. Translated and edited by James Strachey. London: Hogarth, 1953–1974.

JACQUES LACAN

SA Lacan, Jacques. *Anxiety: The Seminar of Jacques Lacan, Book X*. Edited by Jacques-Alain Miller and translated by A. R. Price. London: Polity Press, 2014.

MAURICE MERLEAU-PONTY

PP Merleau-Ponty, Maurice. *Phenomenology of Perception*. Translated by Colin Smith. London: Routledge, 1989.

PAUL RICOEUR

FN Ricoeur, Paul. *Freedom and Nature: The Voluntary and the Involuntary*. Translated by Erazim V. Kohák. Evanston, IL: Northwestern University Press, 2007.

NOTES

INTRODUCTION

1. "Middle term"—a logical term referring to its mediating role in the syllogism—is derived from Aristotelian logic, and it is invoked in almost all accounts of habit referring to this tradition, either directly, or, via Hegel's speculative anthropology of habit that identifies habit as the middle term of the syllogism uniting particularity and universality, subject and predicate. See PM, §410, 410Z; LPS, 154; see notes 6 and 16.

2. PP, 145.

3. PP, 146; Kirill Chepurin, "Subjectivity, Madness and Habit: Forms of Resistance in Hegel's Anthropology," in *Hegel and Resistance: History, Politics and Dialectics*, ed. Rebecca Comay and Bart Zantvoort (London: Bloomsbury, 2018), 111.

4. Italo Testa, "Hegel's Naturalism or Soul and Body in the Encyclopedia," in *Essays on Hegel's Philosophy of Subjective Spirit*, ed. David Stern (Albany: SUNY Press, 2013), 28.

5. William James, "What Pragmatism Means," in *Pragmatism* (Cambridge, MA: Harvard University Press, 1978), 39. Michael Taussig briefly discuss the "fly-wheel" in his *Mastery of Non-Mastery in the Age of Meltdown* (Chicago: University of Chicago Press, 2020), 157, 204n15. In reality, James's use of the fly-wheel analogy in this sentence is more like a ballast that has turned into the sinking deadweight of custom and calling, or, perhaps more vividly, the Beckettian ballast that "chains the dog to its vomit." Sara Ahmed pays close attention to the centrality of overcoming resistance through use that smooths and eases a passage in William James's account of habit. See Sara Ahmed, *What's the Use? On the Uses of Use* (Durham: Duke University Press, 2019), 40–43, 71–75.

6. "The essential element of the syllogism is the unity of the extremes, the *middle term* that unites them and the *ground* that supports them." See SL, 589; ESL §185.

7. I take the phrase "existence at its worst" from Catherine Malabou, "Addiction and Grace: Preface to Félix Ravaisson's *Of Habit*," in Felix Ravaisson, *Of Habit*, trans. Clare Carlisle and Mark Sinclair (London: Continuum, 2008), vii. The term "habit proper" is used here as it is in the vocabulary of phenomenology, such as Merleau-Ponty's term *corps propre*, which draws on Husserl (and earlier formulations of the *Leib/Körper* distinction as first conceptualized by Fichte) and is used to describe habit as a lived-through body that is optimally characterized by pliability and equilibrium.

8. I take the term "revolving door" from "sliding door" in Italo Testa, "Dewey, Second Nature, Social Criticism, and the Hegelian Heritage," *European Journal of Pragmatism and American Philosophy* 9, no. 1 (2017): 4, http://journals.openedition.org/ejpap/990. I suppose *pharmakon* or the "double law of habit" might be other terms for habit as a revolving door. For the double law of habit, see Clare Carlisle, *On Habit* (London: Routledge, 2014), 27-31. For bodily understanding see PP, 139, 140, 144, 146.

9. Walter Benjamin "The Destructive Character," in *Walter Benjamin: Selected Writings, Volume 2, Part 2, 1931–1934*, ed. Michael W. Jennings and Howard Eiland (Cambridge, MA: Belknap Press, 2005), 541–542. Žižek's primary example of a life without habits, the evacuation of all givens, draws on the Cartesian Ego, Hegel's references to war, and revolutionary figures who are at least potentially without habits. See Slavoj Žižek, "Introduction," *Virtue and Terror by Maximilien Robespierre*, ed. Jean Ducange, trans. John Howe (London: Verso: 2007), xviii. Friedrich Nietzsche, *The Gay Science*, trans. Josefine Nauckhoff and Adrian Del Car (Cambridge: Cambridge University Press, 2001), 295: "the most intolerable, the truly terrible, would of course be a life entirely without habits." William James, *Principles of Psychology*, vol. 1 (New York: Henry Holt & Company, 1890; New York: Dover Publications, 1950), 122: "There is no more miserable human being than one in whom nothing is habitual but indecision, and for whom the lighting of every cigar, the drinking of every cup, the time of rising and going to bed every day, and the beginning of every bit of work, are subjects of express volitional deliberation." FN, 285.

10. Alexandre Kojève, *Introduction to the Reading of Hegel: Lectures on The Phenomenology of Spirit*, ed. Allan Bloom, trans. James H. Nichols Jr. (Ithaca, NY: Cornell University Press, 1980), 220. On "processless habit," see PN §375, §375Z; PM §396, §396Z. For other passages in Hegel on death and habit, see PM §410; LPS, 157; EPR, 397n3.

11. Nietzsche, *The Gay Science*, 295; Henri Bergson, *Creative Revolution*, trans. A. Mitchell (London: Macmillan, 1911), 279; Ravaisson, *Of Habit*, 75.

12. For some important accounts of habit that are attentive to these dimensions, see the following: Sarah Ahmed, *What's the Use? On the Use of Use* (Durham, NC: Duke University Press, 2019); Sarah Ahmed, *Willful Subjects* (Durham, NC: Duke University Press, 2014); Tony Bennett, "Mind the Gap: Towards a Political History of Habit," *tOPICS* 6, no. 3 (September 2015): 1–24; Jane Dryden, "Hegel's Anthropology: Training the Body," in *Hegel's Encyclopaedia of the Philosophical Sciences: A Critical Guide*, ed. Sebastian Stein and Joshua Wretzel (Cambridge: Cambridge University Press, 2021), 127–147; Terrance MacMullan, *Habits of Whiteness: A Pragmatist Reconstruction* (Bloomington: Indiana University Press, 2009); Shannon Sullivan, "Reconfiguring Gender with John Dewey: Habits, Bodies, and Cultural Change," *Hypatia* 15, no. 1 (Winter 2000): 23–42; Shannon Sullivan, "Oppression in the Gut: The Biological Dimensions of Deweyan Habit," in *A History of Habit: From Aristotle to Bourdieu*, ed. Tom Sparrow and Adam Hutchinson (New York: Lexington Books, 2013), 255–274; Shannon Sullivan, *Revealing Whiteness: The Unconscious Habits of Racial Privilege* (Bloomington: Indiana University Press, 2006); and Nicholas Mowad, *Meaning and Embodiment: Human Corporeity in Hegel's Anthropology* (Albany: SUNY Press, 2019).

13. PM §410/*Werke* 10 §410: "habit is a form that embraces all kinds and stages of spirit's activity."

14. Habit is also addressed in Hegel's *Lectures on Aesthetics* and as a "*Spiritual mechanism*" in Hegel's *Science of Logic* and *Encyclopedia of Logic*. See, for example, SL, 631/*Werke* 6, 410; ESL §195Z.

15. PM §410/*Werke* 10 §410.

16. PM §410Z/Werke 10 §410Z: "Der Leib ist die *Mitte*, durch welche ich mit der Außenwelt überhaupt zusammenkomme." All accounts of habit that draw on Hegel refer to habit in terms of the syllogism and syllogistic middle term. See, for example, Slavoj Žižek, "Discipline Between Two Freedoms—Madness and Habit in German Idealism," in Markus Gabriel and Slavoj Žižek, *Mythology, Madness and Laughter: Subjectivity in German Idealism* (New York: Continuum, 2009), 107, and Catherine Malabou, *The Future of Hegel: Plasticity, Temporality and Dialectic*, trans. Lisbeth During (London: Routledge, 2005), 37: "Dialectically sublating the anthropological moment of judgment, habit represents an example of the dialectical syllogism, restoring the unity of subject and predicate." Of course, the syllogism is everywhere in Hegel's writings from nature to subjective spirit to objective spirit to absolute spirit, as logic in Hegel is not restricted to the formal aspects of inferential reasoning, but rather it is a metaphysics and an onto-logic. Simply put it is the very movement and inner dynamic (life) of the concept in its unity.

17. PM §411, §411Z, §412, and §412Z.

18. Catherine Malabou, *The Future of Hegel*, 38.

19. PM §410Z; PN §250; SL, 348.

20. See Malabou, "Addiction and Grace," vii–viii.

21. See notes 1, 6, 16.

22. In my account, habit is not the Deweyian "cooperation of organism and environment." See John Dewey, "Human Nature and Conduct: An Introduction to Social Psychology," in *The Middle Works of John Dewey, 1899–1924*, ed. Jo Ann Boydston, vol. 14: 1922, *Human Nature and Conduct* (Carbondale, IL: Southern Illinois University Press, 1983), 15.

23. Stefanos Geroulanos and Todd Meyers, "Integrations, Vigilance, Catastrophe: The Neuropsychiatry of Aphasia in Henry Head and Kurt Goldstein," in *Plasticity and Pathology: On the Formation of the Neural Subject*, ed. David Bates and Nima Bassiri (New York: Fordham University Press, 2016), 131.

24. Theodor Adorno, *Minima Moralia: Reflections from a Damaged Life*, trans. E. F. N. Jephcott (London: New Left Books, 1974), 49. See Rebecca Comay's astute comment about the respective approaches to the normal and pathological in Freud and Hegel in *Mourning Sickness: Hegel and the French Revolution* (Stanford, CA: Stanford University Press, 2010), 95–96. For Freud's succinct statement on how pathological exaggeration and distortions sheds light on "normal phenomena," see SE 14 (1914–1916), "On Narcissism (1914)," 82.

25. See Jacques Lacan, *The Seminar of Jacques Lacan Book XI: The Four Fundamental Concepts of Psychoanalysis*, ed. Jacques-Alain Miller, trans. Alan Sheridan (New York: W. W. Norton, 1998), 23, 25–26, on the "active practitioners of orthopedics" that stitch up the gap that the unconscious shows us. As he notes, when one is dealing with the gap, one is dealing with a (pre-)ontological function. This daemonic power is Freud's characterization of the death drive's compulsion to repeat. See SE 18 (1920–1922), "Beyond the Pleasure Principle (1920)," 21–22.

26. PM §410Z.

27. The dominance of this approach is attested to in even sophisticated accounts of the relationship between habit and pathology. For instance, although Wes Furlotte's important book *The Problem of Nature in Hegel's Final System* is very attentive to the more disruptive aspects of habit, he sees this "proneness" manifested and intensified when habit reverts or "regresses" to pathological states, whereas I see habit as generating these disruptions and collapses in a much more quotidian way. See Wes Furlotte, *The Problem of Nature in Hegel's Final System* (Edinburgh: Edinburgh University Press, 2018), 145: "Without this fluid quality

(of habit), subjectivity would be excessively prone to collapse in the ways highlighted in the extreme of self-feeling's psychopathological fixation." My account is an extreme one where this fluidity is lacking in and as a constitutive desease rather than as a regression or proneness to disease as such.

28. Bruno Latour, *An Inquiry into Modes of Existence: An Anthropology of the Moderns*, trans. Catherine Porter (Cambridge, MA: Harvard University Press, 2013), 269; FN, 284, 298. David Wills has made a similar point noting the lack of an "ethics of automaticity" owing to its perpetual role as the other of the human, free will, and decision. See David Wills, *Dorsality: Thinking Back Through Technology and Politics* (Minneapolis: University of Minnesota Press, 2008), 6. For a good account of the complexity and centrality of mechanism and exteriority in Hegel, see Nathan Ross, *On Mechanism in Hegel's Social and Political Philosophy* (New York: Routledge, 2008).

29. PM §410. The overcoming of resistance, Hegel writes, is when "corporeity (is) rendered completely pervious, made into an instrument ... *without resistance and with ease*" (my emphasis). William James simply notes that "the overcoming of ... resistance is a phenomenon of habituality." See William James, *The Principles of Psychology*, vol. 1, 105. The latter is a quotation taken from Léon Dumont.

30. I am in sympathy with the scholarship on Hegel arguing that resistance is not something generated by critics of Hegel in response to his mobilism but rather that material resistance, antagonism, and excess are at the core of the Hegelian system and crucial to its tempo and cadence. For a collection of essays on this topic, see Rebecca Comay and Bart Zantvoort, eds., *Hegel and Resistance: History, Politics, and Dialectics* (London: Bloomsbury, 2018). Adrian Johnston has, I think, summed up the general thrust of this rethinking of Hegel as a focus on him "as a thinker of discordant material inconsistency rather than harmonious ideational consistency." See Adrian Johnston, *Adventures in Transcendental Materialism: Dialogues with Contemporary Thinkers* (Edinburgh: Edinburgh University Press, 2014), 118.

31. PM §410Z.

32. "Preface to the Second Edition," SL, 17.

33. Here I am paraphrasing a sentence from Comay on a different issue. See Comay, *Mourning Sickness*, 131.

34. Giorgio Agamben, *The Coming Community*, trans. Michael Hardt (Minneapolis: University of Minnesota Press, 1993), 27–29: "Being engendered from one's own manner of being is, in effect, the very definition of habit (this is why the Greeks spoke of a second nature." Agamben also adds: "And this being engendered from one's own manner is the only happiness really possible for humans. ... The impropriety, which we expose as our proper being, manner, which we *use*, engenders us. It is our second happier nature." It should be noted that Agamben's account of habit here and elsewhere is attentive to its disturbing qualities of dispossession and impropriety along with more balanced and redemptive ones, although I would argue that habit plays a primarily political and mediating role between zoe and bios in his writings at the limits of any anthropology. See, for example, *Homo Sacer: Sovereign Power and Bare Life*, trans. Daniel Heller-Roazen (Stanford, CA: Stanford University Press, 1998), 148–153. Agamben goes into more detail about the relationship between habit and use in the final volume of his *Homo Sacer* series, *The Use of Bodies*, trans. Adam Kostko (Stanford: Stanford University Press, 2016).

35. This apocryphal quotation—attributed to the Duke of Wellington—appears in William James's "Habit" in *The Principles of Psychology*, vol. 1, 120, in which he reads it as a further exemplification of the extreme control that habit has on permanently fixing us in

our dispositions and social positions in life. I am taking it in the opposite sense, however, such that habit does not overcome nature through spirit, but rather is an intensification of nature's own instability and excess that is elaborated on rather than stabilized. More recent work on Hegel and habit moves away from aspects of Kojève's "anthropogenetic desire" that places the emphasis on the "*human*, non-biological I" and its overcoming of nature. These accounts pay close attention to Hegel's *Philosophy of Nature* and to how nature's instability, "weakness" (*ohnemacht*), and excesses are carried forth—or always already idealized—as it is further elaborated on in so-called second nature. Here I am thinking of the writings of Wes Furlotte, Adrian Johnston, Jean-Luc Nancy, Catherine Malabou, Slavoj Žižek, and Frank Ruda.

36. Jacques Lacan, "The Mirror Stage as Formative of the I Function as Revealed in Psychoanalytic Experience," in *Écrits*, trans. Bruce Fink (New York: W. W. Norton, 2002), 75–81.

37. Gaston Bachelard, *Intuition of the Instant*, trans. Eileen Rizo-Patron (Evanston, IL: Northwestern University Press, 2013). I return to this passage in chapter 2.

38. Hegel uses the words "abbreviation" (*Abbreviaturen*) and "simplicity" (*Einfachheit*) in the "Preface to the Second Edition" of *Science of Logic* in the sense of a universality that is "summed up in a representation." See SL, 14–15/*Werke* 5, 24. These passages echo the discussion of habit's "adroitness of execution" (*Geschicklichkeit im Exekutieren*) in *Philosophy of Mind* and *Lectures on the Philosophy of Spirit*, in which the words "simplification" and "simple" are also used to indicate the incorporation and universalization of a series of particularities, units, and repetitions. See PM §410, §410Z; LPS, 153–158/VPG, 129.

39. See Rebecca Comay, "Resistance and Repetition: Hegel and Freud," in *Hegel and Resistance: History, Politics and Dialectics*, 44, and Katrin Pahl, *Tropes of Transport: Hegel and Emotion* (Evanston, IL: Northwestern University Press, 2012), 191–194. Pahl's term "desperate analysis" is intended to echo Hegel's claim that the path and movement of the concept in the *Phenomenology of Spirit* is a "path of despair." See PS §78. Comay's "philolytic drive" links this insistent analytics to psychoanalytic notions of the (death) drive.

40. See Christoph Schuringa, "Nature, spirit, and second nature: Hegel and McDowell," *Revista Eletrônica Estudos Hegelianos* 15, no. 25 (2018): 83–84. The passage referred to in Schuringa's text is *Nicomachean Ethics* 1147a21–22. It should be noted that although the notion of second nature has its roots in the crucial role of habit in the formation of virtue and character in Aristotle's *Nichomachean Ethics*, as far as I know the exact term "second nature" never occurs in Aristotle's writings on habit. As Allegra de Laurentiis has noted, perhaps *Nicomachean Ethics* 1152a31–34 is Aristotle's closest definition of habit as second nature: "The reason why habit is also difficult to change is that it is like nature, as Euenus says, 'Habit, my friend, is longtime training, and in the end training is nature for human beings.'" See Allegra de Laurentiis, *Hegel's Anthropology: Life, Psyche, and Second Nature* (Evanston, IL: Northwestern University Press, 2021), 177.

41. Schuringa, "Nature, spirit, and second nature: Hegel and McDowell," 83–84.

42. John Dewey, *Human Nature and Conduct* (New York: Henry Holt & Company, 1922), 24. The full passage reads: "When we are honest with ourselves, we acknowledge that a habit has this power because it is intimately a part of ourselves. It has a hold upon us because we are the habit."

43. On the intimate incommensurability between language and the body, such that the latter is only "given partially" through the former, which is to say, in parts, see Judith Butler, *Senses of the Subject* (New York: Fordham University Press, 2015), 20.

44. PP, 103, 98–147.

45. This passage is elaborated on in many other sections in PS and Hegel's other texts. Jacques Lacan, "Aggressiveness in Psychoanalysis," *Écrits*, trans. Bruce Fink (New York: W. W. Norton, 2002), 93. For Hegel's main statement on the beautiful soul, see PS §658.

46. Lacan, "The Mirror Stage as Formative of the I Function," *Écrits*, 75–81. The words and phrases quoted in the following two paragraphs are derived from this text.

47. PS §28–29, §808. The hyphen here points to the very resistance at the heart of this interiorization.

48. Theodor Adorno, "Aspects of Hegel's Philosophy," in *Hegel: Three Studies*, trans. Shierry Weber Nicholsen (Cambridge, MA: MIT Press, 1993), 4–5.

49. Jacques Lacan, *The Seminar of Jacques Lacan Book II: The Ego in Freud's Theory and in the Technique of Psychoanalysis*, ed. Jacques Alain Miller, trans. Sylvan Tomaselli (New York: W. W. Norton, 1991), 54.

50. FN, 297.

51. See *Hegel and the Human Spirit: A Translation of the Jena Lectures on the Philosophy of Spirit* (1805–6) *with Commentary* by Leo Rauch (Detroit: Wayne State University Press, 1983), 86–87; G. W. F. Hegel, *Jenaer Systementwürfe III: Naturphilosophie und Philosophie des Geistes*, ed. Rolf-Peter Horstmann (Hamburg: Felix Meiner Verlag, 1987), 172–173; LPS, 152/VPG, 123; PM §453/ *Werke* 10 §453.

52. *Hegel and the Human Spirit*, 87.

53. Lacan, "The Deconstruction of the Drive," *Book XI: The Four Fundamental Concepts of Psychoanalysis*, 169–170; LPS, 153.

54. On repetition and habit, see PM §410: "This process of building up the particular and corporeal expressions of feeling into the being of the soul appears as a *repetition* (*Wiederholung*) of them, and the generation of habit as a *practice* (*Übung*)"; LPS, 153: "Habit is acquired through repetition so that the individual is appropriated to universality"; Lacan, "Seminar on the 'Purloined Letter,'" *Écrits*, 33, 39. Lacan makes clear that "insistence" is the essential characteristic of the "compulsion to repeat" (*compulsion de répétition*)/"repetition automatism" (*automatisme de répétition*) that he takes up from Freud's account of the death drive in *Beyond the Pleasure Principle*. On habit's complex relationship to the drive in Hegel (*Trieb*), see PM §410, §410Z; LPS, 155–156; EPR §11, 11Z.

55. PS §32; SA, 86–89, 282.

56. SA, 38, 40, 220.

57. SE 5 (1916–1917), "Introductory Lessons to Psychoanalysis," 27.

58. On Hegel's "circle of circles" that cuts into itself as the figure for speculative movement rather than just a "circle," see SL, 750–751; ESL, §15, §17. In some of the secondary literature on Hegel, this shape and movement is characterized in terms of the "spiral" and "spiraling." I do not have the time or space to list all these secondary sources, so I will just point to one that addresses the wider cultural implications of the spiral, including references to Hegel. See Nico Israel, *Spirals: The Whirled Image in Twentieth-Century Literature and Art* (New York: Columbia University Press, 2015).

59. For the most succinct statements about this fixity and the "fixed subject," see PS §23, §60–§66. Adorno specifically invokes the term "static logic" as something that Hegel is trying to overcome through dialectical mediation. See Adorno, "Skoteinos, or How to Read Hegel," *Hegel: Three Studies*, 116. Werner Hamacher also notes that Hegel's speculative proposition is meant to overcome the "static" relationship between subject and predicate. See Hamacher, *Pleroma—Reading in Hegel*, trans. Nicholas Walker and Simon Jarvis (Stanford:

Stanford University Press, 1998), 5–7. Angelica Nuzzo invokes the term "static logic" to characterize the understanding (*Verstand*) in Hegel. See *Approaching Hegel's Logic Obliquely: Melville, Molière, Beckett* (Evanston: Northwestern University Press, 2018), 29.

60. Malabou, "Addiction and Grace," viii; Tom McCarthy, "Navigation Was Always a Difficult Art," in *The Mattering of Matter: Documents from the Archive of the International Necronautical Society*, Tom McCarthy, Simon Critchley, et al. (Berlin: Sternberg Press, 2012), 145.

61. Fredric Jameson, *The Hegel Variations: On the Phenomenology of Spirit* (London: Verso, 2017), 28. See also Frederic Jameson, "Hegel and Picture-Thinking, or, An Episode in the History of Allegory," *Crisis & Critique* 4, no. 1 (March 2017): 145–159. For two accounts of Hegel that are attentive to the theatrical staginess of Hegel's *Phenomenology of Spirit*, see Comay, *Mourning Sickness* and Pahl, *Tropes of Transport*. The classical Renaissance setup sounds a bit like Adorno's illusionistic "three-walled stage of bourgeois theatre." See Theodor Adorno, "The Position of the Narrator in the Contemporary Novel," in *Notes on Literature*, trans. Shierry Weber Nicholsen, vol. 1 (New York: Columbia University Press, 1991), 33. Clearly, the theatrical "curtain" and its manipulation are intimately related to habit's veiling function.

62. PP, 110.

63. Roland Barthes, *A Lover's Discourse: Fragments*, trans. Richard Howard (New York: Vintage, 2002), 123.

64. See G. W. F. Hegel, *The Philosophy of History*, trans. J. Sibree (New York: Dover, 1956), 42, and PS §546. Weaving/spinning is also another metaphor for habit to which I return in chapter 3. The sense of habit that I am pursuing is more akin to a psychoanalytic passage à l'acte that is not merely an "acting-out" within given symbolic coordinates but rather an attempt to exit them, and it is a sign of habit's unbearability. See SA, 122. Needless to say, this sense of habit as destitution also requires a certain kind of framing and stage machinery, which I explore primarily through *Remainder*.

65. PS §207/*Werke* 3, 163. Pinkard's translation is "this *unhappy and estranged consciousness within itself*."

66. Bruno Latour's account of habit in "Learning to Respect Appearances," *Inquiry into Modes of Existence*, 259–281, has helped me clarify my own views on habit. Clearly, Latour is emphasizing habit's role in constructing a posteriori essences through its "effects of immanence." The nature of the "manual restart's" relationship to "automatic pilot" that Latour emphasizes is related to the vexed issue of the role of understanding and consciousness in relationship to habit, as opposed to its automatic qualities. In chapter 2, I pursue my own take on the relationship between habit and understanding.

67. On the illuminating possibilities of "coarse reduction," "lack of subtlety," and "exaggeration" in Hegel's method, see Comay, *Mourning Sickness*, 95–96; Rebecca Comay and Frank Ruda, *The Dash—The Other Side of Absolute Knowing* (Cambridge, MA: MIT Press, 2018), 3 and 7; and Malabou, *The Future of Hegel*, 148–154.

68. As both Malabou and Žižek have noted, within certain strands of philosophical Modernism, habit shifts from a positive virtue (Aristotle) necessary for human freedom—a tradition carried forth by Hegel and the French philosophers of habit such as Ravaisson—to something purely mechanical—exemplified by Descartes and carried forth by Kant—such that becoming habitual is the opposite of freedom.

69. Gilles Deleuze, *Difference and Repetition*, trans. Paul Patton (New York: Columbia University Press, 1994), 79; Malabou, *The Future of Hegel*, 26. Tom Sparrow, *Plastic Bodies: Rebuilding Sensation After Phenomenology*, foreword by Catherine Malabou (London: Open Humanities Press, 2014), 101; Michael Taussig, *The Mastery of Non-Mastery in the Age of Meltdown* (Chicago:

University of Chicago Press, 2020), 138; Frank Ruda, "The Lost Habit: Elements to a Hegelian Theory of Laziness/Foulness," in *Hegel's Rabble: An Investigation into Hegel's Philosophy of Right* (London: Bloomsbury, 2011), 79, 189n9.

70. In 2016 I invited McCarthy and Fast to engage with me in a focused discussion about habit in *Remainder*. The result was a public conversation between the three of us, "On Habit in Remainder," that took place at The House of Literature (*Litteraturhuset*) in Oslo in November 2016 (https://litteraturhuset.no/arkiv/on-habit-in-remainder/). During this visit, they also graciously came to talk with students in my On Habit, Art and Architecture seminar.

71. PM §410Z.

72. On the speculative word speculative/speculation in Hegel, see ESL §82. The one issue raised by McCarthy but not explicitly by Hegel in his discussion of the word "speculation" is financial speculation. Hegel makes clear in his discussion of the word that philosophy must draw on the storehouse of ordinary language and not invent a new one. Part of Adorno's attempt to unhinge speculation from Hegel's idealism, what he characterizes as "identity thinking," is to see speculation as a way of using the concept to reach beyond the concept. This is precisely where Adorno connects his "non-conceptual" negative dialectics to an emphasis on the "dregs" in psychoanalytic theory, practice, and technique. See Adorno, *Lectures on Negative Dialects, Fragments of a Lecture Course, 1965/1966*, ed. Rolf Tiedemann, trans. Rodney Livingstone (London: Polity Press, 2008), 94–95. But Adorno's basic definition of speculation as moving beyond the given is really just elucidating Hegel's own statement in his Preface to *Elements of the Philosophy of Right* that free thinking, i.e., speculative thinking, "does not stop at what is *given*." See EPR, 11.

73. I return in depth to the speculative sentence in the following chapter.

74. Tom McCarthy, *Empty House of the Stare* (Cambridge, MA: MIT Press, 2019), 28; Michael Marder, *Hegel's Energy: A Reading of the Phenomenology of Spirit* (Evanston, IL: Northwestern University Press, 2021), 81.

75. LPS, 157.

76. PM §410Z.

77. I recall coming across this phrase reading Levinas, although I cannot recall the exact text.

78. Lacan, "The Mirror Stage as Formative of the I Function," 78.

79. Tom McCarthy and Simon Critchley, "Interview: Simon Critchley, March 29, 2001," in *The Mattering of Matter*, 64; Kojève, *Introduction to the Reading of Hegel*, 142. Also see Jean-Clet Martin, *Une Intrigue criminelle de la philosophie: Lire la Phénoménologie de l'Esprit de Hegel* (Paris: Éditions La Découverte, 2009). The language of murderous violence in Hegel is often enabled by the use of speculative words, such as vanishing (*Verschwinden*), i.e., "disappearing."

80. Adorno, "Skoteinos, or How to Read Hegel," 123 and Catherine Clément, *Syncope: The Philosophy of Rapture*, trans. Sally O'Driscoll and Deirdre M. Mahoney (Minneapolis: University of Minnesota Press, 1994), 73.

81. Comay, "Resistance and Repetition," 53.

82. Žižek, Johnston, Comay, Dolar, Pahl, Malabou, Ruda, Clet-Martin, Nancy, and Hamacher are all attentive to the "quasi-automatic" character of the dialectical process. See, for example, Slavoj Žižek, *Less than Nothing: Hegel and the Shadow of Dialectical Materialism* (London: Verso, 2013), 492; Adrian Johnston, *A New German Idealism: Hegel, Žižek, and Dialectical Materialism* (New York: Columbia University Press, 2018), 188–189; Comay, "Resistance and Repetition," 52.

83. The French word démonter, as Roland Barthes has shown, elucidates the logic of breakdown, with its felicitous connotation of taking apart and being violently thrown to the ground.

84. The interpretation of Hegel's *Phenomenology of Spirit* as a bildungsroman of consciousness's coming into being is still prevalent and was put forth in the strongest of terms by Kojève in his *Introduction to the Reading of Hegel: Lectures on The Phenomenology of Spirit*. For recent examples that persuasively argue that it is not a bildungsroman, see Jameson, *Hegel Variations*, 16; Comay, *Mourning Sickness*, 146–147; Pahl, *Tropes of Transport*, 181–210. Not surprisingly, Hegel's account of habit is also often read as a bildungsroman, but that seems to disregard Hegel's critique of any "edifying" role for philosophy. I am more attracted to recent attempts that take seriously the Soul's ongoing immersion in nature, thus paying attention to Hegel's *Philosophy of Nature*, the volume that proceeds his account of habit in *Philosophy of Mind*. These accounts tend to avoid the overly culturological interpretations of habit as a Fichtean self-positing, marking spirit's definitive "break" from its natural grounds. For accounts sensitive to the latter approach, see Adrian Johnston, Wes Furlotte, Slavoj Žižek, Catherine Malabou, Frank Ruda, and Simon Lumsden. For accounts of habit that place a stronger emphasis on this break, see Alfredo Ferrarin and John McDowell.

85. PS §32.

86. G. W. F. Hegel, "Aphorisms from the Wastebook," in *Miscellaneous Writings of G. W. F Hegel*, ed. Jon Stewart (Evanston, IL: Northwestern University Press, 2002), 248; G. W. F. Hegel, "Aphorismen aus Hegels Wastebook (1803–1806)," *Werke* 2, 547: "Die Fragen, welche die Philosophie nicht beantwortet, sind so beantwortet, daß sie nicht so gemacht werden sollen."

87. Tarrying and remaining with the resistances to change—when unhalting flow halts and becomes stuck, when inertia is brought to an extreme instead of fluidified, when the elements or pieces are fixed or fixated and not soluble, when the old persists as mindless repetition—might be the very precondition for change. See Comay, "Resistance and Repetition," 48–54; Žižek, *Less Than Nothing*, 483; Pahl, *Tropes of Transport*, 181–210.

88. See Terry Pinkard, "Translator's Note," in PS, xliv–xlv, on the difficulty and disagreements in translating *die Sache selbst* into English. It is one of the most frequently used terms in Hegel's writing.

89. H. S. Harris, *Spirit: Chapter Six of Hegel's Phenomenology of Spirit* (Indianapolis, IN: Hackett Publishing, 2001), viiin1, viiin2; Rocío Zambrana, "Subjectivity in Hegel's Logic," in *Oxford Handbook of Hegel*, ed. Dean Moyer (Oxford: Oxford University Press, 2017), 291n1; Jameson, *The Hegel Variations*, 39.

90. Terry Pinkard, "Translators Note," in PS, xliv–xlv. See, for example, PS §4, §408–§417 for some examples of where he has used "the crux of the matter" to translate *die Sache selbst*. A. V. Miller translates these same passages as "heart of the matter" or "matter in hand." See PS 1977.

91. PS §17. The complete sentence reads as follows: "In my view, which must be justified by the exposition of the system itself, everything hangs on grasping and expressing the true not just as *substance* but just as much as *subject*."

92. ESL §24, A2: freedom is "to be at home with oneself in one's other."

93. PM §409.

94. PM §409, §410.

95. On the legacy and inheritance of Hegel's notion of habit, subject, and substance in a rethinking of the humanistic legacy of anthropology, see Frank Ruda, "Hegel's Mother,"

in *Inheritance in Psychoanalysis*, ed. Joel Goldbach and James A. Godley (Albany: SUNY Press, 2018), 85–108.

96. See Terry Pinkard's "Translator's note," PS, xlii, concerning Hegel's use of the word *Entäußerung*, which, along with its cognates, appears numerous times in *Phenomenology of Spirit*.

97. PS §753.

98. SA, 161, 178.

99. PP, 153.

100. SL, 539/*Werke* 6, 287.

101. Frank Ruda offers a brief but intriguing account of Hegel's philosophy of the hand in "The Lost Habit: Elements to a Hegelian Theory of Laziness/Foulness," in *Hegel's Rabble: An Investigation into Hegel's Philosophy of Right* (London: Bloomsbury, 2013), 82–85. Sarah Ahmed engages in a compelling discussion of hands, body parts, and grasping that manifest a resistant, persistent and deviant will of their own in relationship to literature, with a select few references to Hegel, throughout her important book, *Willful Subjects* (Durham, NC: Duke University Press, 2014).

CHAPTER 1

1. On the gerund, see Tom McCarthy, "Recessional, or the Time of the Hammer," *Typewriters, Bombs, Jellyfish: Essays* (New York: New York Review of Books, 2017), 99–124 and Tom McCarthy, *Recessional—Or, the Time of the Hammer*, ed. Elisabeth Bronfen (Zurich/Berlin: Diaphenes, 2016), 18, 19, 22, 28.

2. For the term "neurofiction," see N. Katherine Hayles, "The Costs of Consciousness: Tom McCarthy's *Remainder* and Peter Watts's *Blindsight*," in *Unthought: The Power of the Cognitive Unconscious* (Chicago: University of Chicago Press, 2017), 86–112. For instance, the following sentence from Malabou's *The New Wounded* might seem like a succinct encapsulation of the stakes in *Remainder*, whereby senseless, contingent, and external traumas to the brain result in "cognitive and affective disturbances, such as affective and libidinal deficits, disruption of habits, the tragic loss of life skills and evidenced by an inability to make decisions and display behaviors of indifference or disaffection." See *The New Wounded: From Neurosis to Brain Damage*, trans. Steven Miller (New York: Fordham University Press, 2012), 4. Although my account declines to read the novel through Malabou's compelling notion of destructive plasticity, as that relates to what she calls "the neurological novel," I have learned a lot from her work—particularly *The Future of Hegel*—and her firm and clear positions have helped me articulate my own. For a compelling reading of *Remainder* that resonates with Malabou's theories of plasticity and the catastrophic effects of neurocognitive trauma, but that pursues its own particular argumentation, see Hayles, "The Costs of Consciousness," 86–96. Needless to say, my account differs from her framing of the novel in fundamental ways. Indeed, McCarthy himself thanks two individuals in his acknowledgments for sharing their experiences of "(post)-trauma" with him, and the novel's narrator explicitly refers to damage inflicted on the part of his brain that controls motor functions on the right side of his body, and he subsequently engages in "rerouting" training to help remedy the loss of function attributable to the accident (Rem, 309,19).

For Adrian Johnston's pithy summary of Malabou's notion of "the new wounded," see Adrian Johnston, *Adventures in Transcendental Materialism: Dialogues with Contemporary Thinkers* (Edinburgh: Edinburgh University Press, 2014), 279.

3. PS §37: "However much this negative now initially appears as the inequality between the I and the object, still it is just as much the inequality of the substance with itself. What seems to take place outside of the substance, to be an activity directed against it, is its own doing, and substance shows that it is essentially subject." See also PS§18.

4. Gaston Bachelard, *Intuition of the Instant*, trans. Eileen Rizo-Patron (Evanston, IL: Northwestern University Press, 2013), 32.

5. Tom McCarthy and Simon Critchley, "Joint Statement on Inauthenticity," in *The Mattering of Matter: Documents from the Archive of the International Necronautical Society*, Tom McCarthy, Simon Critchley, et al. (Berlin: Sternberg Press, 2012), 232.

6. McCarthy and Critchley, "Joint Statement on Inauthenticity," 232; LPS, 153. See Simon Lumsden, "Between Nature and Spirit: Hegel's Account of Habit," in *Essays on Hegel's Philosophy of Subjective Spirit*, ed. David S. Stern (Albany: SUNY Press, 2013), 126.

7. Henri Bergson, *Matter and Memory*, trans. N. M. Paul and W. S. Palmer (New York: Zone Books, 1990), 82–83. Bergson is contrasting the "motor mechanism" of habit to the "independent recollections" of memory that are represented with their "outline, their color, and their place and time."

8. See, for example, SL, 347–348/*Werke* 6, 26–27.

9. SL, 51.

10. Theodor Adorno, "Skoteinos, or How to Read Hegel," in *Hegel: Three Studies*, trans. Shierry Weber Nicholsen (Cambridge, MA: MIT Press, 1993), 121.

11. See PM §409/*Werke* 10 §409: "But this abstract realization of the soul in its corporeal vehicle is not yet the self." Petry's translation of this sentence from §409 is slightly different: "This abstract being-for-self of the soul in its corporeity (*Leiblichkeit*) is not yet ego." See M. J. Petry, *Hegel's Philosophy of Subjective Spirit*, vol. 2, Anthropology (Dordrecht, Holland: D. Reidel Publishing Company, 1978), 389.

12. "Trauma is not something that affects the subject, the ultimate trauma is the rise/explosion of subjectivity itself." See Slavoj Žižek, *Incontinence of the Void* (Cambridge, MA: MIT Press, 2017), 27. This notion is repeated throughout Žižek's writings.

13. Jean-Luc Nancy, *Being Singular Plural*, trans. Robert Richardson and Ann O'Byrne (Stanford, CA: Stanford University Press, 2009), 19. In other places, Nancy calls this the "expiration of the subject."

14. McCarthy, "Get Real, or What Jellyfish Have to Tell Us About Literature," *Typewriters, Bombs, Jellyfish*, 69.

15. McCarthy, "Get Real," 70–71.

16. I have benefited from the following work on grammatical form, typography, punctuation, and a more generalized stigmatology: Peter Szendy, *Of Stigmatology: Punctuation as Experience*, trans. Jan Plug (New York: Fordham University Press, 2018); Giorgio Agamben, "**Se*: Hegel's Absolute and Heidegger's *Ereignis*" and "Absolute Immanence," in *Potentialities: Collected Essays in Philosophy* (Stanford, CA: Stanford University Press, 2000), 116–137, 220–142; David Wills, "Living Punctuations: Cixous and Celan," in *Inanimation: Theories of Inorganic Life* (Minneapolis: University of Minnesota Press, 2016), 111–152; Rebecca Comay and Frank Ruda, *The Dash—The Other Side of Absolute Knowing* (Cambridge, MA: MIT Press, 2018); Theodor W. Adorno, "Punctuation Marks," in *Notes to Literature*, ed. Rolf Tiedemann, trans. Shierry Weber Nicholsen (New York: Columbia University Press, 1991), 91–98; Hélène Cixous, *Stigmata: Escaping Texts* (London: Routledge, 1998).

17. On the notion of the "asynchronous present tense" that is relevant to this sentence in *Remainder*, see Armen Avanessian and Anke Hennig, *Present Tense: A Poetics* (London: Bloomsbury Press, 2015), 70–93.

18. See the discussion of the grammatical dash in Comay and Ruda, *The Dash*, 85.

19. Tom McCarthy's explicit interest in complex modes of time and temporality in relationship to matter are in evidence throughout all his writings.

20. This passibility is highly relevant both to habit itself and to the writing of habit that emphasizes the author of an action as simultaneously the recipient of that action.

21. On the formation of the subject *and* its inability to narrate its own formation, see Judith Butler's *Senses of the Subject* (New York: Fordham University Press, 2015), 1–22. A similar sentiment, directly in relation to the structure and movement of the Hegelian speculative sentence, is put forth by Werner Hamacher, *Pleroma: Reading in Hegel*, trans. Nichols Walker and Simon Jarvis (Stanford, CA: Stanford University Press, 1998), 4.

22. SL, 348.

23. The most sustained explication of the "speculative sentence/proposition" (*spekulativer Satz*) is found in the Preface to *Phenomenology of Spirit*, §60–§66/*Werke* 3, 58–59, although its implications permeate every aspect of Hegel's philosophy. The relationship of the speculative sentence/proposition to judgment, logic, and the "predicative proposition" is elaborated in the "Judgment" and "Syllogism" sections of the *Science of Logic* and Encyclopedia Logic. The speculative sentence has been the focus of a lot of exciting work in recent years, which has influenced my own reading of *Remainder*. See, for instance, Jean-Luc Nancy, "Preamble" and " The Speculative Proposition," in *The Speculative Remark (One of Hegel's Bons Mots)*, trans. Céline Surprenant (Stanford, CA: Stanford University Press, 2001), 1–19, 75–101; Katrin Pahl, "Speculative Rhythm," in *Hegel and Language*, ed. Jere O'Neill Surber (Albany: SUNY Press, 2006), 233–248; Katrin Pahl, "Juggle," in *Tropes of Transport: Hegel and Emotion* (Evanston, IL: Northwestern University Press, 2012), 100–119; Hamacher, *Pleroma*, 5–8; Daniel Heller-Roazen, "Collapsing Sentences," in *No One's Ways: An Essay on Infinite Naming* (New York: Zone Books, 2017), 188–191; Malabou, *Future of Hegel*, 10–12, 134, 167–183; Frank Ruda, "Hegel, Resistance and Method," in *Hegel and Resistance: History, Politics and Dialectics*, ed. R. Comay and B. Zantvoort (London: Bloomsbury, 2018), 15–33; Comay and Ruda, "The Dash, or How to Do Things with Signs," in *The Dash*, 53–61; Fredric Jameson, *The Hegel Variations: On the Phenomenology of Spirit* (New York: Verso, 2010), 6–26. I address the related notion of the "infinite judgment" in the following chapter.

24. PS §62.

25. PS §60/*Werke* 3, 57.

26. PS §60/*Werke* 3, 57–58. Miller translates *geht zugrunde* as "perishes" and *schwankt* as "shaken." See PS 1977 §60.

27. Hegel is explicit that philosophy must draw on the storehouse of ordinary language and not invent a new one. But just as philosophical usage must pay attention to the everyday language from which it is twisted, not every appearance of the word "speculation" will be philosophically pertinent. See ESL §82. For a brief but informative discussion of ESL §82, see Nancy, *The Speculative Remark*, 188n22.

28. I take the phrase "speculative attitude" from Frank Ruda, who claims that such a belief is necessary in order to identify and read a speculative sentence because it is not a separate category of sentence, and thus it can also be read in a grammatically proper or ordinary way. See note 29. "Punctuating differently" is, clearly, part of that speculative attitude/reading. See Frank Ruda, "Hegel, Resistance and Method," 24.

29. PS §63/*Werke* 3, 60.

30. Katrin Pahl usefully notes that Hegel's speculative sentence is a way of writing and reading "with subject matter" rather than "above" or "about" it. See Pahl, "Speculative Rhythm," 243.

31. SL, 68: "In this connection, we must observe right at the beginning that the proposition, in the form of *a judgment*, is not adept to expressive speculative truths." See also Pahl, *Tropes of Transport*, 119. I return more directly to issues of understanding and judgment in relation to habit, Hegel, and *Remainder* in the following chapter.

32. PS §63, §64, §66.

33. PS §63; PS 1977 §63/*Werke* 3, 60.

34. "Preface," EPR, 11.

35. PS §66: "From this side, too, there is an obstacle based in the habit (*Gewohnheit*) of grasping the speculative predicate according to the form of a proposition instead of grasping (*fassen*) it as concept and essence."

36. LPS, 154/VPG, 125–126.

37. PM §409.

38. PS §64.

39. "Preface," PS §60–§66. As Pahl has put it, the speculative rhythm is clearly not a clichéd and comforting "regular three-step" dialectical rocking movement. See Pahl, *Tropes of Transport*, 101.

40. Deland Scott Andersen, *Hegel's Speculative Good Friday: The Death of God in Philosophical Perspective* (Atlanta, GA: Scholars Press, 1996), 23.

41. Hamacher, *Pleroma—Reading in Hegel*, 7.

42. On the origins of the word "hypostasis" as "sediment," see Giorgio Agamben, "Theory of Hypostases," *The Use of Bodies*, trans. Adam Kotsko (Stanford, CA: Stanford University Press, 2015), 135–145 (particularly 136). For Hegel's account of the *hypokeimenon* in regard to (verbal) disputes about whether a predicate does or does not belong to a subject, see SL, 551–552.

43. LPS, 153.

44. LPS, 153.

45. See Adorno, *Hegel: Three Studies*, 7, 16, 50. Overly culturological accounts of habit tend to associate habit with a Fichtean self-positing claiming that is where second nature makes a definitive break from its natural grounds.

46. See Gilles Deleuze and Félix Guattari, *A Thousand Plateaus: Capitalism and Schizophrenia* (Minneapolis: University of Minnesota Press, 1987), 17.

47. For an articulation of the claim that the "subject is residuum" from a Hegelian perspective, see Slavoj Žižek, *Absolute Recoil: Towards a New Foundation of Dialectical Materialism* (London: Verso, 2014), 29.

48. PM §410: "Habit on ampler scale, and carried out in the strictly intellectual range, is recollection and memory, whereof we shall speak later." This "whereof we shall speak later" refers to the paragraphs on Memory ("mechanical memory") in the "Psychology" subsection of the *Philosophy of Mind* (§461–§464). Comay and Ruda, *The Dash*, 81.

49. PS §60/*Werke* 3, 57–58. The term "fixed subject" is from PS §62. This logic of breakdown also has connotations of falling/perishing and can be written as *Zugrundegehen*. Written another way, *zu Grunde gehen* suggests a return to ground or fundamentals.

50. SA, 319.

51. PS §62.

52. Adorno, *Hegel: Three Studies*, 8–9.

53. Rebcca Comay, "Resistance and Repetition: Hegel and Freud," in *Hegel and Resistance: History, Politics and Dialectics*, ed. Rebecca Comay and Bart Zantvoort (London: Bloomsbury, 2018), 53.

54. SL, 748.

55. Pahl, "Speculative Rhythm," 241; *Tropes of Transport*, 111–112.

56. PS §32. The more familiar A. V. Miller translation of this sentence is "it [Spirit] wins its truth only when, in utter dismemberment, it finds itself" (*Er gewinnt seine Wahrheit nur, indem er in der absoluten Zerrissenheit sich selbst findet*). See PS 1977 §32/*Werke* 3, 36. I explore the Dionysian and sparagmatic implications of this "utter dismemberment" in the following chapters.

57. For a sustained treatment of mechanism in relationship to grammar and the speculative sentence, see Nancy, *The Speculative Remark*. Nancy notes that "long sentences with multiple reversals … signal the most characteristic syntax of Hegelian discourse," (70). I might add that Hegelian discourse is also characterized by some very short sentences with massive implications coiled within them, for example: "The *being of spirit is a bone*"; "The *thing is* I"; "What is rational is actual; and what is actual is rational." See PS §343, §791; "Preface," EPR, 20. The short-circuiting between long and short sentences is also characteristic of McCarthy's writing.

58. Tom McCarthy, *Empty House of the Stare* (Cambridge, MA: MIT Press, 2019), 28.

59. Michael Marder, *Hegel's Energy: A Reading of the Phenomenology of Spirit* (Evanston, IL: Northwestern University Press, 2021), 181: "Much in dialectics happens as replay and a replay of the replay, but there is always a difference factored into the repetition."

60. LPS, 157.

61. PS §668.

62. Bruno Latour, *An Inquiry into Modes of Existence: An Anthropology of the Moderns*, trans. Catherine Porter (Cambridge, MA: Harvard University Press, 2013), 264–272.

63. SA, 172. Here I am paraphrasing Lacan's critique of the professor who teaches on teaching—snips into teaching—but does not emphasize the cut enough in his collage work.

64. PS §60.

65. Pahl, *Tropes of Transport*, 102.

66. On the necessity of mechanism and mechanical activities in the domain of the spiritual, with specific references to reading, writing, and grammar, see ESL §195Z; SL, 631; PM §410Z; PS §507.

67. McCarthy is clearly influenced by a Joycean approach to language that, as Deleuze and Guattari note, engages in an atomization and subdivision into infinitely small units. See Deleuze and Guattari, *A Thousand Plateaus*, 308. McCarthy has written and lectured extensively on Joyce. See "Why *Ulysses* Matters," *Typewriters, Bombs, Jellyfish*, 21–48. On Lacan's treatment of Joyce, see Tom Eyers, *Lacan and the Concept of the 'Real'* (Basingstoke: Palgrave Macmillan, 2012), 144–153.

68. Linda Ben Zvi, *Women in Beckett: Performance and Critical Perspectives* (Urbana, IL: University of Illinois Press, 1992), 6.

69. McCarthy and Critchley, "Calling All Agents," *Mattering of Matter*, 180–182.

70. See Jacques Lacan, *The Seminar of Jacques Lacan Book XX: On Feminine Sexuality, the Limits of Love and Knowledge*, ed. Jacques-Alain Miller, trans. Bruce Fink (New York: W. W. Norton, 1998), 34–36, and Jean-Claude Milner, *L'amour de la langue* (Paris: Seuil, 1978), 91–92. On the voice and its "waste scraps," see SA, 251.

71. Alain Badiou and Barbara Cassin, *There's No Such Thing as a Sexual Relationship: Two Lessons on Lacan*, trans. Susan Spitzer and Kenneth Reinhard (New York: Columbia University Press, 2017), n4, 73.

72. David Metzger, "Interpretation and Topological Structure," in *Lacan: Topologically Speaking*, ed. Ellie Ragland and Dragan Milovanovic (New York: Other Press, 2004), 142.

73. See McCarthy, "*Tristram Shandy*: On Balls and Planes," *Typewriters, Bombs, Jellyfish*, 84–85.

74. McCarthy, "*Tristram Shandy*," 77–78. On the dash in *Tristram Shandy*, see Szendy, "The Point of (No) Monument, or Tristram's Cut," in *Of Stigmatology*, 17–22.

75. McCarthy, "*Tristram Shandy*," 85.

76. On the Hegelian dialectic as a processing machine, see Žižek, *Less Than Nothing: Hegel and the Shadow of Dialectical Materialism* (London: Verso, 2013), 492; on Nancy's characterization of the Hegelian dialectic as a hypersystem, see Alain Badiou and Jean-Luc Nancy, *German Philosophy: A Dialogue*, trans. Richard Lambert (Cambridge, MA: MIT Press, 2018), 22.

77. Tom McCarthy, "*Tristram Shandy*," 87. The geometrical and topological figurations of this *ricorso* are always in play in McCarthy's "plotting."

78. Comay and Ruda, *The Dash*, 83.

79. Peter Sloterdijk, *You Must Change Your Life*, trans. Wieland Hoban (London: Polity Press, 2017), 26; PS §409.

80. FN, 296.

81. Jacques Lacan, "Of Structure as the Inmixing of an Otherness Prerequisite to Any Subject Whatever," in *The Structuralist Controversy: The Languages of Criticism and the Sciences of Man*, ed. Richard Macksey and Eugenio Donato (Baltimore: John Hopkins University Press, 1977), 188.

82. Giorgio Agamben, *Homo Sacer: Sovereign Power and Bare Life*, trans. Daniel Heller-Roazen (Stanford, CA: Stanford University Press, 1998), 153. This is not, of course, his last word on habit, and he has some very interesting things to say about the "riveting" of being and having in *The Use of Bodies* that are highly relevant to the aesthetics of habit in *Remainder*.

83. SL, 515. See also ESL §166; PS §439.

84. SL, 515.

85. The articulation of the relationship between being and having is persistent throughout all discussions of habit across very different philosophical perspectives. The stress on one or the other is a significant indication of a thinker's broader philosophical project. One striking example is the contrasting emphasis on "having" in Lacan and "being" in Deleuze.

86. Latour, *Inquiry into Modes of Existence*, 268.

87. This passage is from a public lecture held in Louvain in 1972 and filmed by Jacques-Alain Miller. It clearly formulates Lacan's notion of the subject as the bearer or support of the unconscious. See Jacques-Alain Miller and Jacques Lacan, "Jacques Lacan: Conférence de Louvain," *La Cause du Désir* 96, no. 2 (2017): 7–30, https://www.cairn.info/revue-la-cause-du-desir-2017-2-page-7.htm.

88. SA, 89. In particular, see the chapter "Not Without Having It" (85–99). Émile Benveniste, "'Être' et 'avoir' dans leurs fonctions linguistiques," *Problèmes de linguistique générale* (Paris: Gallimard, 1966), 1:187–207. Lacan makes a direct link between habit and anxiety in SA, 75–76. For Lacan, habit is suffused with the nonmediatory qualities of anxiety that he pursues throughout this seminar. As Brian Robertson usefully notes: "All three [read Kierkegaard, Jean Wahl, and Lacan] understand the affective dimension of anxiety in relation with an absolute that stubbornly resists any form of social or symbolic mediation." See *Lacanian Antiphilosophy and the Problem of Anxiety: An Uncanny Little Object* (New York: Palgrave Macmillan, 2015), 85. I assume Hegel is omitted here because of Lacan's explicit claim that Hegel's logic is a bulwark against anxiety. It is more to the point that Hegel's speculative dialectic generates anxiety through and through. For specific references to anxiety in Hegel, see PS §80, §194.

89. Lacan's account of the nonrelationship of being and having is fundamental to his topological critique of phenomenological accounts of habit, understanding, and intentionality. See, for instance, SA, 100–102 (on the "object behind desire"); 96, 136 (on the ant and the moebius strip).

90. Benveniste, "'Être' et 'avoir,'" 198; PM §410, §410Z/LPS, 153–157.

91. FN, 297.

92. FN, 297. Adrian Johnston, *Žižek's Ontology: A Transcendental Materialist Theory of Subjectivity* (Evanston, IL: Northwestern University Press, 2008), 60: "The body, right from the start, is a source of distress (and therefore, experiences bringing the subject back into too excessive a proximity with his or her body generate an alarm associated with this distressing drive-body)." Habit is what enacts and perpetuates this anxiety, as it generates this drive-body and rivets us to it in its very attempt to create a "gap" within this proximity of self-feeling.

93. Rethinking Hegel's dialectic in relation to the Freudian death drive is a feature of Hegel scholarship in the work of Rebecca Comay, Frank Ruda, Slavoj Žižek, Adrian Johnston, Mladen Dolar, and Alenka Zupančič. It should be noted that scholars have long been attuned to the atomizing and mortifying powers of the understanding (*Verstand*) as opposed to reason (*Vernunft*) in Hegel's work.

94. PS §32.

95. See, for example, PN §375; PM §410; EPR §151Z.

96. PM §410. The variation on this in EPR §151Z reads: "Human beings even die as a result of habit." In other English translations of this quotation, it is "killed by Habit."

97. McCarthy, "INS Founding Manifesto (1999)," *Mattering of Matter*, 53.

98. Comay and Ruda, *The Dash*, 25.

99. McCarthy, "INS Founding Manifesto (1999)," 53.

100. McCarthy, *Matter of Mattering*, 53, 252.

101. LPS, 154; ESL §173Z. In this passage, Hegel is contrasting sickness, which is a "simple-negative judgment," with death, which is a "negative-infinite judgment": "in death, as one would say, body and soul separate from one another, i.e. subject and predicate fall completely outside one another."

102. For the term "strange conatus," see Comay, "Resistance and Repetition," 43.

103. Gilles Deleuze, *What Is Philosophy?* trans. Hugh Tomlinson and Graham Burchell (New York: Columbia University Press, 1994), 158.

104. Gilles Deleuze, *Cinema 2: The Time-Image*, trans. Hugh Tomlinson and Robert Galeta (Minneapolis: University of Minnesota Press, 1989), 100.

105. Tom McCarthy, *Empty House of the Stare* (Works from "la Caixa" Collection of Contemporary Art), ed. Lydia Lee and Nimfa Bisbe with Candy Stobbs (London and Barcelona: Whitechapel Gallery and "la Caixa" Collection, 2019), 17–19.

106. PS §545/*Werke* 3, 403.

107. PS §545; PS 1977 §545; Denis Diderot, *Le Neveu de Rameau*, ed. Jean Fabre (Geneva: Droz, 1950), 82. The standard English translation of *Rameau's Nephew* renders "patatras!" as "wallop! down goes the idol." See *Rameau's Nephew and D'Alembert's Dream*, trans. Leonard Tancock (New York: Penguin, 1966), 101. *Rameau's Nephew* plays an important role in Hegel's *Phenomenology* that is not isolated to this specific section. For two texts attentive to *Rameau's Nephew* and its aesthetico-political import, see Giorgio Agamben, "The man of Taste and the Dialectic of the Split," *The Man without Content*, trans. Georgia Albert (Stanford: Stanford University Press, 1999), 13–27; Michael Marder, "Rameau's nephew for the 21st Century," in *Dump Philosophy: A Phenomenology of Devastation* (London: Bloomsbury, 2021), 135–142.

108. PS §545.

109. Rebecca Comay, *Mourning Sickness: Hegel and the French Revolution* (Stanford, CA: Stanford University Press, 2011), 105.

110. Comay, *Mourning Sickness*, 25.

111. PM §410Z.

112. PM §410Z; PN §365Z. Both English translations use the word "seizure" to translate *Begreifen* in the *Philosophy of Nature* and *Bemächtigung* in *Philosophy of Mind*.

113. McCarthy, "Why Ulysses Matters," *Typewriters, Bombs, Jellyfish*, 29.

114. McCarthy, *Empty House of the Stare*, 18.

115. SL, 539.

116. Christoph Menke, "Hegel's Theory of Second Nature: The 'Lapse' of Spirit," in "Normativity and Freedom," special issue, *Symposium* 17, no. 1 (Spring 2013): 42.

CHAPTER 2

1. In reference to the narrator of *Remainder*, N. Katherine Hayles specifically describes a loss of "kinaesthetic fluidity," suggesting that he has also lost empathy, probably owing to damage to mirror neurons. See N. Katherine Hayles, "The Costs of Consciousness: Tom McCarthy's *Remainder* and Peter Watt's *Blindsight*," in *Unthought: The Power of the Cognitive Unconscious* (Chicago: University of Chicago Press, 2017), 89. Hayles's account of *Remainder* resonates with aspects of Malabou's work on destructive plasticity and the "new wounded."

2. Henri Bergson, *Matter and Memory*, trans. N. M. Paul and W. S. Palmer (New York: Zone Books, 1990), 86–87; PP, 98–153.

3. PP, 102–103. As Merleau-Ponty describes it, with kinaesthetic sensation, "I have no need to look for it (my body), it is already with me—I do not need to lead it towards the movement's completion."

4. The term "reparative plasticity" comes from Malabou. See Catherine Malabou, *What Should We Do with Our Brain?*, trans. Sebastian Rand (New York: Fordham University Press, 2008), 25.

5. PM §410Z.

6. John Dewey, *Experience and Nature* (Mineola, NY: Dover, 1958), 281.

7. William James, *Principles of Psychology* (New York: Henry Holt & Company, 1890), 114. These hydraulic metaphors might suggest a blissful unawareness of the chemical and "electrical" nature of neurons and synapses, so crucial to contemporary neuroscience's Hebbian Plasticity, named after the pioneering research of Donald Hebb. Hebb's pithy saying encapsulates his position: "Cells that fire together wire together." On Donald Hebb and neuroplasticity, see Joseph LeDoux, *The Synaptic Self* (New York: Penguin, 2002). On the other hand, as Tristan Garcia has pointed out, the connections between electrical and hydraulic metaphors of intensity are not so inimical. According to Garcia, "apparently there was little difference between what we decided to call 'electrical intensity' and the current of a river." See Tristan Garcia, *The Life Intense: A Modern Obsession* (Edinburgh: Edinburgh University Press, 2018), 24–25.

8. Charles Darwin, *The Works of Charles Darwin:Vol.16: On the Origin of Species*, 1876, ed. Paul H. Barrett and R. B. Freeman (London: Routledge, 1992), 150.

9. PP, 142.

10. PM §410Z/*Werke* 10 §410Z. Th example Hegel uses here is learning to write and its accomplishment as an activity that has become a habit.

11. LPS, 154, 157/VPG, 126, 129.

12. Ann Graybiel, "The Neural Architecture Underlining Habit Learning: An Evolving View," accessed May 20, 2022, https://studyres.com/doc/6338040/the-neural-architecture-underlying-habit-learning--an-evo, 8. Cognitive psychologist George Miller introduced the term "chunking" in a well-known 1956 paper. Like *Remainder*, Miller's paper is preoccupied with numbers, grouping bits of information, sequences of acts in short-term memory, and motor learning. Remarkably, despite all the advances in the understanding of neuroplasticity, the basic structure for discussing habit formation has remained firmly couched in the language of cut and continuity. For instance, a recent article on chunking in the journal *Neuron* discusses motor chunking as a rhythm consisting of two parts. First, the "parsing process" is more involved in the learning phase when actions are broken down into discrete sequences. Second, the "concatenation process" consists of the inculcation of a habit, marked by automaticity, speed, dexterity, abbreviation, and fluidity. See Nicholas F. Wymbs, Danielle S. Bassett, Peter J. Mucha, Mason A. Porter, and Scott T. Grafton, "Differential Recruitment of the Sensorimotor Putamen and Frontoparietal Cortex During Motor Chunking in Humans," *Neuron* 74, no. 5 (June 2012), 936–946. *Remainder*'s emphasis on the "mechanical" and "numerical" account of steps, stages, parts, and units in habit formation are also qualities that Hegel explicitly relates to the understanding (*Verstand*) as opposed to reason (*Vernunft*). For instance, see *Hegel*, PN §345Z: "Numerical determinations, [are] also characteristic of the understanding," or SL, 540: "We have already shown that number is a form unsuited to conceptual determinations." For Hegel, the number, with the unit as its principle, turns what is being counted into totally separate units indifferent to each other. Interestingly, Hegel claims that "higher mathematics," which deals with the infinite, "falls back on *pictorial representation*," SL, 544–545.

13. Hayles, "The Costs of Consciousness," 96.

14. See Tom McCarthy, "Toke My Asymptote—or, the Ecstatic Agony of Appearance," *Diaphanes*, Special Issue on Authenticity and Feedback, vols. 8–9 (Winter 2019/2020): 27.

15. Andreja Novakovic, *Hegel on Second Nature in Ethical Life* (Cambridge: Cambridge University Press, 2017), 35. On the "habit of gliding across the keyboard," see Gaston Bachelard, *Intuition of the Instant*, trans. Eileen Rizo-Patron (Evanston, IL: Northwestern University Press, 2013), 38. Merleau-Ponty refers to an organist, not a pianist. See PP, 145: the organist "settles into the organ as one settles into a house."

16. PM §410/*Werke* 10 §410. Notice the translation of fluidity as ease.

17. Petry, Hegel's *Philosophy of Subjective Spirit*, vol. 2, §410/*Werke* 10 §410.

18. LPS, 157/VPG, 129.

19. LPS, 153.

20. PS §33/*Werke* 3, 37. A.V. Miller's translation of this passage is "to bring fixed thoughts into a fluid state." See PS 1977 §33. Adorno captures this dialectic well, noting that "contradiction itself—the contradiction between the fixed concept and the concept in motion—becomes the agent of philosophizing." See Theodor Adorno, "The Experiential Content of Hegel's Philosophy," in *Hegel: Three Studies*, trans. Shierry Weber Nicholsen (Cambridge, MA: MIT Press, 1993), 70. Remaining stuck within the realm of the fixed concept is what Hegel calls "picture-thinking" (*vorstellendes Denken*). This phrase, in turn, is another feature of understanding (*Verstand*) as opposed to reason (*Vernunft*), as it remains mired in the sundering, dividing, and abstraction of the accumulation of parts and shapes rather than seeing their dialectical/circular inner-connectedness and their "plastic exposition."

21. PS §2. Hegel repeats this sentiment in PN §250Z.

22. PN §371/*Werke* 9 §371. This is stated much more directly in the following section, §372Z: "We have seen that the Notion of disease is that the organism separates itself into its separate moments." In disease the organism becomes a "fixed self" and "a single determinateness ... takes possession of the whole organism."

23. EPR §278/*Werke* 7 §278. See also EPR §286, which reiterates §278.

24. LPS, 156/VPG, 128.

25. LPS, 156/VPG, 128–129.

26. PM §410Z/*Werke* 10 §410Z. The phrase "being-at-home-with-oneself" is repeated throughout Hegel's writings. It serves to articulate a balance between particularity and universality involving a "reflecting" or "turning back" that speculatively incorporates externality, division, and contradiction. In German, it is rendered through a variable set of words, terms, and sentences. These are thoroughly accounted for by Robert Williams in a footnote accompanying his translation of the *Lectures on the Philosophy of Spirit*. See LPS, 143n233.

27. For instance, see LPS, 141: "I obtain the totality through overcoming the particularity. I make that particular ideal, and I am at home with myself (*qua* totality)."

28. PM §410Z, §410. The word "mechanism" here is meant to indicate that the immediacy of self-feeling is overcome through a mediated immediacy self-posited by habit that *breaks* or *breaches* with our immersion in self-feeling so that we are neither distinguished from our particulars and determinations nor absorbed in them; we move in them without consciousness. It is a "second nature"—or as William James aptly calls it, a "secondary automaticity"—because now it is an "immediacy created by the soul, impressing and moulding the corporeality."

29. On the quotations from Hegel, see PM §409, §409Z, §410, §410Z; LPS, 153. Berthold-Bond, in *Hegel's Theory of Madness* (Albany: SUNY Press, 1995), translates *Verrücktheit* as "madness," as do many others. Furlotte prefers to render *Verrücktheit* as "derangement": "We believe there is something fundamentally correct in Petry's choice of 'derangement' for *Verrücktheit*, because it denotes the radical *disruption* of an established order that is crucial to Hegel's account of acute psychopathology. This nuance is entirely lost, for instance, in Berthold-Bond's repeated use of 'madness' in his *Hegel's Theory of Madness*." See Wes Furlotte, *The Problem of Nature in Hegel's Final System* (Edinburgh: Edinburgh University Press,

2018), 105n11. Berthold-Bond made one of the first strong and sustained cases for Hegel's anthropology as prefiguring many of Freud's insights about the unconscious and the drives and even to particular terms such as "fixation." Kirill Chepurin suggests the word "displacement" as another inflection of *Verrücktheit*. See Kirill Chepurin, "Subjectivity, Madness and Habit: Forms of Resistance in Hegel's Anthropology," in *Hegel and Resistance: History, Politics, and Dialectics*, ed. Rebecca Comay and Bart Zantvoort (London: Bloomsbury Academic, 2018), 109. In a key passage on the beautiful soul in the *Phenomenology of Spirit*, Miller translates *Verrüktheit* as "*disordered* to the point of madness." See PS 1977 §668. Pinkard translates the same passage as "*shattered* into madness." See PS §668.

30. John McCumber, "Hegel on Habit," *Owl of Minerva* 21, no. 2 (1990): 158.

31. PM §410Z.

32. Alain, *Idées*, Champs essais (Paris: Éditions Flammarion, 1983), 200. This passage has been quoted in many discussions of habit since it was cited by Malabou. See Catherine Malabou, *The Future of Hegel: Plasticity, Temporality, and Dialectic*, trans. Lisabeth During (London: Routledge, 2005), 36.

33. Michael Ondaatje, "Her House," *The Cinnamon Peeler: Selected Poems* (New York: Vintage, 1997), 153. This connection between inhabit and habit, *bewohnen* and *Gewohnheit*, is a strong feature of philosophical accounts of habit—Merleau-Ponty and Bachelard come to mind here. This poem is also an instance of "how gendered and raced habits are not merely phenomenologically and psychoanalytically, but also biologically embodied," in ways that map and sync the internal with the external, bodies with environments, inhabitation with domesticity. See Shannon Sullivan, "Oppressions in the Gut: The Biological Dimensions of Deweyan Habit," in *A History of Habit: From Aristotle to Bourdieu*, ed. Tom Sparrow and Adam Hutchinson (New York: Lexington Books, 2013), 256–257.

34. PM §408Z/*Werke* 10 §408Z. This term is translated as "sinking-into-self" or "self-sunkenness." Hegel often uses the verb/adverb *versenkt*, in both negative and positive terms, which is translated as "absorbed," "sunken," or "immersed." See, for example, PS §58/*Werke* 3, 56; ESL §34/*Werke* 8 §34. This Hegelian sense of absorption can render a much different sense of that word than we are used to in discussions of habit.

35. Vilém Flusser, "Taking up Residence in Homelessness," *Vilém Flusser: Writings*, ed. Andreas Strohl, trans. Erik Eisel (Minneapolis: University of Minnesota Press, 2002), 100–101. Also see "Habit: The True Aesthetic Criterion," in the same edited volume (51–57).

36. PN §337Z.

37. "Translator's Preface," EPR, xliii.

38. The narrator's getting caught or snagged on the corner of the kitchen counter is reminiscent of Hamacher's account of nausea and the impulse to vomit (*Ekel*) in Hegel. There, the word is recognized as being part of an etymological family of the word *Eg* or *Eck*, signifying "corner" or "edge." For Hamacher, these connections relate to the pressing and stabbing sensation experienced in the stomach during nausea. Needless to say, nausea typically results in retching or vomiting rather than digesting, incorporating, or smoothing over. See Werner Hamacher, *Pleroma—Reading in Hegel*, trans. Nicholas Walker and Simon Jarvis (Stanford, CA: Stanford University Press, 1998), 248–249.

39. Tom Sparrow, *Plastic Bodies: Rebuilding Sensation After Phenomenology* (London: Open Humanities Press, 2015), 208. In this passage, Sparrow is drawing on and extending Alfonso Lingis's work on sensation and imperatives. PP, 143.

40. "For it can *literally* (*à la lettre*) be said that something is not in its place only of what can change places—that is, of the symbolic. For the real, whatever upheaval we subject it

to, is always and in every case in its place; it carries its place stuck to the sole of its shoe, there being nothing that can exile it from it." Jacques Lacan, "Seminar on the Purloined Letter," *Écrits*, trans. Bruce Fink (New York: W. W. Norton, 2002), 17. McCarthy specifically refers to this well-known passage from Lacan in "Get Real, or What Jellyfish Have to Tell Us About Literature," *Typewriters, Bombs, Jellyfish: Essays* (New York: New York Review of Books, 2017), 69.

41. PS 1977 §589/*Werke* 3, 436. Pinkard translates this as "fury of disappearing." PS §589.

42. This "cog-wheel rigidity" is one of the autonomic symptoms of trauma that the narrator manifests later in the novel, intensified by his reenactment "addiction." It is also a common manifestation in Parkinson's disease.

43. For a further elaboration of McCarthy's discussion of bullfighting, the bull, and stigmatization drawing on Michel Leiris's essay "Literature Considered as a Bullfight," see McCarthy, "Get Real, or What Jellyfish Have to Tell Us About Literature," *Typewriters, Bombs, Jellyfish*, 67–69. On the etymology of stigma, derived from the verb *stizein*, see Peter Szendy, *Of Stigmatology: Punctuation as Experience*, trans. Jan Plug (New York: Fordham University Press, 2018), 4.

44. PN §371Z

45. PN §354Z/*Werke* 9 §354Z: "blood-globules (*Blutkügelchen*) only appear when blood is dead, when it is exposed to the atmosphere." This viscous, sluggish, and globular blood is evident throughout the film, and it shares traits with a myriad of other sticky substances that sediment and stain.

46. See PN §354–§365. See PS §162 on the "universal bloodstream." Also see Werner Hamacher's account of blood in Hegel, as related to digestion and respiration in *Pleroma—Reading in Hegel*, 244–248.

47. I shall return in depth to this per-severing hand—which is always a "second-hand" in *Remainder*—in chapter 3.

48. PS §658.

49. McCarthy's main reference here is to Derrida's article on Francis Ponge, which he links to other thinkers and writers whom he sees as attentive to unsublatable matter (Joyce, Stevens, Melville, Bataille, Carroll, etc.). See McCarthy, *Typewriters, Bombs, Jellyfish*, 31–36, 70–76. For the direct references to Hegel and blotting up matter in concepts, see Tom McCarthy and Simon Critchley, "Joint Statement on Inauthenticity," in *The Mattering of Matter: Documents from the Archive of the International Necronautical Society*, Tom McCarthy, Simon Critchley, et al. (Berlin: Sternberg Press, 2012), 64–66, 141–144, 157, 223–226.

50. PN §298A. Some of the characteristics of the sponge also echo Hegel's account of the polyp, which he specifically describes in one-sided topological terms, as it disrupts given notions of inside and outside. See PN §365Z. For two passages in *Remainder* that explore matter as "full of tiny pores," holes and cracks, that resonate with Hegel's account, see Rem, 278, 294.

51. McCarthy's consistent references to sponges and jellyfishes signify a writerly way of being conducive to the materiality and permeability of an uncontainable kind of writing that spills and stains (Jean-Luc Nancy might characterize it in terms of "exscription" that is characterized as "spilled sense."). Like a psychoanalyst practicing evenly suspended attention, attuned to the senseless matter of *lalangue* at the heart of *la langue*, McCarthy lets matter, sounds, words, and phrases spill through him and stain the already pulpy matter of the page.

52. Jonathan Cole, *Pride and a Daily Marathon* (Cambridge, MA: MIT Press, 1995), 62, 185n4. This is a term used by the neuropsychologist Alexander Luria following Henry Head.

53. Here I am twisting Donald Phillip Verene's notion of a "vacuous actuality." Verene uses that term to refer to the substance that has not become subject. I am using the term "evacuating actuality" to account for the kenotic spilling over effected in *Remainder*. See Donald Phillip Verene, *Hegel's Recollection: A Study of Images in the Phenomenology of Spirit* (Albany: SUNY Press, 1985), 113. To return to the previous chapter, this drilling also pertains to the senseless signifiers that are generated at the level of the sentence and grammatical marks in *Remainder* through acts of writing that resonate with psychoanalytic techniques of evenly suspended attention and scanding.

54. Given the nature of this scene, with its overturned cup, it is worth recalling that Lacan equates anamorphosis to an eye as a kind of bowl that overflows with excesses of the gaze that are beyond any specular defense mechanisms that would "tame" it. See Jacques Lacan, "Anamorphosis," *The Seminar of Jacques Lacan Book XI: The Four Fundamental Concepts of Psychoanalysis*, ed. Jacques-Alain Miller, trans. Alan Sheridan (New York: W. W. Norton, 1998), 89. The "underside" in this scene also invokes Lacan's claim that that "the gaze is that underside of consciousness" (83).

55. PN §354Z. Ultimately, for Hegel, mechanism is about exteriority. See SL, 631: "This is what constitutes the character of *mechanism*, namely, that whatever the connection that obtains between the things combined, the connection remains one that is *alien* to them, that does not affect their nature, and even when a reflective semblance of unity is associated with it, the connection remains nothing more than *composition*, *mixture*, *aggregate*, etc." Hegel's definition of habit as the "mechanism of self-feeling" indicates not only that habit is a second nature and, thus, automatic—it also indicates that habit is always shot through with an intractable exteriority. This is made clear in a passage that almost immediately follows the quote I cite above from SL, 631: "*Spiritual* mechanism, like its *material* counterpart, also consists in the things connected in the spirit remaining external to one another and to spirit. A *mechanical mode of representation, a mechanical memory, a habit, a mechanical mode of acting*, mean that the pervasive presence that is proper to spirit is lacking in what spirt grasps or does."

56. PN §354Z. The blood's "endless process of division and this suppression of division, which leads to another division, is an expression of the Notion in its self-moving movement and its mediation of immediacy." Also see PS §162: "This simple infinity, or the absolute concept, is to be called the simple essence of life, the soul of the world, the universal bloodstream, which is omnipresent, neither dulled nor interrupted by any difference, which is instead itself both every difference as well as their sublatedness."

57. LPS, 105; PN §362Z.

58. SA, 327. The issue of (im)possible breathing is more pressing than ever in regard to issues of racialized violence and capitalism, biopolitical conditions of the COVID pandemic, and ecological injustice. See Achille Mdembe, "The Universal Right to Breathe," trans. Carolyn Shread, *Critical Inquiry* 47, no. 52 (Winter 2021), https://www.journals.uchicago.edu/doi/full/10.1086/711437; and Athena Athenasiou, "(Im)possible Breathing: On Courage and Criticality in the Ghostly Present," *Redescriptions: Political Thought, Conceptual History and Feminist Theory* 23, no. 2 (2020): 92–106.

59. Here, we should pay attention to what Lacan calls the "*pulsative* function" of the unconscious that is gapped through an on-off rhythm of appearance and disappearance, fading, and cutting out. See, for example, Lacan, *Book XI: The Four Fundamental Concepts of Psychoanalysis*, 43.

60. Wes Furlotte's account of habit tends to emphasize its claim to cure the deranged body of self-feeling *and* to highlight that nothing guarantees it will accomplish that task. As a result, Furlotte notes that it is a "perpetual possibility" that habit is prone to "regress" or "relapse" back into the diseased states in which the body and the mind are mired in nature and the drives. Much less attention is paid to a more robust and insistent account of the odd materiality that habit constantly generates and which, in turn, creates perpetual, persistent, persevering, and quotidian disturbances and autoperturbations of the body. See Furlotte, *Problem of Nature*, 149. Although at times Adrian Johnson also uses the language of "proneness" and "regression," his account of habit's "second-nature" and its elaborations of weak "first-nature" is more attentive to the generative, ongoing, and constitutive everyday realm of the autoperturbations in habit. See Adrian Johnston, "The Weakness of Nature: Hegel, Freud, Lacan, and Negativity Materialized," in *Hegel and the Infinite: Religion, Politics, and Dialectics*, ed. Slavoj Žižek, Clayton Crockett, and Creston Davis (New York: Columbia University Press, 2011), 169–170. The phrase "weakness of nature" is derived from Hegel's *die Ohnmacht der Natur*. See *Werke* 9 §250, §250A /PN §250, §250A. Miller translates *Ohnmacht* as "impotence." Comay and Ruda translate it as "malfunction." See Rebecca Comay and Frank Ruda, *The Dash—The Other Side of Absolute Knowing* (Cambridge, MA: MIT Press, 2018), 24–25.

61. LPS, 154.

62. LPS, 153–154.

63. PN §250Z: "The *immediately* concrete thing is a group of properties external to one another and more or less indifferently related to each other." PM §410.

64. SL, 17/*Werke* 5, 27.

65. Elisa Magri, "The Place of Habit in Hegel's Psychology," in *Hegel's Philosophical Psychology*, ed. Susanne Herrmann-Sinai and Lucia Ziglioli (London: Routledge, 2016), 75.

66. ESL §154/*Werke* 8 §154.

67. Alain Badiou, *The Century*, trans. Alberto Toscano (London: Polity Press, 2007), 108–109.

68. FN, 291; Leo Bersani, *Thoughts and Things* (Chicago: University of Chicago Press, 2020), 9. Bersani is quoting a line by Galoup in Claire Denis's film *Beau Travail*.

69. LPS, 153; PM §410Z.

70. PM §410Z.

71. Adrian Johnston, *Žižek's Ontology: A Transcendental Materialist Theory of Subjectivity* (Evanston, IL: Northwestern University Press, 2008), 60.

72. LPS, 156.

73. Bachelard, *Intuition of the Instant*, 47.

74. On issues of privilege, hierarchy, heteronormativity, racism, ageism, and ableism embodied in notions of ease, fluidity, and dexterity in habit see Sarah Ahmed, *Willful Subjects* (Durham, NC: Duke University Press, 2014), 147–149, and Jane Dryden, "Hegel's Anthropology: Transforming the Body," in *Hegel's Encyclopedia of the Philosophical Sciences: A Critical Guide*, ed. Sebastian Stein and Joshua Wretzel (Cambridge: Cambridge University Press, 2021), 136–146.

75. PM §410.

76. PP, 144.

77. PP, 138–139.

78. This position perhaps receives its most blunt formulation in Gilbert Ryle's notion of "knowing how" as a "disposition, but not a single-track disposition like a reflex or habit." He goes on to note: "In short he has to innovate, and where he innovates he is not operating from habit. He is not repeating hackneyed moves." The narrator in *Remainder* is obsessively repeating "hackneyed moves." See *The Concept of Mind* (London: Hutchinson's University Library, 1949), 46–47.

79. Maurice Blanchot, *The Infinite Conversation*, trans. Susan Hanson (Minneapolis: University of Minnesota Press, 1992), 308.

80. William James, *Psychology: Briefer Course* (Cambridge, MA: Harvard University Press, 1892), 286; Giorgio Agamben, *Profanations*, trans. Jeff Fort (Princeton, NJ: Princeton University Press), 13. Also see Peter Sloterdijk, *You Must Change Your Life*, trans. Wieland Hoban (London: Polity Press, 2017) for another account of genius in relationship to habit.

81. On extimacy (*extimité*), see Jacques Lacan, *The Seminar of Jacques Lacan Book VII: The Ethics of Psychoanalysis*, ed. Jacques-Alain Miller, trans. Dennis Porter (New York: W. W. Norton, 1997), 171; Jacques-Alain Miller "Extimité," in *Lacanian Theory of Discourse: Subject, Structure, and Society*, ed. M. Bracher, M. W. Alcorn Jr., R. J. Cortell, and F. Massardier-Kenney (New York: New York University Press, 1994), 74–87.

82. Catherine Malabou, "Addiction and Grace: Preface to Félix Ravaisson's *Of Habit*," in Félix Ravaisson, *Of Habit*, trans. Clare Carlisle and Mark Sinclair (London: Continuum, 2008), viii.

83. Charles Sanders Peirce, "A Survey of Pragmatism," *Collected Papers*, ed. Charles Hartshorne and Paul Weiss, vol. 5 (Cambridge, MA: Harvard University Press, 1932–1958), 491. Interestingly, Elisa Magri has offered a solution to this dilemma that echoes Peirce's in an important essay, "The Place of Habit in Hegel's Psychology": "Yet concrete universality can be attained through speculative thought by dialectically reconstructing both the meaning of universality and the logical process in which it is involved." See Elisa Magri, "The Place of Habit in Hegel's Psychology," in *Hegel's Philosophical Psychology*, ed. Susanne Herrmann-Sinai and Lucia Ziglioli (London: Routledge, 2016), 84.

84. PM §396, §396Z.

85. Nathan Ross, *On Mechanism in Hegel's Social and Political Philosophy* (New York: Routledge, 2008), 96.

86. Henri Bergson, *The Creative Mind: An Introduction to Metaphysics*, trans. Mabelle L. Andison (New York: The Citadel Press, 1946), 231–232. Bergson is paraphrasing Ravaisson from *On Habit*. The denigration and fear of automaticity is particularly robust in the French discourse on habit from Ravaisson to Bergson to Merleau-Ponty to Ricoeur. Although there is a recognition in Hegel of the danger of automaticity—and a notion of willing that is never really absent in even the most primary dispositions—there is an import given to automatism and mechanism in Hegel's speculative philosophy that is crucial to its strange tempo, movement, and materiality from his philosophy of nature to Absolute Knowledge.

87. PP, 110, 146. Here Merleau-Ponty is critical of Ravaisson's notion of habit as the fossilized residue of a spiritual activity. See PP, 142.

88. David Farrell Krell, *Contagion: Sexuality, Disease, and Death in German Idealism and Romanticism* (Bloomington: Indiana State University Press, 1998), 148. Although, in this context, Krell is talking about infection, the "feigned immediacy" behind which a complex transformation is in place holds true for magic as well.

89. PM §410Z.

90. PM §410Z; Ravaisson, *Of Habit*, 57. One might put this passage into conversation with Merleau-Ponty's sense of habit as the "motor grasping of a motor significance." See PP, 143.

91. Wendy Hui Kyong Chun notes this emphasis on consciousness in habit change: "Intriguingly, almost all the literature, from the psychological to the philosophical, assumes that consciousness drives habit change and, further, that conflict/crisis drives this consciousness." See Wendy Hui Kyong Chun, *Updating to Remain the Same: Habitual New Media* (Cambridge, MA: MIT Press, 2017), 85.

92. Tom McCarthy, "Interview: Melissa McCarthy, March 30, 2001," *Mattering of Matter*, 107. Paul de Man, "Semiology and Rhetoric," *Allegories of Reading: Figural Language in Rousseau, Nietzsche, Rilke, Proust* (New Haven, CT: Yale University Press, 1979), 11–12. This passage is important to McCarthy's critique of authenticity, and his notions of buffeting and buffering. He elaborates on these ideas using some different texts from de Man and Baudelaire in "Toke My Asymptote—or, the Ecstatic Agony of Appearance," *Diaphanes*, Special Issue on Authenticity and Feedback, vols. 8–9 (Winter 2019/2020): 31.

93. ESL§21, 21Z. Freud raises a similar warning about "mental activities such as thinking something over" and the "sheering off into intellectual discussion" rather than pursuing the "way" of knowing in his discussion of psychoanalytic technique. See SE 7 (1911–1912), "Recommendations to Physicians Practicing Psycho-Analysis (1912)," 119.

94. ESL §10. This thinking over that cleaves apart knowing and understanding from the object's own movements—and the self-satisfaction taken from this kind of explaining away—are forcefully articulated in PS§133, §166.

95. Hayles, "The Costs of Consciousness," 90–91. McCarthy seems to be arguing for something akin to this state, in which consciousness runs ahead of experience creating a "buffering" and "buffeting" condition that is explored in his novels. Both resonate to a degree with Mark Hansen's notion of "feed-forward," in which consciousness is far slower than bodily responses and subperceptual experience, and thus we need to feed-forward that data so that it can be presented post factum to a consciousness that is too slow to grasp it directly. See Mark Hansen, *Feed-Forward: On the Future of Twenty-First-Century Media* (Chicago: Chicago University Press, 2014). In relation to Hansen's notion of feed-forward, I have benefited from reading Michael Haworth's *Neurotechnology and the End of Finitude* (Minneapolis: University of Minnesota Press, 2018), 97–98.

96. PS §32. The issue of *Verstand* is raised throughout Hegel's writings, and I call attention to many of these instances in what follows.

97. Here, I am using Pahl's translation of PS §32/*Werke* §32. See *Tropes of Transport: Hegel and Emotion* (Evanston, IL: Northwestern University Press, 2012), 191-192. Pinkard's translation is slightly different: "The activity of separating [*Die Tätigkeit des Scheidens*] is the force and labor of the *understanding*, the most astonishing and greatest of all the powers, or rather, which is the absolute power."

98. See, for example, "Preface to the First Edition," SL, 10: "The *understanding determines*, and holds the determinations fixed. *Reason* is negative and *dialectical*, since it dissolves the determinations of the understanding into nothing; it is *positive*, since it generates the *universal*, and comprehends the particular therein." See also ESL: "Reason's battle consists in overcoming what the understanding has rendered rigid" (§32); the speculative "is explicitly what contains those oppositions at which the understanding stops short … and contains them as something sublated within itself and precisely by this means proves itself to be concrete and a totality" (§82).

99. Hegel consistently characterizes understanding by its "abstraction," "one-sidedness," "rigidity," "fixity," and isolating tendencies. See, for instance, "Preface to the Second Edition," ESL, 11. In contrast to the understanding, reason is the capacity to turn all external, impassible finite "limits" into interior "borders" that have already been crossed. On the issue of "limit" and "border" in relation to understanding and reason, see Mladen Dolar, "Voice and Topology: The Tiny Lag," in *New Conceptions of Geometry and Space in Freud and Lacan*, ed. Michael Friedman and Samo Tomsic (Bielefeld: transcript Verlag, 2016), 68.

100. Ross, *On Mechanism in Hegel's Social and Political Philosophy*, 67. Since, throughout Hegel's speculative philosophy, mechanism stands for "exteriority," it is always linked to *Verstand* in its resistance to mediation, interiorization, vitality, and life. Similar statements to Ross's can be found in other accounts of *Verstand*'s relationship to *Vernunft* in Hegel. For instance, see Karin de Boer, *Thinking in the Light of Time: Heidegger's Encounter With Hegel* (Albany: SUNY Press, 2000), 223: "[Hegel] proposes that precisely when the fixating, discursive understanding gets *stuck*, space opens up for the speculative reason to understand the concepts that were fixated by the understanding as independent entities, as subordinate moments of a single movement." This "stuckness" is a major feature in the writings on Hegel by Žižek, Dolar, Ruda, Johnston, and Comay.

101. SL, 540.

102. ESL §24/*Werke* 8 §24.

103. PS 1977 §32.

104. Pahl's sections on the *Verstand* in *Tropes of Transport* are illuminating in terms of its mortifying dimensions.

105. PS 1977 §32.

106. Comay and Ruda, *The Dash*, 81: "In this light, we should also reconsider the infamous hyphen in *Er-innerung* [*The Phenomenology of Spirit*, §808]. Even while graphically emphasizing the intensification of interiority, the mark registers a split within the self-remembering self. The hyphen negates the inwardness it simultaneously underscores."

107. PN §365Z: "Understanding will always hold to the mediations as such, regarding them as external relationships mechanical and chemical in nature; but they are nonetheless subordinate in comparison with free vitality and self-feeling. The understanding pretends to know more than speculative philosophy and loftily looks down on it, but it remains confined within the sphere of finite mediation, and vitality as such is beyond its grasp." Also see PN §337Z for a similar statement about understanding's inability to do justice to the unity of life, a point repeated again in ESL §216, §216Z.

108. PN §365Z

109. PP, 153.

110. PS §20, §538. On the latter passage, see Pahl, *Tropes of Transport*, 182, 186, 195. This breaking of bones continues all the way through the *Phenomenology*. In the first section (§1) of the preface, understanding is likened to an anatomist, which is reiterated slightly differently later on (§51). Next, in the "Phrenology" section, the account of "observing reason" contains the Infinite Judgement "The *being of spirit is a bone*" (§343). Finally, in the passage just cited (§538), and in "Absolute Knowing (§808)," where the term "skull place" (*Schädelstätte*) is translated as "Golgotha" by Pinkard, i.e., "the Golgotha of Absolute Spirit," in a passage that appears right before Hegel's rewording of Schiller's poem "Friendship" that ends the *Phenomenology*. On this *Schädelstätte*, see Pahl, "Hegel's Tears," in *Tropes of Transport*, 85–90. Comay also discusses Schiller's poem at length in *The Dash*, 65–85.

111. Andrew Cole's *The Birth of Theory* features a brief but interesting section about habit in relation to Heidegger's distinction between "ready-to-hand" and "present-at-hand" that resonates with *Remainder*. The latter demands that we *attend* to an object *qua* object or a "tool as a tool," which is constructed in a certain way, which must be mentally disassembled before any actual disassembly takes place before repair" (63). But it is clear that the narrator in *Remainder* is not really interested in "repairing" anything in any standard sense of making something functional again. See Andrew Cole, *The Birth of Theory* (Chicago: University of Chicago Press, 2014), 63.

112. Johnston, *Žižek's Ontology*, 60.

113. LPS, 154.

114. See, for example, Žižek, *Less Than Nothing: Hegel and the Shadow of Dialecticcal Materialism* (London: Verso, 2013), 496.

115. PP, 144.

116. Panofsky clearly emphasizes that it was not the notional or theological *content* of scholastic thought that was shared by architecture and scholastic philosophy. Rather, its *modus operandi*, its "way of operating," resulted in analogous approaches to thinking and acting in both domains. See Erwin Panofsky, *Gothic Architecture and Scholasticism* (*Wimmer Lecture*, 1948) (Latrobe, PA: The Archabbey Press, 1951).

117. SL, 751.

118. PS 1977 §32/*Werke* 3, 36. See, for example, Georges Bataille, "Hegel, Death and Sacrifice," in *The Bataille Reader*, ed. Fred Botting and Scot Wilson (London: Blackwell Publishing, 1977), 294n5.

119. Tom McCarthy, *Recessional—Or, the Time of the Hammer*, ed. Elisabeth Bronfen (Zurich/Berlin: Diaphenes, 2016), 64.

120. G. W. F Hegel. *Lectures on the Philosophy of World History: Introduction*, trans. H. B. Nisbet (Cambridge: Cambridge University Press, 1975), 89. For other references to the cunning of reason, see EPR §344, §348; SL, 662–669; ESL §25; *Hegel and the Human Spirit: A Translation of the Jena Lectures on the Philosophy of Spirit* (*1805–6*) *with Commentary* by Leo Rauch (Detroit: Wayne State University Press, 1983), 103–104. As Adorno well noted, cunning permeates Hegel's philosophy as a whole.

121. EPR §344, §348.

122. On the roots of cunning in classical mechanics and the lever principle—directly related to habit, repetition and anthropotechnics—see Sloterdijk, *You Must Change Your Life*, 199; Sloterdijk, "The Other Logos, or the Reason of Cunning: On the Intellectual History of the Indirect," *What Happened in the 20th Century: Towards a Critique of Extremist Reason*, trans. Christopher Turner (London: Polity Press, 2018), 187–212. Habit is one of the primary instances of what Jean-Luc Nancy has called the "mechanics always at work in speculation," in which the movement of spirit is always subjected to the "lever" and "leverage" of mechanical repetition. See Jean-Luc Nancy, *The Speculative Remark* (*One of Hegel's Bons Mots*), trans. Céline Surprenant (Stanford, CA: Stanford University Press, 2001), 70.

123. *Hegel and the Human Spirit*, 103.

124. Hegel specifically notes that the cunning of reason consists in the activity of mediating. See ESL §209Z.

125. ESL §80; SL, 539.

126. I do not have enough time to go into how octopi think and act, but simply put they are not characterized by a central intelligence focused in the brain. Rather, their nervous system is spread throughout the body, mostly in the arms that act relatively independently. See, for example, Peter Godfrey-Smith, *Other Minds: The Octopus and the Evolution of Intelligent Life* (London: Williams Collins, 2017). Of course, these arms always seem to get their "wires crossed" in the novel.

127. PM §405Z: "a magical power is one whose action is not determined by the interconnection, the conditions and mediations of objective relations." The actual section on animal magnetism begins on PM §406.

128. PM §405Z, §410Z.

129. Hayles, "The Costs of Consciousness," 89–90. Again, there is ample evidence for such an interpretation as Naz is described in the novel as being completely onside and involved as the narrator, but for entirely different reasons, as well as an addict, like the narrator, although addicted to a different drug. See Rem, 234, 264.

130. Mikkel Borch-Jacobsen, "The Sorcerer and his Magic," *Lacan: The Absolute Master*, 157–167; PM §410: "The soul's making itself an abstract universal being … is habit."

131. Hayles, "The Costs of Consciousness," 89–90.

132. Ravaisson, *Of Habit*, 63.

133. PM §410, §410Z. Malabou reiterates this point. See *Future of Hegel*, 37. The issue of habit embodying the unity of subject and predicate is clear in LPS, 154; PM §410, §410Z.

134. Habit always remains stuck circulating arounds its status as a judgment, which is always a form of partition and division—not to mention disruption—that is well-captured by the German word for judgment, *Urteil*, which Hegel understands as *Ur-teil*, an "originitive division." See SL, 552 and ESL §166: "The *judgment* is the concept in its particularity." On the issue of judgment in relationship to the speculative sentence, see Pahl, *Tropes of Transport*, 104; Angelica Nuzzo, *Approaching Hegel's Logic, Obliquely: Melville, Molière, Beckett* (Albany: SUNY Press, 2018), and Daniel Heller-Roazen, "Collapsing Sentences," in *No One's Ways: An Essay on Infinite Naming* (New York: Zone Books, 2017), 172–173.

135. LPS, 156, 157/VPG, 128–129; SL, 347/*Werke* 6, 25–26. *Entzweiung* can be more literally translated as "two-ness" or "duality."

136. ESL §173; PS §346.

137. For some accounts of the infinite judgment, see Heller-Roazen, "Collapsing Sentences," 167–191; Pahl, *Tropes of Transport*, 110–111, 118–119, 194–199; Johnston, *Žižek's Ontology*, 229–234; Slavoj Žižek, *The Sublime Object of Ideology* (London: Verso, 1989), 206–209; Slavoj Žižek, *Absolute Recoil: Towards a New Foundation of Dialectical Materialism* (London: Verso, 2014), 32–33; Mladen Dolar, "The Phrenology of Spirit," in *Supposing the Subject*, ed. Joan Copjec (New York: Verso, 1994), 64–83.

138. See, for example, ESL §173, SL, 567, PS §340.

139. ESL §173; SL, 567: "It ought to be a *judgment*, and hence contains a connection of subject and predicate; but any such connection should ought not *at the same time to be* there." Mladen Dolar's classic essay, "The Phrenology of Spirit," takes up the unyielding and extreme logic of the infinite judgment that manifests itself not only in the obvious and explicit instances it is named, but also permeates Hegel's speculative philosophy as a whole. See "The Phrenology of Spirit," 64–83. This extension of the logic of the infinite judgment into other realms of nonrelation and post-Hegelian materialism are pursued in his more recent essays, such as "Hegel and Freud," *e-flux Journal*, no. 34 (April 2012): 1–14.

140. PS §343.

141. ESL §80Z. This notion is repeated three times in PS §340. For example: "this last stage of observing reason is its very worst, and for that reason its complete reversal is necessary."

142. See Žižek, *Absolute Recoil*, 32; *Less Than Nothing*, 483.

143. ESL §22.

144. PS §790, §791.

145. Ravaisson, *Of Habit*, 63.

146. FN, 297.

147. FN, 297, 299–300.

148. SA, 236–237: "Freud tells us—*anatomy is destiny*. … It becomes true if we give anatomy its strict, and if I may, etymological meaning that emphasizes *ana-tomy*, the function of the cut."

149. PS §340. At this point, Hegel notes, if spirit does not reflect itself from this moment of extreme contradiction, "the mediating middle where it stands is the unsanctified void." In using the word "explosion," I am referring to Adorno's claim that the pervading logic of Hegel's notion of mediation is "a kind of permanent explosion ignited by the contact of extremes." See Adorno, "The Experiential Content of Hegel's Philosophy," *Hegel: Three Studies*, 82.

CHAPTER 3

1. See PS 1977 §80; PS §80/*Werke* 3, 74. Miller translates *unaufhaltsam* as "unhalting," while Pinkard renders it as "unrelenting." The resonances between *halten*-derived terms are a feature of Hegel's philosophy, as it speculatively accounts for the relationship between fixity and fluidity, i.e., unhalting movement or progress (*unaufhaltsam*), impeded (*aufgehalten*), held or held up (*gehalten*), holding together (*Zusammenhalt*), holding fast (*festhält*), and comportment/carriage/posture (*Haltung*).

2. Bruno Latour, *An Inquiry into Modes of Existence: An Anthropology of the Moderns*, trans. Catherine Porter (Cambridge, MA: Harvard University Press, 2013), 270.

3. Catherine Malabou, *The New Wounded: From Neurosis to Brain Damage*, trans. Steven Miller (New York: Fordham University Press, 2012), 48.

4. Giorgio Agamben, *The Time That Remains: A Commentary on the Letter to Romans*, trans. Patricia Dailey (Stanford: Stanford University Press, 2005), 40. Ricoeur also notes the "bent of habit drifting towards waste activity." See FN, 291.

5. Adrian Johnston, *Adventures in Transcendental Materialism: Dialogues with Contemporary Thinkers* (Edinburgh: Edinburgh University Press, 2014), 274–294.

6. Malabou, *The New Wounded*, 5, 214.

7. PP, 130. Merleau-Ponty specifies that the notion of "sediment" in relation to bodily habit is not to be taken in the sense of an "inert mass." He further argues that there may be a drift towards inertia, but that in the movement of habit proper there is a dialectical balance between "sedimentation" and "spontaneity" that is definitive of our "world-structure."

8. See Tom McCarthy, "Toke My Asymptote—or, the Ecstatic Agony of Appearance," *Diaphanes*, Special Issue on Authenticity and Feedback, vols. 8–9 (Winter 2019/2020), 27–32, where he tracks his interest in cybernetics and "feedback loops" from literature to Norbert

Weiner to Lacan. Much of his language about the impossibility of immediacy, hyperactive feedback loops, and relentless remediation resonates with my account of Hegel and habit.

9. On "meaningless sound," see PS §23/*Werke* 3, 26. On "murmuring" and "water," see PN §300A/*Werke* 9 §300A: "Water, being without cohesion, makes no sound, and its movement, as merely *external* friction of its freely displaceable parts, yields only a murmuring sound (*Rauschen*)."

10. On "swallowing a mouthful of water," see PS§590. On the issue of language and vanishing into air as its mode of persisting and universalizing itself, see PS§507.

11. Brian Robertson, *Lacanian Antiphilosophy and the Problem of Anxiety: An Uncanny Little Object* (New York: Palgrave Macmillan, 2015), 205. For the voice as a stain and a "left-over" of the signifying process and "stuck words" that are endlessly replayed in the "topology of saying," see Mladen Dolar, "Voice and Topology: The Tiny Lag" in *Psychoanalysis: Topological Perspectives (New Conceptions of Geometry and Space in Freud and Lacan*, ed. Michael Friedman and Samo Tomšič (Blelefeld: transcript Verlag, 2016), 73–74, 80, 91.

12. PS §39: "truth is not a stamped coin issued directly from the mint and ready for one's pocket ... it is not truth in the sense that would just discard inequality, like discarding the slag from pure metal." See also Jacques Lacan, "The Function and Field of Speech and Language in Psychoanalysis," Écrits, trans. Bruce Fink (New York: W. W. Norton, 2002), 209: "Indeed, however, empty his discourse may seem, it is so only if taken at face value—the value that justifies Mallarmé's remark, in which he compares the common use of language to the exchange of a coin, whose obverse and reverse no longer bear but eroded faces, and which people pass from hand to hand 'in silence.' This metaphor suffices to remind us that speech, even when almost completely worn out, retains its value as a *tessera*."

13. Tom McCarthy, "Why *Ulysses* Matters," *Typewriters, Bombs, Jellyfish: Essays* (New York: New York Review of Books, 2017), 27, 33.

14. N. Katherine Hayles, "The Costs of Consciousness: Tom McCarthy's *Remainder* and Peter Watts's *Blindsight*," in *Unthought: The Power of the Cognitive Unconscious* (Chicago: University of Chicago Press, 2017), 86–96.

15. One finds the following striking passage in the "Preface: On Stigmatexts by Hélène Cixous," in Hélène Cixous, *Stigmata: Escaping Texts*, trans. Eric Prenowitz (New York: Routledge, 1998), n.p.: "The person who is properly or figuratively stigmatized has traits of the saint (Saint Francis of Assisi) and the outlaw, of the martyr and the condemned."

16. PS §693/*Werke* 3, 509, and PS §725.

17. On "buffeting," see Rebecca Comay, "Afterword: Antinomies of Resistance," in *Hegel and Resistance: History, Politics and Dialectics*, ed. Rebecca Comay and Bart Zantvoort (London: Bloomsbury Academic, 2018), 195–200. On "buffeting" from a Deleuzian perspective, see Brian Massumi, *The Power at the End of the Economy* (Durham: Duke University Press, 2005), 9. In McCarthy's subsequent novel, *Satin Island*, "buffeting" is pursued more in terms of "buffering," a perpetual lag in which information is never quite equated with its absorption in experience. This logic of buffering is also in play in *Remainder* in regard to information-overload, noise, feedback loops, temporal lag, trance-like states, and narrative breakdown. See McCarthy's comments on buffering in *Recessional—Or, the Time of the Hammer*, ed. Elisabeth Bronfen (Zurich/Berlin: Diaphenes, 2016), 35–36, 52–53. Also see chapter 2, n. 92.

18. See Jacques Rancière, "Divided Beauty (Dresden, 1764)," *Aisthesis: Scenes from the Aesthetic Regime of Art*, trans. Zakir Paul (London: Verso, 2013), 1–20. Ruda offers some interesting comments concerning "air" and "wind" in his chapter on habit in *Hegel's Rabble*. See

"The Lost Habit: Elements to a Hegelian Theory of Laziness/Foulness," in *Hegel's Rabble: An Investigation into Hegel's Philosophy of Right* (London: Bloomsbury, 2011), 85–87. I would argue that habit's intransitive transitivity, paralyzed unrest, and mobilized inertia cannot be equated with an aesthetics of standstill and stagnation, although both those terms are used by Hegel. For examples of the term "standstill" (*stehenbleiben*), see PS §795/*Werke* 3, 580; PM §410Z/*Werke* 10 §410Z; LPS, 140/VPG, 108.

19. PN §350Z. I derive the term "infra-buffeting" from Massumi, *The Power at the End of the Economy*, 9. See note 17.

20. Thomas Venker, "Background Noises, Dirt and an Energy Saving Lamp: The Sound World of *Remainder*" (LP Liner Notes). Tom McCarthy, "Why *Ulysses* Matters," *Typewriters, Bombs, Jellyfish*, 42. There are numerous references to waves and the wake in this essay.

21. PN §282Z. Freud and Lacan emphasize the close connection between the traumaticity of birth, breathing, and anxiety. The language of "engendering" when it comes to "second nature" (a beginning again for the first time) makes clear how habit is also intimately engaged with these conditions.

22. PS §11.

23. See SE 20 (1925–1926), *Inhibitions, Symptoms and Anxiety* (1926), 96–97, 101. See SA, 327.

24. See Lacan, "On My Antecedents," Écrits, 52. On the relationship of the gust effect, drive, and fetish object, see Robertson, *Lacanian AntiPhilosophy and the Problem of Anxiety*, 39.

25. William James, "The Sentiment of Rationality [1879, 1882]," *The Will to Believe and Other Essays in Popular Philosophy* (Cambridge, MA: Harvard University Press, [1897] 1979), 9, 67–68.

26. SL, 81/*Werke* 5, 113.

27. Two choice instances where trembling (*Zittern*) features in the *Phenomenology of Spirit* are found in §162, §194. On key accounts of "trembling," see Jean-Luc Nancy, *Hegel: The Restlessness of the Negative*, trans. Jason E. Smith and Steven Miller (Minneapolis: University of Minnesota Press), 44–45: "Trembling is the act of being-affected—a passive acting that merely makes the body vibrate, that unsettles substance"; "Negativity makes all determinateness tremble." See Katrin Pahl, "Trembling," in *Tropes of Transport: Hegel and Emotion* (Evanston, IL: Northwestern University Press, 2012), 162–163: "Trembles and shakes are bodily modes of unsettling the body." Pahl also raises the issue of "textual trembling" that is addressed in this book's previous chapter on the speculative sentence in Hegel and *Remainder*.

28. PS §162, §163, §194; PN §354Z.

29. SL, 347–348/*Werke* 6, 27–28.

30. PS §194: "This consciousness was not driven with anxiety about this or that matter, nor did it have anxiety about just this or that moment; rather, it had anxiety about its entire essence. It felt the fear of death, the absolute master. In that feeling, it had inwardly fallen into dissolution, trembled in its depths, and all that was fixed within it had been shaken loose." In *Seminar on Anxiety* and *Television* Lacan, in a "backhanded" way, acknowledges that the mood of Hegel's philosophy is shaken by anxiety precisely in his claim that speculative dialectics wards off anxiety.

31. PS §171.

32. PP, 145.

33. Tom McCarthy, "Navigation Was Always a Difficult Art," in *The Mattering of Matter: Documents from the Archive of the International Necronautical Society*, Tom McCarthy, Simon Critchley, et al. (Berlin: Sternberg Press, 2012), 131–137.

34. McCarthy, "General Secretary's Report," 133.

35. McCarthy, "General Secretary's Report," 135.

36. McCarthy, "Toke My Asymptote," 28–29.

37. McCarthy, *Recessional*, 19.

38. See, for example, SA, 25, 54, 75–77, 89, 160, 174, 327; Jacques Lacan, *The Seminar of Jacques Lacan Book XIX: … or Worse*, ed. Jacques-Alain Miller, trans. A. R. Price (London: Polity Press, 2018), 32.

39. McCarthy briefly comments on this scene from Beckett's *Happy Days* in *Recessional*, 43–44, in which he describes her repetitive gestures as "re-enacting a re-enactment."

40. Samuel Beckett, *Proust and Three Dialogues with Georges Duthuit* (London: John Calder, 1976), 16.

41. On the suffocating weight of anxiety that chokes off speaking and communicating, see Robertson, *Lacanian AntiPhilosophy and the Problem of Anxiety*, 81.

42. PS §507.

43. On the "circuit breaker" analogy in Hegel, see Catherine Clément, *Syncope: The Philosophy of Rapture*, trans. Sally O'Driscoll and Deirdre M. Mahoney (Minneapolis: University of Minnesota Press, 1994), 63–64. Clément is well aware that "logical movement goes forward by jolts" but ultimately observes that the "negation of negation fulfills its work of circuit breaker (*échangeur routier*) and meaning gets underway again."

44. Alain Badiou, *In Praise of Theatre* (London: Polity Press, 2015), 84. This is precisely the role that habit does *not* play for Badiou. The "situation" comprises given habits that the event ruptures. Badiou seems unwilling to account for the immanent, evential and disruptive status of habit itself, although habit plays an important role *post festum* as a fidelity to the event.

45. PM §411Z/*Werke* 10 §411Z. This is elaborated on in LPS, 160: "This willing to stand becomes habit, but the habit always depends on the will to stand." Robert R. Williams translates *absolute Gebärde* as "primary gesture."

46. PS §32.

47. PS §78. Miller translates this as "the way of despair." See PS 1977 §78.

48. PP, 103, 108, 143–144, 153, 170.

49. Pahl, *Tropes of Transport*, 104.

50. Pahl, *Tropes of Transport*, 47, 104.

51. PS §315.

52. LPS, 160/VPG, 133; PM §411/*Werke* 10 §411. For "tool of tools," see PM §411Z/*Werke* 10 §411Z. Miller translates it as "this instrument *par excellence*," but I have translated it more literally as it better captures the repetition here as well as the Aristotelian reference.

53. The term "second-hand" is repeated many times in *Remainder*. See, for instance, 24–25, 54, 67. Again, McCarthy's privileged way of getting at issues of repetition, materiality, temporality, and ontology is through a critique of authenticity.

54. SE 5 (1901), "Bungled Actions." The book title in German is *Zur Psychopathologie des Alltagsleben: Über Vergessen, Versprechen, Vergreifen, Aberglaube und Irrtum*.

55. Berthold-Bond's section on "The Anatomy of Un-Intentionality" is attentive to the fact that all intentionality is subject to the recoil of action. I extend these insights not only to the act and actuality of gestures—their externalization in a deed or purposive act—but also to habit's very capacity to unify and ground those actions in the first place. See Daniel Berthold-Bond, *Hegel's Theory of Madness* (Albany: SUNY Press, 1995), 122–125.

56. On the prefix ver- in Hegel and Freud, see Katrin Pahl, *Tropes of Transport*, 183, 258n6, and "The Way of Despair," in *Hegel and the Infinite: Religion, Politics, and Dialectic*, ed. Slavoj Žižek, Clayton Crockett, and Creston Davis (New York: Columbia University Press, 2011), 143; Mladen Dolar, "Hegel and Freud," *e-flux Journal* 34 (April 2012): 9–14; Rebecca Comay, *Mourning Sickness: Hegel and the French Revolution* (Stanford, CA: Stanford University Press, 2011), 64, 66, 96, 123; Rebecca Comay and Frank Ruda, *The Dash—The Other Side of Absolute Knowing* (Cambridge, MA: MIT Press, 2018), 44–47; Slavoj Žižek, *Absolute Recoil: Towards a New Foundation of Dialectical Materialism* (London: Verso, 2014), 387–388, and *Less Than Nothing: Hegel and the Shadow of Dialectical Materialism* (London: Verso, 2013), 492–496; and Elizabeth Rottenberg, *For the Love of Psychoanalysis: The Play of Chance in Freud and Derrida* (New York: Fordham University Press, 2019), 57, 75–77.

57. SL, 347.

58. SA, 79: "This *understumble*, untranslatable in French, incorporates *stumble* into *understand*."

59. Dolar, "Hegel and Freud," 9–14. These five Ver- words for negation are: *Verneinung* (negation), *Verdrängung* (repression), *Verwerfung* (foreclosure), *Verleugnung* (disavowal), and *Verschiebung* (displacement). The ver- words in *The Psychopathology of Everyday Life* are *Versprechen, Verschreiben, Verlesen, Vergessen*, and *Vergreifen*. In his *Introductory Lectures* of 1916 and 1917, he adds *Verhören, Verlegen*, and *Verlieren*. See SE 6 (1901), 307. The notion of *sich vergreifen* as "to commit an assault" occurs in SE 6 (1901), 230n7. For an excellent account of *Vergreifen* in *The Psychopathology of Everyday Life*, see Elizabeth Rottenberg, *For the Love of Psychoanalysis*, 53–59, 75–77. With regard to falling, tripping, stumbling, and slipping—the primary manifestations of the bungled actions occurring in everyday life—we might add Heidegger's term *Verfallen* (falling), often characterized as being *caught up* in the everyday, in the sense of being "ensnared" or "entangled" in it. The compulsive repetitions of habit generate such entanglements.

60. PS §472/*Werke* 3, 351.

61. ESL 216Z and EPR 270Z. For other references to Hegel's philosophy of the hand, see PN §248Z, §350Z; ESL §160Z; LPS, 160–161; PM §411, §411Z; PS §315. Here I am referring to sections that specifically mention the hand's status as a "cut off" in relationship to the whole, organic unity, and actuality.

62. PS §32. "Death, if that is what we wish to call that non-actuality." In other instances, Hegel describes the "non-actual" as what is separated, abstract, vanishing, and as a kind of virtuality.

63. PN §371.

64. PP, 144; Walter Benjamin, "Rastelli's Story," *Walter Benjamin: Selected Writings*, ed. Howard Eiland and Michael W. Jennings, vol. 3, 1935–1938 (Cambridge, MA: Belknap Press, 2002), 96–98. Benjamin's Rastelli features in a chapter of Michael Taussig's *The Mastery of Non-Mastery* and is central to the book as a whole as it pertains to issues of automaticity, proprioception, habit, and possession. See Taussig, "The Alpha and Omega of All Mastery," in *The Mastery of Non-Mastery in the Age of Meltdown* (Chicago: University of Chicago Press, 2020), 133–143.

65. PP, 144.

66. Here I am drawing on some passages on the plant and its flowering from PN §348Z. Contrary to my vitalistic wording, for Hegel the plant is not organized "organically."

67. See Andreja Novakovic, *Hegel on Second Nature in Ethical Life* (Cambridge: Cambridge University Press, 2017), 35. PP, 145–146.

68. I italicize *matter at hand* to call attention to the fact that it is one of the English translations of Hegel's "subject matter" (*die Sache selbst*).

69. SA, 216–217. In this passage, Lacan is addressing the functions of causality as that relates to bodily experience, with direct reference to Maine de Biran's position. Here it is worth considering the role of the arm in G. E. M. Anscombe's classic book *Intention* (Cambridge, MA: Harvard University Press, 2000).

70. SA, 177, 219; PM §410.

71. PP, 144.

72. See SE 20 (1925–1926), *Inhibitions, Symptoms Anxiety* (1926a), 89–90. Of course, there are many examples of such eroticized "organs," which impair organic totality and purpose in Freud's work: the bowels, throat, etc. This also holds true for anxiety in Freud and Lacan, e.g., the lungs. And of course, the classical part-objects in Lacan, such as the gaze and voice.

73. SA, 10–11, 319. See also Robertson, *Lacanian Antiphilosophy and the Problem of Anxiety*, 76.

74. SA, 10.

75. SA, 214.

76. SA, 215.

77. See note 53.

78. Freud notes that its normal meaning is "to climb too high." SE, 4, 214n7.

79. PS §80.

80. Robertson, *Lacanian Antiphilosophy and the Problem of Anxiety*, 193. On the *dompte-regard*, see Lacan, *The Four Fundamentals Concepts of Psychoanalysis*, 105, 111, 114–115.

81. SA, 136, 206.

82. PS §343: "However much it is otherwise said of spirit that it is, it has *a being*, it is a *thing*, a singular *actuality*, still it is not thereby *meant* that it is something we can see, or take in our hands, or push around and so forth, but that is what is *said* of it, and what in truth the foregoing has been saying may be expressed in this way: The *being of spirit is a bone*." And ESL §160Z: "We cannot grasp the concept as such with our hands and, when it comes to the concept, we generally have to take leave of seeing and hearing."

83. PS §578. See also the relevant passages on the spirit is a bone and its elaboration in terms of the infinite judgment of the I is a thing and thing is an I in PS §791.

84. SA, 214.

85. What is variably characterized as letting go, releasing, self-relinquishing, self-divestiture, releasement, or self-emptying, captures the movement of the concept that is the logic of the not yet within grasping, and it is intrinsic to the kenotic nature of Hegel's speculative philosophy. For some accounts that are attentive to kenotic insistence in Hegel, see Nancy, *Hegel: The Restlessness of the Negative*, 55–65; Catherine Malabou, *The Future of Hegel: Plasticity, Temporality, and Dialectic*, trans. Lisabeth During (London: Routledge, 2005), 155–158; Comay, *Mourning Sickness*, 109–117, 145–149; Žižek, "Hegel and Shitting: The Idea's Constipation," in *Hegel and the Infinite*, 221–232; Pahl, "Release," in *Tropes of Transport*, 83–99;

Alex Dubilet, *The Self-Emptying Subject: Kenosis and Immanence, Medieval to Modern* (New York: Fordham University Press, 2018), 92–147.

86. PS §47/*Werke* 3, 46.

87. PN §247Z; PS §726.

88. PS §407–§409, §439.

89. PS §47, §785.

90. SL, 81/*Werke* 5, 113.

91. PS §162. See also PN §354 and §354Z for further elaborations of the term "pulsation" (*Pulsieren*) in Hegel. For the relationship of "pulsation" to punctuation in Hegel, see Peter Szendy, "Punctum Saliens, or The Pulsating Point" and "The Point of the Overcast Stitch" in Peter Szendy, *Of Stigmatology: Punctuation as Experience*, trans. Jan Plug (New York: Fordham University Press, 2018), 59–72.

92. On the language of diffusion and pervasion that usually accompanies the word "infection" (*Ansteckung, Infektion, Infizieren, infiziert*), see PS §545. The vocabulary of "infection" or "contagion" in Hegel is central to the "unmediated" temporality, materiality, and spatiality of spirit in Hegel and is central to the universalizing of the particular in habit. For key passages on infection, see PN§345A, §346Z, §365A; PS §196, §507, §545; PM §405Z, §410Z. On the temporality of infection in Hegel, see Stephan Gregory, "Patience and Precipitation: Two Figures of Historical Change," in *Cultural Techniques: Assembling Spaces, Texts & Collectives*, ed. Jörg Dünne, Kathrin Fehringer, Kristina Kuhn, and Wolfgang Struck (Berlin: De Gruyter, 2020), 277–294. Also see the short conversation between Karen Ng and Andreja Novakovic: "Ansteckung/contagion," 5 Minuten Hegel, video, August 2020, https//5minutenhegel.de/ansteckung. On the "vanishing of vanishing," see PS §407–§409. The issue of vanishing, addressed throughout the *Phenomenology of Spirit*, is central to my account of the kenotic anaesthetics of habit in *Remainder*. See chapter 4, n. 16, for a list of sections in the *Phenomenology of Spirit* that address vanishing.

93. On the "*pulsative* function" of the unconscious as it is grasped through the on-and-off rhythm of appearance and disappearance, fading in and fading out, see Lacan, "Of the Network of Signifiers," in *The Seminar of Jacques Lacan Book XI: The Four Fundamental Concepts of Psychoanalysis*, ed. Jacques-Alain Miller, trans. Alan Sheridan (New York: W. W. Norton, 1998), 43., and SA, 217–218, 238, 285. Essential to Lacan's notion of pulsatility is the word "vanishing." I return to the issue of pulsatility and vanishing with regard to Joan of Arc's left hand in Jules Bastien-Lepage's painting.

94. PS §37.

95. SA, 10.

96. In the film there is an ironing scene captured by CCTV cameras during the Madlyn Mansions reenactment. Another ironing scene that also addresses habit and repetition are the soldiers from the French Foreign Legion collectively ironing in Claire Denis's film *Beau Travail*. Related to this, the notion of the fold or folding is also relevant and particularly notable in the French language. For example, *un mauvais pli* (a bad habit).

97. Hélène Cixous, "Without end, no, State of Drawingness, no, rather: The Executioner's taking off," *Stigmata: Escaping Texts*, 22–23.

98. McCarthy, *Recessional*, 54, 50.

99. SA, 122.

100. Jacques Lacan, "Anamorphosis," in *The Seminar of Jacques Lacan Book XI: The Four Fundamental Concepts of Psychoanalysis*, ed. Jacques-Alain Miller, trans. Alan Sheridan (New York: W. W. Norton, 1998), 89; Dolar, "Anamorphosis," *S: Journal of the Circle for Lacanian Ideology Critique*, no. 8 (2015): 129. Žižek articulates the distinction between reality and the Lacanian Real as follows: "Reality is … the external limit, while … the Real is the *internal* limit, … the unseizable boundary that prevents it from becoming itself, of attaining its identity-with-itself, the twist that causes it to return in on itself, to turn in circles." Slavoj Žižek, *The Most Sublime Hysteric: Hegel with Lacan* (Cambridge: Polity, 2014), 57.

101. Rottenberg is attuned to the complexities of the relationship of *Vergreifen* to *begreifen* in Freud's *Psychopathology of Everyday Life*. See *For the Love of Psychoanalysis*, 76–77.

102. This is also the counter-marionette to interpretations that implicitly or explicitly evoke this figure in suggesting that the narrator pulls himself up and together by vision and understanding given his loss of proprioception.

103. Merleau-Ponty, "Eye and Mind," in *The Primacy of Perception and Other Essays on Phenomenological Psychology, the Philosophy of Art, History and Politics*, ed. James Edie (Evanston: Northwestern University Press, 1964), 163. This is worded in a slightly different fashion in PP, 98: "my whole body for me is not an assemblage of organs juxtaposed in space. I am in undivided possession of it and I know where each of my limbs is through a *body image* in which all are included."

104. Merleau-Ponty, "Eye and Mind," 185.

105. For accounts of virtuality in habit see PP, 111; Malabou, *Future of Hegel*, 45, 49–50, 54–56, 71, 146; Žižek, "Discipline between Two Freedoms–Madness and Habit in German Idealism," 103–104, 109, 112, 121.

106. Gilles Deleuze, *Difference and Repetition*, trans. Paul Patton (New York: Columbia University Press, 1994), 99–102.

107. Ben Lerner, 10:04: *A Novel* (New York: McClelland & Stewart, 2014), 9–10. Subsequent quotes refer to these pages. In the novel, only the detail of Joan of Arc's hand is reproduced along with the hand from the film *Back to the Future*, from which the title of the novel is derived. A special thank you to Bruce Barnhart for introducing me to 10:04 and encouraging our Temporal Experiments research group at the University of Oslo to read it.

108. PM §406Z.

109. Comay, *Mourning Sickness*, 116; PS §658.

110. For one example among many that links spinning, habit, domesticity, and gendered inhabitation, see Vilém Flusser, "Taking up Residence in Homelessness," in *Vilém Flusser: Writings*, ed. Andreas Ströhl, trans. Erik Eisel (Minneapolis: University of Minnesota Press, 2002), 95: "The secret codes of homes are not made of conscious rules, but rather spun from unconscious habits. What characterizes the habit is the fact that one is not conscious of it."

111. PS §546.

CHAPTER 4

1. William James, *Principles of Psychology*, vol. 1 (New York: Henry Holt, 1890; New York: Dover Publications, 1950), 104.

2. Tom McCarthy, *Recessional—Or, the Time of the Hammer*, ed. Elisabeth Bronfen (Zurich/Berlin: Diaphenes, 2016), 54, 71, and "Get Real, or What Jellyfish Have to Tell Us About Literature," in *Typewriters, Bombs, Jellyfish* (New York: New York Review Books, 2017), 71.

3. The issue of hylomorphism is often raised and featured in scholarship on Hegel's account of habit as a manifestation of soul in his philosophy of subjective spirit that emphasizes his indebtedness to Aristotle's concept of the soul, substance, and metaphysics, which Hegel forthrightly acknowledges, and which literally bookends his *Philosophy of Mind*. See PM §378, §577. Allegra de Laurentiis mobilizes a qualified use of hylomorphism to characterize the ontology of Hegel's soul. See Allegra de Laurentiis, "The Aristotelian Metaphysics of Hegel's Soul," in *Hegel and Ancient Philosophy: A Re-Examination*, ed. Glen Alexander Magee (London: Routledge, 2020), 115–131, and "Hylomorphism and Hegel's Account of the Soul," in *Jahrbuch für Hegelforschung*, ed. Helmut Schneider (Sankt Augustin: Academia Verlag, 2017), 247–265. I have preferred to get at the strange materiality generated by habit through my reading of *Remainder* and from a psychoanalytic perspective. Here, I have been influenced by Lacan's critique of Aristotle's notions of soul, substance, ethics, and habit that is an insistent thread through his seminars and essays, despite his clear reverence for and indebtedness to the philosopher. This is fundamentally related to Lacan's critique of Aristotle's "science of happiness," that although paving the way for a jouissance of being, remains within the tempered logic of the pleasure principle. See, for example, Jacques Lacan, *The Seminar of Jacques Lacan Book VII: The Ethics of Psychoanalysis*, ed. Jacques Alain Miller, trans. Dennis Porter (New York: W. W. Norton, 1997), 318. *The Seminar of Jacques Lacan Book XX: On Feminine Sexuality, the Limits of Love and Knowledge*, ed. Jacques-Alain Miller, trans. Bruce Fink (New York: W. W. Norton, 1998).

4. PM §389. "Corporeity saturated by soul" is Petry's translation of a sentence from PS §411 Z that Wallace translates as "unresistingly pervaded."

5. Tom McCarthy, "Recessional, or the Time of the Hammer," *Typewriters, Bombs, Jellyfish: Essays* (New York: New York Review of Books, 2017), 111. Here, he is talking about Blanchot.

6. PP, 98, 110, 153. The English translation renders Merleau-Ponty's *Schéma corporel* as "body image."

7. SL, 539/*Werke* 6, 287.

8. Jean-Luc Nancy, *The Speculative Remark (One of Hegel's Bons Mots)*, trans. Céline Surprenant (Stanford, CA: Stanford University Press, 2001), 70.

9. Online Etymology Dictionary, s.v. "Relish," updated June 25, 2021, https://www.etymonline.com/word/relish.

10. Lacan uses the terms "repetition function" and "restitutive function" to characterize the disturbing and unsettling Freudian death drive and the homeostatic nature of the pleasure principle, respectively. See Lacan, *Book II: The Ego in Freud's Theory*, 63, 79–80.

11. Tom McCarthy, "Why *Ulysses* Matters," *Typewriters, Bombs, Jellyfish*, 29.

12. PS §808.

13. For instance, see Andrew Cole, "How to Think a Figure; or, Hegel's Circles," *Representations*, no. 140 (Fall 2017): 49; Katrin Pahl, *Tropes of Transport: Hegel and Emotion* (Evanston, IL: Northwestern University Press, 2012), 83; Rebecca Comay, *Mourning Sickness: Hegel and the French Revolution* (Stanford, CA: Stanford University Press, 2011), 130; Dubilet, *The Self-Emptying Subject: Kenosis and Immanence, Medieval to Modern* (New York: Fordham University Press, 2018), 116–122.

14. See McCarthy, "Recessional," *Typewriters, Bombs, Jellyfish*, 99–124.

15. On the infinitization of kenosis in Hegel, see Dubilet, *The Self-Emptying Subject*, 169.

16. The issue of vanishing is addressed throughout *Phenomenology of Spirit* and is central to my account of the kenotic anaesthetics of habit in *Remainder*. For important manifestations

of this term, see PS §47–48, §165, §195, §206, §341, §361, §404, §407–§409, §430, §439, §507, §545, §589, §657–§659, §729, §788–§789, §795, §808. I have benefited from reading Casey Ford's PhD dissertation on vanishing in Hegel and Deleuze. See Casey Ford, "The Logic of Vanishing: Becoming in Hegel and Deleuze," PhD diss. (University of Guelph, 2016).

17. PN §589.

18. *Hegel and the Human Spirit: A Translation of the Jena Lectures on the Philosophy of Spirit (1805–6) with Commentary* by Leo Rauch (Detroit: Wayne State University Press, 1983), 86–87. For the German, see G. W. F. Hegel, *Jenaer Systementwürfe III, Naturphilosophie und Philosophie des Geistes*, ed. Rolf-Peter Horstmann (Hamburg: Felix Meiner Verlag, 1987), 172.

19. SL, 745.

20. See, for example, SA, 217–218, 238, and Lacan, *Book XI: The Four Fundamental Concepts of Psychoanalysis*, 43, 206–207, 223.

21. The issue of vanishing has also been raised by McCarthy within the realm of the International Necronautical Society. For an example, see the discussion of anamorphosis in Holbein's Ambassadors and related issues of appearance and disappearance in literature in Tom McCarthy, "Navigation Was Always a Difficult Art," in *The Mattering of Matter: Documents from the Archive of the International Necronautical Society*, Tom McCarthy, Simon Critchley, et al. (Berlin: Sternberg Press, 2012), 121–122.

22. SA, 136.

23. McCarthy, "Why *Ulysses* Matters," 28.

24. PS §658. See also §659 ("the feeble essentialities of evaporated life") and §361 ("vanish like a lifeless fog").

25. McCarthy, "Stabbing the Olive: Jean-Philippe Toussaint," in *Typewriters Bombs Jellyfish*, 186.

26. McCarthy, "Stabbing the Olive," 186.

27. PP, 145–146.

28. The inner eight is the moebius strip as cut. For a few examples of Lacan's discussion of the "inner eight" or "interior eight," see Jacques Lacan, "Science and Truth," in *Écrits*, trans. Bruce Fink (New York: W. W. Norton, 2002), 731; Lacan, *Book XX: On Feminine Sexuality, The Limits of Love and Knowledge*, 136; Lacan, *Book XI: The Four Fundamental Concepts of Psychoanalysis*, 155–156, 274. Like Lacan, McCarthy's interest in the figure eight also registers the importance of structuralism for a "very particular mode of the subject for which the only index I have found is topological." Lacan, "Science and Truth," 731.

29. On "the double-circuit topology of the hole," see Pierre Skriabine, "Clinic and Topology: The Flaw in the Universe," in *Lacan: Topologically Speaking*, ed. Ellie Ragland and Dragan Milovanovic (New York: Other Press, 2004), 79. To bring this account back to Hegel's discussion of habit in the anthropology of the soul, it is interesting to note that Nancy characterizes the soul as an "internal outside." Jean-Luc Nancy, *Corpus II: Writings on Sexuality*, trans. Anne O'Byrne (New York: Fordham University Press, 2013), 84.

30. SL, 631.

31. PN §337Z.

32. SA, 89.

33. PS §62; ESL §17.

34. ESL §81 Z.

35. Giorgio Agamben, "Habitual Use," *The Use of Bodies*, trans. Adam Kotsko (Stanford, CA: Stanford University Press, 2015), 61.

36. Agamben, "Habitual Use," 61.

37. In mathematics, an inflection point on a curve is the place where the sign of the curvature changes direction, going from concave to convex or vice versa.

38. Gilles Deleuze, *Difference and Repetition*, trans. Paul Patton (New York: Columbia University Press, 1994), 100. Žižek puts this in another way in *Less Than Nothing: Hegel and the Shadow of Dialectical Materialism* (London: Verso, 2013), 549. "The 'drive' is in many ways almost the photographic negative of the 'will': It is the push to eject its object, to lose it, to introduce a gap, not to overcome it. Thus, we could even say that the will is a countermovement to the drive, an attempt to re-inscribe the "asubjectal" drive into the economy of the ego as the agency of control and domination."

39. SL, 751.

40. SL, 751.

41. Theodor Adorno, "Aspects of Hegel's Philosophy," in *Hegel: Three Studies*, trans. Shierry Weber Nicholsen (Cambridge, MA: MIT Press, 1993), 51.

42. PS §802. For one account of the "point" in relationship to habit and the issue of simplification and abbreviation, see Catherine Malabou, "The Blunt Tip of Meaning," in *The Future of Hegel: Plasticity, Temporality, and Dialectic*, trans. Lisabeth During (London: Routledge, 2005), 148–150.

43. On the rotary movement of the drive, see Žižek, *Less Than Nothing*, 376.

44. Lacan, "Of the Network of Signifiers," in *Book XI: The Four Fundamental Concepts of Psychoanalysis*, 50–51.

45. McCarthy, "Get Real, or What Jellyfish Have to Tell Us About Literature," *Typewriters, Bombs, Jellyfish*, 67–68.

46. Félix Guattari, *Chaosmosis: An Ethico-Aesthetic Paradigm*, trans. Paul Bains and Julian Pefanis (Bloomington: Indiana University Press, 1995), 17–18, 75.

47. Guattari, *Chaosmosis*, 71.

48. On the "circuit breaker" analogy in Hegel, see chapter 3, n. 43.

49. Dubilet, *The Self-Emptying Subject*, 116.

50. Dubilet, *The Self-Emptying Subject*, 92–122. Casey Ford makes a similar point in noting that the problem of vanishing is not terminated with the "vanishing of vanishing." The gerund "vanishing" persists (a point that Ford emphasizes). See Ford, "The Logic of Vanishing," 120.

51. Butler, *Senses of the Self* (New York: Fordham University Press, 2015), 94.

52. My account of temporality in *Remainder* runs counter to Fredric Jameson's account of it in his essay "The Aesthetics of Singularity," which is an elaboration of a previous essay, "The End of Temporality." Fredric Jameson, "The Aesthetics of Singularity," *New Left Review*, no. 92 (March–April, 2015): 101–132; Fredric Jameson, "The End of Temporality," *Critical Inquiry* 29, no. 4 (Summer 2003), 695–718. Both essays explore the shrinkage of time to the present and the body in late capitalism. *Remainder* is one of the literary/aesthetic examples mobilized in "The Aesthetics of Singularity" to advance the notion that "singularity is a pure present without past or future." Jameson links this "aesthetic of singularity" to the

heterogenous temporality of the financial derivative, a new and more intense form of fictitious capital that dissolves the past and future, thus imprisoning us in the present. All the components for such an analysis are certainly there in *Remainder*, but I think a very different and more disruptive sense of temporal volatility is at stake in *Remainder* due to its "not yet" logic of breakdown in and through repetition and habit.

53. The syntax here is my own and is derived from listening to the film.

54. Lacan, "The Function and Field of Speech and Language in Psychoanalysis," in *Écrits*, 209.

INDEX

Page numbers in italics refer to figures.